TWENTY THOUSAND
YEARS
IN SING SING

WARDEN LEWIS E. LAWES

TWENTY THOUSAND YEARS IN SING SING

LEWIS E. LAWES

edward

WARDEN OF SING SING PRISON

Ray Long & Richard R. Smith, Inc.

New York · 1932

4-24-47

Copyright, May, 1932, by
LEWIS E. LAWES

All rights reserved

PRINTED IN THE UNITED STATES OF AMERICA

TO

THOSE TENS OF THOUSANDS
OF MY FORMER WARDS
WHO HAVE JUSTIFIED MY
FAITH IN HUMAN NATURE

CONTENTS

LIST OF ILLUSTRATIONS

ix

TWENTY THOUSAND
YEARS
IN SING SING

PROLOGUE: A BROADCAST

I HAVE been directed to kill lawfully one hundred and fifty men and one woman.

It is my legal duty to be present physically in the death chamber. But actually I have never seen an execution.

My experience has convinced me of the futility of capital punishment. History would seem to confirm this viewpoint.

It is related of Boswell that when troubled with digestive disturbances he would seek relaxation by a stroll through the public highways in the neighborhood of a gallows, hoping to find solace at a "hanging." Rather a gruesome way to work up an appetite! Imagine a Rotarian dinner or a Kiwanis celebration preceded by a spicy execution as a sort of psychological appetizer. The hardiness of our forbears was coincidental with public enforcement of punitive judgments. Not only were gallows set up in public squares, but meaner forms of chastisement such as stocks, pillories, whipping posts and ducking stools were among the outstanding examples of civic efficiency. And the quaint but effective (!) disciplinary judgments, such as lashing, branding, maiming, and the like were enforced openly either as additional degradations to the convicted or as "examples" to those "who might have been" or "might still be." Whether such displays whetted the public appetite for excitement must ever remain a subject for animated discussion among present day psychologists and psychiatrists.

With the advancement of civilization and the soften-ing influences of human progress men began to abhor the practice of killing or maiming on the public square. They preferred to isolate culprits. Dungeons and pris-ons became the vogue. Like the housewife who "cleans" house by sweeping the rubbish under the bed or in hidden corners, so modern society complacently "rids" itself of misfits by hiding them from public view, re-gardless of moral filth lurking in those dark recesses.

Probably because of its intense emotional appeal an execution, whether by gallows, guillotine or knife, was the greatest of all punitory attractions. Frequently, order among the eager populace had to be maintained by troops. More often the "killing" was made the occasion for family outings, with lunches and drinks for adults and sweetmeats for the youngsters. Doubt-less many a cultured and respected citizen would hide surreptitiously among the sight-seers to feast his eyes upon the performance and, like Boswell, return home cured of a headache, with restored and sharpened appetite. In many instances these public exhibitions served to glorify the victim who became the self-esteemed heroic, dying contentedly amid the cheers or jeers of friends or foes.

We must not forget that these performances were supposed to influence the mean and lowly folk for good. Like the cure-all fakir who exhibits to his gullible audience the positive recuperative powers of his pills, through the testimony of a "cured" subject to whom he points with pride, so did authority through these exhibitions of dire punishments design to cure the on-lookers of evil tendencies. It is interesting, however, to know that as these public spectacles grew in number and virulence, offences increased.

Of particular interest are the numerous instances of culprits who were among the first victims of the punitive structures they themselves planned and built.

It is difficult to determine the exact period of transition in popular reaction against public punishments. It seems, however, that with the advent of personal comforts and luxurious living, and the gradual ascendency of brain over brawn, these public demonstrations became less and less popular and gradually lost favor altogether. Punishment was inflicted behind prison doors. Every warden felt as did the bard of old when he affirmed that "I am forbid to tell the secrets of my prison house." And so it came to pass that executions, like all other serious judgments, were carried out in prison yards or specially constructed cells or houses. No longer the public display. Only a limited number of witnesses were permitted to attend the final ceremonies. But human nature is ever captious. No sooner were these executions hidden from public view than curiosity sought to know the details of each killing; the reactions of the victim were and still are the subjects of long, varied, intimate and sensational reports read with an avidity equal to that of the sight-seers of old. Our sensibilities do not permit us to witness the infliction of the death sentence, but most of us scan the details of the proceedings in the death chamber. There is an influential school of thought that insists upon the publicity of these happenings as effective deterrents. "Let men know what they must face," they maintain, "and they will be more circumspect."

These people would not for a moment countenance

the return to public executions, but to broadcast the dire retributive consequences of wrongdoing might well be within the scope of their theories of prevention and deterrence.

Taking them at their word I visualized the possibility not only of reporting the procedure in the death chamber at a legal killing, but of utilizing modern mechanics to their utmost in really broadcasting an execution. Why not? We would be spared the horror of actually witnessing the agonies of the victim. But there would be all the "warnings" that were thought to go with the old fashioned killings.

Religion, seeking broader fields of influence, makes frequent use of the radio; education, in all its manifold activities, looks to the radio for ever widening scholastic interests; sports broadcast their events to enthusiastic but home loving audiences. The world is becoming radiophile and prefers all its mental and intellectual pabulum attractively synthesized through the medium of a broadcasting agency. The radio is supplanting the newspapers as a news carrier and even the police are depending, in a large measure, on the ether to acquaint the public with the latest and more important crime wave. Pugilists do not confine their fistic exhibitions to their immediate audiences. Their every move and feint are reported instantaneously to eager millions comfortably ensconced in the quiet of their dwellings. Beyond question, the radio has become an important factor in social development.

The reactions of various types of listeners-in would be especially interesting, and my purpose here is to spy imaginatively on characteristic groups with the

view of ascertaining the forceful effect of such broadcasting upon minds and characters.

Those who still believe in the efficacy of capital
punishment should urge the desirability of bringing
home, in the most vivid manner, not only the news of
the accomplished fact of an execution, but also the
actual procedure followed in carrying out the death
sentence. Our sensibilities may recoil from witnessing
the death dealing act, whether hanging or electrocution, but hearing the ceremony (!) would be less disconcerting and probably just as effective—if the death
penalty is in reality the deterrent its enthusiasts claim
it is.

The proceedings usually commence at eleven o'clock
at night, an hour when children of tender years are
asleep, so that the gruesome program will be heard
only by grown-ups. There will be interesting groups.
A "death house" broadcast will find a wide and varied
audience. Many modern "Boswells" will discover
therein the elusive thrill so vainly sought as a pallia-
tive; some would listen in to gather material for ser-
mons and preachments; others would find solace in
acknowledging the finality of the law, its majesty and
effective judgment; still others would enjoy a half
hour's entertainment to edge off a wearisome night.

The program is not unduly extended. Station XYZ
clears the air a little before the hour. The sound waves
ply their osmotic way through the air and the voice of
the announcer is heard.

"This is Station XYZ, ABC announcing, talking
from the death house at Sing Sing Prison. You are
about to follow with me the details leading up to the
execution of a man convicted of the crime of murder

5

in the first degree. He took a human life and is about to pay the penalty fixed by law. While we are waiting for the proceedings to commence I shall describe the surroundings so that you may have an idea of the local setting. Though we are within the walls of Sing Sing Prison the death house is really a prison within a prison. It has its own kitchen, hospital, exercise yards, visiting room, and so forth. There are two wings of twelve cells each for the men, with separate wings of three cells for women (rather complimentary to the women it seems), six cells in the hospital section and six cells in the pre-execution chamber to which the condemned men are removed on the morning of the day of the execution. This section, referred to as the 'dance hall' by the condemned, is connected by a corridor 'in-back' (the pet name for the execution chamber), and the 'ice-box' or morgue adjoining. The building is well but not brilliantly lighted.

"From my point of vantage I can see entering a number of gentlemen. With two or three exceptions they are civilians and of serious mien. They are being shown into the execution chamber and seated in pew-like benches facing a large, square chair, to which are attached a number of leather straps. They seem strained, as at a funeral waiting for the dirge. They are now all seated and I shall ask your indulgence while I leave the room to attend the march of the condemned, his death march, from the cell in the pre-execution chamber to the chair. I shall walk with him and give you my impressions along the line of march.

＊　　　＊　　　＊　　　＊

"And now, ladies and gentlemen of the radio audience, I am in the pre-execution chamber, directly in

6

front of the cell of the man who is the central figure of this proceeding.

"In his cell I see another gentleman, evidently praying with the condemned. Their words are low and indistinct. Several tall, husky, uniformed guards quietly approach the cell, and with the rattle of a key the steel barred cell door swings open. No word is spoken. At a nod from the leader of the uniformed guards, the prisoner rises. A guard bends down, knife in hand. With a deft stroke he slits the right trouser leg. Silently the march begins. The condemned man is a young fellow not over twenty-five, pale, tired looking. Flanked by the guards, with the clergyman keeping step and praying, the prisoner marches on with a steady tread. There is a curious eagerness in his step.

"The procession moves on—a door opens and we are in the execution chamber. One cannot look at the witnesses while concentrating on the activity around the chair. The prisoner is seated, two guards stoop to adjust the straps, quickly pinioning the arms and legs and torso.

"It will soon be over. The man in the chair seems dazed. His eyes follow the feverish activities of the men who are fumbling at the straps. He regards it all impersonally. Does he realize that every twist and turn and pull is bringing him closer to eternity? The guards straighten up, finally. They have adjusted the electrode to the right leg. It is attached at the spot inside the open slit. One of them is lifting a hood over the prisoner's head. The man in the chair looks up at it. The adjustment of that hood is the final act of preparation. It will shut out forever all that remains to him of life and living.

"The condemned man lifts his eyes toward the guard who is holding the hood. They carry a silent appeal. The hood remains aloft. The prisoner looks around the room. Wait a moment, please. He is speaking. The witnesses sit erect and stare at the condemned man.

"'May I say a few words?' was what the prisoner said. All heads turn inquiringly toward the Warden. He nods. Guards stand still at their posts, waiting.
. . .

"'Please do all you can to do away with capital punishment. I don't fear death. None of the boys who are to follow me fears death either. I was convicted on circumstantial evidence. Thanks to all the officers for being considerate. Good-bye. . . everybody. Maybe we'll meet again. . . . Who knows?'

"The prisoner smiled as he spoke. Silence again. The hood is being placed on his head. The face is now covered. The guards stand aside.

"A slim, gray haired gentleman approaches the chair with a nervous, jerky tread. He bends low to examine the electrode on the right leg; makes the final adjustments of the hood and steps rapidly away to the instrument panel, ten feet to the rear of the chair.

"Now there is a sputtering drone; maybe you can hear it through the air. The body of what a moment ago was a living human being leaps forward as if to break its bonds. A thin, gray wisp of smoke curls slowly up from under the hood—there is a faint odor of burning flesh.

"The hands turn red, then white, and the cords of the neck stand out like steel bands. As I talk the drone increases in volume, the body is still straining at the straps. The hands grip the arms of the chair in an ever tightening grasp. The raucous droning continues. Now there is a general subsidence and the body relaxes. One of the men, apparently a physician, approaches the inert body, applies his stethoscope, shakes his head and steps back. The droning is heard again and simultaneously the body assumes rigidity and seemingly tries to burst its bonds. Again a subsidence, another examination. . . . A voice is heard. . . . 'Warden, I pronounce this man dead.'

"Three guards are now rapidly unstrapping the body. They lift it on a waiting litter and wheel it through a side door beyond which a white enameled operating table is visible. It is the autopsy room.

"The witnesses, I now count twelve, are rising from their seats. There is a low, subdued whispering. They move toward the exit, all eager to get out, and now I am alone with the chief guard.

"Ladies and gentlemen of the radio audience, you have listened to an actual occurrence. You have been witnesses to an execution of a human being whose life was forfeited to the State pursuant to law because he took life regardless of law. You may not have enjoyed the broadcast. I hope, however, it was instructive. Good night."

*　　*　　*　　*

Assuming that this broadcast from the death house was actually made, how would the listeners-in react to it? Human nature hasn't changed with the years.

There would be—

The modern Boswell, reincarnated, intellectual dyspeptic who needs an appetizer. He would turn from

9

the radio and remark to his wife: "Mary, any cold chicken left in the refrigerator? I'm famished."

And the preacher: "Bess, I've got a corking good sermon for next Sunday. The Wages of Sin is Death— in the Electric Chair."

And the committeeman for the enforcement of the death penalty: "That'll head them off. No mercy on those killers. A few more and we'll have them licked."

And the judge who pronounced the judgment of death: "Too bad."

And the "Chief" in his favorite night club, his lips twisted into a slight smile: "Well, we save on the silver casket." And after a pause, "These are hard times, too."

And the widow of the victim of the condemned: "That man's wife. I'm sorry for her."

And the tired business man at the club as he dealt the cards to his three cronies: "They do those things quickly nowadays. Competent fellows up there."

And the young fellow, slim, sleek-haired, deep-set eyes, as he sat alone in his luxurious apartment: "The sap. A first rate bungler."

The door of a bedroom of an apartment on the third floor closes softly. Young Ted climbs quietly into his bed. Ted is fifteen. An impressionable youngster. He had been ordered to bed an hour ago, but he hadn't missed a word of that broadcast through the slit of the partly opened door. Now he is lying back on his pillow, his eyes staring into the darkness. His mind reviews the story. "Gee, but he was a brave fellow, all right."

But wait! It's eleven thirty. The radio is still on. Station XYZ. The final news of the day. The announcer seems excited. "United Press reports a daring robbery on Broadway a little after eleven o'clock. The Climax Theatre safe was blown open and the total receipts of the evening—several thousand dollars—taken. The police surprised the robbers as they were leaving.

"Shots were exchanged. But the bandits escaped in a high powered car. A policeman was wounded and is believed to be in a critical condition. Detectives say they have picked up several valuable clues."

CHAPTER 1: ROOKIE DAYS

"TREAD softly and carry a big stick," was my first lesson in penology, on my arrival at Clinton Prison on March 1st, 1905. It was to be followed literally. When I reported for duty that night, I was handed a pair of sneakers and a club. The sneakers, to enable the guard to make his rounds noiselessly, so as not to disturb the sleeping forms within the dark cells, and the club to be used in emergencies should any of those forms become unduly active. I had rather a hard time of it on that first tour of duty.

Listening to the crescendo of snores that broke the otherwise dead silence of the old cell block was hardly measuring up to my conception of the duties of a prison keeper. In my younger days, at Elmira, New York, I had seen something of prison life. The house where I was born stood only a half mile from the New York State Reformatory. We lived there until I reached the age of seventeen. Our crowd, the boys in the neighborhood, grew up in the tradition that the prisoners up there on the hill, behind those walls, were the State's bad boys. We were cautioned not to approach too near the Reformatory grounds. Something might happen. Yet, nothing could keep us from there on a Saturday afternoon, when the shooting of the cannon announced the usual weekly military drill. The Reformatory band's martial music was impressive and inspiring. We would listen with rapt attention to the commands of the officers and the steady march of the "soldier boys," and never left until, with the bugle call at sunset, the flag was lowered and the day was done. It was our weekly treat.

From a safe distance, I used to watch some of the Reformatory boys work on the front lawns of the institution, or on the farms. They didn't look so dangerous. Nor did they seem unhappy. They joked among themselves and appeared rather neat and clean. I admired, too, the neatly uniformed officers.

It may be that my youthful fancy developed in me a keen desire to become a part of that show. It is more than likely that the urge to wear a uniform prompted me to be among the first to offer myself, at the age of fifteen, for enlistment in the regular United States Army, at the outbreak of the Spanish American War. But they wouldn't have me. Too young, they said. It took me two years to make the grade. In the meantime I developed a sympathetic attitude towards newspaper men. For while attending the Elmira Free Academy, I worked with the Elmira Telegram on Fridays, Saturdays and Sundays. Finally, within two months of eighteen, I joined the Regular Army.

Soldiering in 1901 was a drab affair. Nothing exciting happened in all the three years of my army service. There were no wars, except for a few skirmishes in the Philippine Islands, no strikes and no extraordinary calls for special duty anywhere in the world. I won no medals, but it was great training. One learns precision and is hardened, physically, in the great outdoors that is the soldier's life. If one has imagination, the job of being a soldier can be very satisfying. It was to me. I had plenty of leisure, which I utilized both for physical recreation and for intellectual pur-

13

suits. The former led me to an Army football game in Madison Square Garden and resulted in a casualty— a fractured collar-bone and a dislocated shoulder. I began to ponder about a career. It was probably in one of those inspired moments that I determined to try the civil service examination for reformatory and prison guard. Three months before my discharge from the Army, I took the test.

It was long after I had my discharge, when I was already launched in the insurance business in my home town, Elmira, that the mail brought me the notice of my appointment as a guard. But instead of the Reformatory that had captured my imagination as a youngster, I was directed to report at Clinton Prison at Dannemora, then known as the Siberia of America. Thus did my youthful ambitions lead me far afield from the place of my early enthusiasm.

Friends ridiculed my appointment. "Why don't you wait?" one laughed. "You might get a job as dog catcher, or you might get into the circus as an animal trainer." I had hoped to succeed in the insurance business; the range of my early ambition reached to the presidency of the Company. I was that ambitious. But the call was there and I decided to make the trip to Dannemora to see what it was all about.

I remember well the day of my arrival at Dannemora. I stood upon the dingy platform of the Village railroad station, after a tedious journey. I was the only passenger. The desolate atmosphere, the wildness of the country with dense forests and high mountains on every side, lent no encouragement to my contemplated profession. I felt disheartened. It was a far jump from the busy town of Elmira that I had known

14

for twenty-one years and the rather enticing atmosphere of the Reformatory overlooking it, with its weekly dress parade and fine band, to this dreary little town nestling high up in the mountains. The fact that it was only twenty miles from the Canadian border meant nothing in those days. Volstead had just entered Congress, and had not yet attained national fame. I inquired of the Station Master as to train schedules, intending to take the next train back to Plattsburg and then home. Perhaps I would have resumed my work in the insurance field, or waited for that "dog catcher's" job. The Station Master apparently sensed my trouble. "Nothing doing, son, no train until tomorrow morning. Why don't you go up and look 'em over?" What else could one do?

The prison impressed me no better than the town. It was my first experience within prison walls. It was all very depressing. Clinton Prison was then run, as were all other prisons in the State, on the silent system. My informant, who showed me around the grounds, explained the rules: No talking in shops, or at mess, or during the march to mess or shops; limited rations of tobacco, hardly any recreation and a hundred and one other rules. The striped uniform was then in vogue, except for the first offenders; two stripes for the second, three for the third and subsequent offenders. Incorrigibles, so called, wore four stripes. The latter were supposed to be the toughest men—zebras they were called, signifying their many stripes. They were not allowed to work, and except for short exercise periods, were always locked up. These men, I was told and believed, were bad and had to be handled with an iron hand. But if they violated the rules,

15

there was surely no hope for them. They were beyond all redemption.

Prisoners wore gray uniforms, with caps to match. Little round caps that sat on the crown of their heads. They did not walk with steady swinging gait. They shuffled their feet. They looked toward me and my guide with furtive glances, as though they dared not meet our eyes. There was an air of oppression all over the prison that did not appeal to my young and enthusiastic mind, fresh from the open and care free world. I felt that these men were of another world. Something different from mine. I could sense danger in every corner. Talk about the Army! Wars and battles and strike duty, and Central American revolutions. They didn't compare with this job. I nearly returned the next morning, but being young and filled with the spirit of adventure, I decided to try it out. I was told to report that night for duty.

Rookies were always assigned to the night shift. And so I found myself on the night of March 1, 1905, sitting at the end of the corridor that opened on the third tier of the old cell block, watching intently in the dim light. At intervals I strolled soundlessly along the gallery in soft sneakers, peering into each pitch-dark cell, to make sure that its occupant was there, listening at every cell door for the steady breathing of the man inside, and the raucous snores of others who stirred uneasily on their cots from time to time. Every half hour I made my rounds. "Tread softly and carry a big stick." Thus was I initiated into the prison service of the State of New York.

Rookies in any public service are generally frowned upon by the old timers. I met with the same experience. I was probably the youngest man in the service, and on the day of my arrival a number of the older hands took me aside and whispered things.

"Tough place," said one. "Toughest place in the State. We've got the most dangerous criminals here. You never know what they're up to. So you've got to watch your step. They haven't any respect for the new guards."

"You've got to have eyes in the back of your head," cautioned another, "it's nothing for one of them to hit you on the back of the head when you're not looking."

"Don't trust any of them," a white haired, solemn looking keeper warned me. "Like as not, they'll put a knife into you if they get a notion."

I was too excited to ask them how they had managed to get by during their years of service. But I was rather obstinate in those days, and wasn't particularly afraid of things. The more they harped on the dangers of the job, the more determined I was to stay and find out. I was all keyed up by the time I reported for duty on that first night. I was nervous, but alert.

My assignment was to the West Cell Block, where the third termers were confined. They were regarded as among the most dangerous prisoners. I gazed curiously at the sleeping forms, unable to believe that they were so utterly hopeless. I held a tight grip on my club and felt continuously for the gun at my side, prepared for any emergency. I had been well schooled in the use of arms in my three years in the Army, but the club—well, I didn't know exactly what to do with it. Suddenly, as I passed along the tier, something banged me on the head. I almost died of fright. I gripped the club with both hands ready for service.

For the moment I thought I was being attacked by one of those ruffians, who had somehow left his cell. I stood ready to protect myself as well as to inflict severe punishment on the offender. I felt rather foolish when I discovered that my assailant was only an owl that had flown in through an open window.

I confess that before I joined the prison staff at Clinton Prison, my ideas of prisoners were on a par with those entertained by the average citizen today. I thought that the prisoners were a desperate lot and had to be treated accordingly. I was determined to be hard boiled, to show no quarter and ask for none.

The job of prison keeper in those days was no sinecure. The pay was fifty-five dollars a month; and the hours twelve hours every day in the year, except for two weeks' vacation, which was more than set off by extra duty to fill in for vacation relief. Fourteen hours' duty was a frequent occurrence.

Prisons were then run almost entirely on a political basis. Every keeper, regardless of political affiliation, was forced to pay the dominant party twenty-five dollars as an annual levy to insure his job. When another employee and I refused to contribute, we were declared "out." We daily expected our walking papers, but somehow managed to hold on. I was beginning to think lightly of the job. Nothing to do but make my half-hourly trips along the tier, punch the button to register my tour of duty, and try to keep awake the balance of the time.

Often we had a hard time to keep awake. One night I was roused by a sudden commotion along the corridor leading to my gallery. It seemed to me that hell was breaking loose. Someone trying to get out, I thought.

I jumped from my chair, prepared for any eventuality. "All right, Son," a voice called. It was the night Captain on his tour of inspection. He was a rather kindly soul, who understood the weakness of the flesh, and suspected that the early morning hours were not made for wakefulness, especially among the younger men on watch. He didn't want to catch anyone asleep on the job. He had his peculiar method of warning us of his approach. He'd stub his toes against all the cuspidors in his way, so that they rolled along the floor with enough noise to startle us out of any drowsiness. The racket served its purpose. The Captain never found it necessary to report a man for sleeping on the job. Great fellow, that night Captain! Beloved by all his men. His method may not have been ideal from a disciplinary standpoint. Certainly, as Warden, I could not approve of such informality on my staff. But he was human, and that counted.

I soon discovered that it wasn't always hard to keep awake. Toward midnight of the third night of my service, pandemonium suddenly reigned in my gallery. From the interior of one of those darkened cells, there came forth the strains of the Marseillaise, sung in a good strong voice. And almost simultaneously, there was a shrieking and yelling from every cell on the tier. "Lay down, you . . ." "Pipe it." And a hundred other calls and epithets, demanding silence. But the singing continued, and rose above all the clamor of the other prisoners. I was at the moment at the end of the gallery, my post being separated from the tier by a solid door, with a wicket for watching.

I was dumbfounded for the moment. I grasped my club, felt for my gun, and prepared for trouble. I

19

cannot say my heart didn't beat a little faster. I peeped through the wicket expecting to see—well, I wasn't quite sure. . . . But something unusual anyway. There was no one on the tier but my partner on the watch. A 375-pound officer, naturally slow of motion, with a keen sense of Irish humor and a round face in which two small, beady eyes twinkled merrily. He was standing still and looking placidly on at the turmoil. I took courage and went in to see what it was all about. My fat friend pointed to a cell well along the gallery. I approached the cell door and stared in amazement. A prisoner stood at his cell door, naked, except for a red blanket over his shoulders, cut out like a dress used for monkeys; orange skin on his head, and his face painted with various colors. He was singing at the top of his voice. Over and over again, he sang the Marseillaise, in what I thought was good French. It was the most grotesque thing I had ever seen. He was deaf to all threats. There seemed to be no end to his lung power. We decided to remove him, or there would be no peace that night, either for us, or for the other prisoners on the tier.

My placid partner and I opened the cell door and then our troubles began in earnest. Frenchy yelled and kicked and resisted all efforts to drag him out. But we succeeded finally in lodging him elsewhere for the night, to be dealt with in the morning in the ordinary routine. I was convinced that the man had suddenly become demented. In my young and inexperienced heart, I felt sorry for the fellow. But I was disillusioned by my rotund friend as we were returning to the gallery after depositing the "freak" in a cell far away from the other prisoners.

"Frenchy is a bad egg," he remarked, "and he's very dangerous. Let's look through his cell." What we found gave me my first impression of a prisoner's ingenuity. Hidden in a corner were a number of keys, made to fit several doors of the institution. And in another corner we found a blackjack, a weapon made of sand filled into a sock, an instrument that could be used with effectiveness. I found out more about Frenchy next day. Frenchy Menet, he was called. A hunchback, not over five feet four inches in height, with a face like a weasel and the mind of a jackal. He was doing twenty years for murder, and had been in prison since 1902. He was a real "bad man." Tried twice to escape while awaiting trial; tried again when he reached Sing Sing, and actually broke away from Clinton Prison. He was recaptured and given an additional term of three years.

No one could understand how he was able to fashion those keys. They were made of wood, and fitted snugly into the locks for which they were intended. Nor could they understand how he managed to smuggle that blackjack into his cell, until it was recalled that it was done during recreation periods while walking or drilling in the prison courtyard.

He had a way of stooping while walking. No one paid any attention to his stoop, and the occasional grains of sand which he picked up. But he saved every one of those particles. Took them in with him and deposited them in his sock. It took him a long time to fill that sock. He worked patiently until, on the night of his exhibition, he had a weapon that could, if given the opportunity, accomplish the desired purpose. Had any one of us entered his cell alone that night, he would very likely have been clouted. Frenchy would have jumped over the limp body to the open gallery. It might have led to serious consequences.

Frenchy was an ingenious sort of fellow. When he arrived at Clinton Prison he was searched carefully. He was passed as O. K. Yet, all the while, he had six small saws concealed on his body. Only by a fortunate circumstance were they discovered. A few days after his parole in 1924, he called at the Dutchess County Jail to see a prisoner. His astuteness had not left him. On a hunch, he was stripped and searched. A saw was found concealed in the sole of his shoe.

Generally, however, the nights at Clinton Prison were dull and dreary. I made up my mind to change to day duty. But I was still the rookie, and the thing didn't seem hopeful. I began to look around. The only one who could make the change was the Principal Keeper's assistant. And he was hard boiled to the officers as well as to prisoners. One didn't dare just ask him for anything. "No," was his favorite answer. He was a little fellow, weighed about 110 pounds, but mentally hard as nails. He had one ·weakness. His daughters. His name—it doesn't really matter. Old Tommy Ahearn is near enough.

Dannemora is a village today. In 1905, it was just a cluster of houses. Everyone in sight worked either in the prison or for the prison. All prison keepers lived in the village. It was more like a big family. Gossip and scandal occupied both the prison staff and inmates. Everybody knew everything about everybody. I soon learned about Tommy's daughters. A small town is not the best place to bring up daughters. Friendships are scarce and possibilities limited. One day I saw one of the officers, who worked with me, walking down the village main street with a woman companion. He winked at me as I passed him. I thought nothing of it until the following week, when that officer was taken off night duty and transferred to the day shift. I made diplomatic inquiries and learned that the young lady he had escorted the day I met him was none other than the Assistant Principal Keeper's daughter. It was brought home to me that the only way to gain the old man's favor was to get acquainted with one of his daughters. Unfortunately neither inclination nor circumstances warranted such indulgence on my part. But I made a close friend of that swain. He married the girl and I made the day shift.

I did not begin to get my feel of prison life and routine until I was transferred to day duty. Instead of the endless vigil over men whose faces I never saw, and whose sleeping forms were without special significance as individuals, I began to see life; to witness the workings of minds and intellects. I saw men at work. What had been to me shadows and inert shapes, now assumed purpose and animation. The hang-dog look of the newly admitted prisoner, the sullen mien of the old timer, the eager step of the man bound for the world outside, home and kin and things—all these aroused new sensations. They were the aspects of prison life to which I had given but little thought. Somehow they were out of tune with everything that had gone before. In those days, stolidity was the order of the day in all prisons. The official force went about their duties with humdrum monotony. The prisoners did their tasks with dull indifference. The result was an oppressiveness that hung low and dense over the entire prison.

Hate, distrust and malice seemed to exude from every eye. Prisoners were allowed very little recreation outside their cells. Only a few moments of marching in the courtyard. Just aimless treading across a barren waste of ground surrounded by high walls. Men talked in whispers, if they talked at all, and their every movement was under the watchful eye of keepers, who held their clubs ready for instant use.

Under these circumstances, it is not surprising that officers were irritable and nervous. On my first day with the day shift, I was given yard duty. My nerves were taut. The atmosphere seemed to have gripped me, as it probably did every new officer. I had been instructed to be on the alert and watch for trouble. "Don't hesitate to use your club," I was told time and time again by the older guards. "And when you bring it down, strike hard, otherwise you might get the worst of it." I looked for trouble. I found it soon.

I noticed, during one of my patrol rambles, a crowd of men who seemed anxious to screen something in their midst. It looked like a fist fight to me, and I made my way warily toward them. The men paid little attention to me; they were intent on what was going on. No one shouted. It was a silent, desperate battle—a test of brute strength. I knew my duty. I was pushing my way toward the combatants, when I saw a homemade knife raised aloft over the heads of the fighters. I didn't hesitate a moment, lifted my club high and brought it down hard on the head of—the man who was being attacked. I struck the wrong man. The fellow who wielded the knife wasn't touched. Luckily the stricken prisoner pulled through. But I learned something from the experience. I began to understand that

24

in handling men one must have a discerning eye. The punishment cannot be indiscriminate. That the club, though a traditional weapon behind the walls, may do as much harm as good. The rules of the prison compelled me to carry the club as a measure of protection, but I never made use of it again. It was my emblem of authority, but somehow I never had to bang it after that. I was something of a Bible student in those days. And I remembered the anger that was God's, when Moses lashed at the well-spring out there in the desert instead of "talking" to it, as directed from On High. I, too, decided to use words instead of my club. I sought every opportunity to get acquainted with my charges. But I still retained my early impressions of the viciousness of prisoners. Nor were they modified when I was assigned to the company in the stone shed. The men in that company were a tough looking bunch, probably the worst in the whole prison. Those days were before psychiatry and psychology in prison work. Little or no attention was given to a prisoner's mental condition, except in cases of definite insanity. There were no such things as borderline cases, subnormal or any of the other many classifications of present day mental clinics. A man was either crazy, demented, or he was sane.

Under the leadership of the late Dr. J. B. Ransome, the Hospital for the Tubercular, at Dannemora, had become one of the finest institutions of its kind in the country. Close by was also the State Hospital for the Criminal Insane. All hopeless mental cases were confined in that hospital. The prisoner who was merely the mental defective was permitted to remain in the various institutions to mingle with the normal men. Prisons were hard put to solve this intermingling of all grades of mentalities. Quite often men with mental ages of 6 or 7 were assigned to tasks that required the mentalities of 12 or over. The result was anything but satisfactory to ordinary prison administration. It led to frequent disorders in many institutions. Clinton Prison attempted to solve this problem by assembling all the prison "bugs" in one company—that of the stone shed. And in order to train new officers—rookies—in the service, and to test their metal, the company in the stone shed was the one to which these newcomers were invariably assigned. I was no exception. Old Tommy was very nice about it.

"All you've got to do is to hold your head," he said to me unsmilingly, "they are all really harmless. Just a bunch of kids—not in years, but here." And he tapped his forehead. "Whatever happens, don't forget you've got your club."

It was the club I had decided never to use again. But it gave me a sense of security. I had heard a lot about this gang of "nuts." But no one had actually told me with what I would have to contend. I soon found out.

Immediately upon my arrival at the stone shed, a shower of rocks of all sizes came flying my way. I stood my ground and ignored the attack, really too dazed and shocked to do anything else. I found out about it later. That was how they greeted a new officer. If he stood the gaff, he was marked O. K. If he showed resentment, and ducked too quickly, or tried to threaten men with his club, he was treated accordingly. Apparently they marked me right, for I never had any further trouble with that crowd. But I did with others.

Prisons in those days were generally the playthings of politicians. Wardens came and went with every

change of administration. Prison policies had no definite basis. One political boss advocated the harshest
kind of discipline and the most rigorous routine, while
the other insisted upon lenient rules and regulations.
It was all a matter of individual preference. Wardens'
and Superintendents' reports are alike in pointing out
the beneficent results of their pet theories of administration. This shuttlecock policy from without, found
its reflection in the attitude of the officers within. There
was little cooperation among the keepers and their
superiors. As a result there were cliques who spied on
one another. The Warden had his special stool pigeons,
the Principal Keeper his favorites who kept him well
informed, and his assistant had his spies. One incident
brought this state of affairs squarely before me.

I was then stationed in the State Shop, where all
clothing was made for the inmates. I gave a task to a
fellow by the name of Frank. He was a suave, oily sort
of an individual, ingratiating, and, as I found out later,
a double crosser. He looked rather young to be a third
offender, but he wore the three stripes.

Frank refused to do his task—a pair of felt soled
shoes. "I'll have to take you to the P. K.'s office," I
told him. He seemed quite willing to go. I did not then
understand that he really wanted to leave the shop. I
found out later that he was the Principal Keeper's
man. Apparently he had a message to deliver to his
"master." Routine orders demanded that I take him
to the office with a report of his misconduct. The Principal Keeper directed me to put him back to work. I refused to do it; and laid the matter before the Warden,
who insisted that the fellow be punished. Well, the
prisoner was not allowed to remain in the shop. I had

apparently been sustained. But the next day I was told to report elsewhere for duty. I was put on relief, doing odd jobs around the prison. It was my duty to accompany prisoners who were assigned to special tasks.

It was on one of these jobs that I got my first jolt in prison psychology. I was with a plumber, a murderer, who had been commuted from the chair. He crawled underneath the flooring of the hospital building to repair some pipes, and I crawled in after him. It was a dark spot. He had an electric torch, and I had my gun. Suddenly, while resting after a particularly hard tug with his Stillson wrench, he turned to me and asked with a smile, "Got your gun with you?" I answered with a nervous, "Yes, of course." "What would you do," he asked, "if I were to take it from you?" I glanced at the tools he held in his hands. He sensed my excitement. "Don't worry," he laughed, "I'm not that kind of a guy. You're a square shooter yourself. I'm doing time and all I want is to get through with it in peace." And when I didn't answer, he added: "But they're not all like that. You're a new man. Take a tip from me, and don't trust any of 'em too much."

Not long after that, I had occasion to remember his advice. There was a big fellow known as Yegg Foster. He tried to make himself particularly agreeable to me. He was a fourth offender, and a very powerful man. I noticed him in the crowd because he had one finger missing. He was the shoemaker in the State Shop. He was world-wise and stir (prison) wise; the smart-Aleck type who thinks he can break down any other fellow, especially the new officer who hails from the country. The city-bred guard is often spoiled before he gets on the job. In larger communities, people seem to look

28

upon graft, large or small, as a part of the game. But I was country bred. Yegg Foster would always give me a pleasant greeting which I would return. One day he brought me a pair of sneakers. "Wear 'em," he said, "I made 'em especially for you." I accepted them and thanked him for his thoughtfulness. I had no idea at the time that they were made crookedly and against the rules. Several days later, he approached me with a smirk and a smile.

"My wife is very ill," he confided, "and this is an important letter that I would like you to send out to her."

"Why can't you send it through the regular channels?" I asked him.

He had his ready answer. "There is something very private in this letter, that I wouldn't want anyone to read."

I refused absolutely. His face flushed with anger.

"Don't be so high and mighty, Mister," he said. "Want me to tell about those crooked sneakers I made for you?" I thought quickly and asked him to give me the letter and I would try to attend to it. The next morning I turned both the letter and the sneakers over to the Principal Keeper. I remembered the advice of the prisoner-plumber, the murderer.

I floundered along during the next few months encouraged now and then by some human response from a prisoner, disappointed and discouraged more frequently by the trickery and sheer cussedness of others.

For one member of the official family in the Clinton Prison of those days, Dr. Walter N. Thayer, Jr., who was then the Assistant Physician, I have retained an enduring and continuing respect. Always the courteous gentleman with the prisoners, sympathetic and patient. Popular with officers and men. He was the serious student of prison problems. The honors that came to him in later years, culminating in his appointment as Commissioner of Correction of the State of New York, were well deserved.

There was one prisoner in that motley lot, for whom I have ever retained a feeling of thankfulness and regard. Old Chappleau, we called him. He was a first termer and the first man sentenced to die in the electric chair, whose sentence was later commuted to life imprisonment. He had been in prison sixteen years. He was of French extraction, slow of speech, pure white hair, with the saddest eyes I have ever seen. He was the bookkeeper of the State Shop, and a fine penman. He rarely mingled with the other prisoners in his shop, who were mostly third termers.

Joseph Chappleau was fifty-five years old when I first knew him. He had killed a neighbor, Tabor, in a quarrel over some cows that were poisoned. Tabor, it was alleged, had hurled sarcastic comment at Chappleau who threatened to "shut his mouth forever." This was later accomplished on the Tom Miller road just outside of Plattsburg. Witnesses expressed the view that Chappleau was of good character and had lived with his family on a rented farm for ten years. According to the records Chappleau was a college graduate (though he never mentioned it), temperate and had no previous convictions. Rumor had it that the motive of the murder was not the poisoning of the cows but an affair of a sort between Tabor and Chappleau's wife. Old Chappleau never spoke of it. He was a gentle soul, respected alike by officers and fellow prisoners. Death finally released him from the burdens of life in 1911. He died in the prison hospital at Clinton.

I owe a great deal to Old Chappleau. He knew more about finding one's prison oats than any officer I met in those days. We are often cautioned that familiarity breeds contempt. If familiarity really breeds contempt, there is generally a good reason for that contempt. My association with this aged prisoner, his philosophic point of view, the interest he took in the new rookie and his willingness to help, were thought-provoking. I began to realize that stripes alone, whether they designate the first or fourth offender, were not the true measure of a man's emotions. The prison garb proclaimed this man a misfit. No provision had been made to indicate a change of heart and vision that came with the years. Any satisfaction that I have been able to achieve through the twenty-seven years of my prison service, I owe, strangely enough, to two lowly individuals—both prisoners. In their days one was probably a confirmed criminal, the other a victim of fate. Yet I found something in the hearts of those two men that has carried me through every circumstance and enabled me to regard my wards as men with human instincts, responsive to sober influence. One of these men was the life termer at Clinton Prison, my prisoner of rookie days, and the other was no less a personage than Mike the Rat Catcher, whom I first knew as a prisoner at the New York City Reformatory on Hart's Island.

CHAPTER 2: A PRISON
WITHOUT WALLS

My apprenticeship in the service ended on March 1st, 1906, when I left Clinton Prison for Auburn. I came down from the mountains in the wilds of the North Woods, fully convinced of my capabilities as a prison keeper. The urge was twofold. I had been married in Elmira. Home and hearth called me. And the pay was higher—$61.00 a month instead of $55.00. The extra six dollars had considerable purchasing power in those days.

Old Copper John greeted me as I approached the prison gate at Auburn. He was a dignified gentleman, patient and all seeing. He stood in the belfry over the entrance of the prison, watched men as they entered and bade them good-bye as they left. Copper John was a mute witness to many human tragedies and, I believe, also enjoyed life's comics. Copper John was not concerned with what went on behind him. He stood with his back toward the prison. I fancy he gazed upon the faces of the prisoners as they entered. "Good riddance," his metal tongue would say, "get thee behind me and be damned." It seemed to me he begrudged the release of any prisoners. "I'll be seeing you again," was the message that radiated from his iron head. He did, all too often.

I shall never forget my first impression of that silent figure. I could have sworn he sneered at me. There was cynicism in that cold face.

"Keeper of men," he seemed to say, "or slave driver —which are you? Hard boiled or sentimental? This is the cradle of the present prison system of America. The famous Auburn System. Supposed to make men over. New minds for old; clean thoughts for filth. It repairs visions and hearts. It's the latest thing in directing human behavior. The cure-all for crime and delinquency. Come in," I imagined his scornful gesture, "and do your part."

I tried it for six months. I worked companies, locked and unlocked them. I watched prisoners at work, marched them in squad formation several times a week for recreation. Mr. George W. Benham was then the Warden. He was a strict disciplinarian, but a capable administrator. Later he served with distinction as Parole Commissioner. But Warden Benham could do little with the penal policy then in vogue.

The underlying principle of the so-called Auburn System was silence. The prison in those days was actually the city of silent men. The sign language prevailed. During mess the prisoner used his fingers. If a second helping of bread was wanted he would raise one finger; an extra tin of soup, two fingers; another plate of potatoes, three fingers. In the shop, for an interview with the keeper in charge, two fingers; for permission to leave his task for a few moments, one finger.

There was no analyzing of prisoners' minds. They were either sane or definitely insane. For the insane there was the State Hospital for the Criminal Insane at Dannemora. All the others were retained in Auburn and put to work. Dark cells, bread and water diets and other repressive measures helped along. There was little opportunity for contact with the outside world; infrequent visitation; limited correspondence.

Obedience to prison rules was forced into the hearts and minds of prisoners by ever present clubs and guns. All officers were required to carry revolvers while on duty within the prison. A regulation long since discarded. Silence was the symbol of authority. It was the hush of repression. It countenanced no smile, no laugh. Where men cannot laugh, they frown. The frown invariably deepened into a scowl. Features became frozen, metallic like Copper John's. And nerves were frayed. I was made painfully aware of this one night during a terrific electric storm. Lightning jabbed into every cell; sharp and incessant thunder shook the very foundations of the cell blocks. The whole prison was in a sudden uproar. Half the population prayed, the others cursed. God or the devil. There was no middle path.

Praying or cursing! Thus the prisoner spent his days. Praying for relief. Cursing his hard luck. He had practically no recreation period. All he saw of the sun was in the few minutes it took to pass from one shop to another. The brain sought forced outlets. Some succeeded, most did not. "Joe, the Bug," was among the more fortunate ones. He had been in prison twenty-seven years. He gradually developed a keen interest in baseball, although he had never seen a ball game. His favorite team was the Syracuse Stars. His one absorbing pastime was to watch the scores of his team. If they lost, he would moan about his hard luck. When they won, he would be the radiant Joe. This interest helped him to maintain his sanity. Not all prisoners were so fortunate.

One afternoon as I was leaving the prison after my twelve hours' duty, I turned to look up at my old friend Copper John. There he was, still intent upon his vigil. The frozen sneer haunted me all the way home. "It's a hopeless task, you have," he seemed to say. "All negative. No constructive planning. The Auburn System. Bah! It's a makeshift. I don't know what's going on in there behind my back. But I see men as they leave. They have forgotten how to laugh. Their smile is forced, wooden. They have lost their steady, swinging gait. They shuffle along, lock-stepping their way back to life. They'll never catch up. You're wasting your time. You are still young. Why not try elsewhere?"

I did. A few months after I took the civil service examination for Reformatory Guard, I received my appointment at Elmira. I reported for duty on a Saturday afternoon, the day of the dress parade, the martial music, the sharp, military commands, and the steady soldierly march of the prisoners that I had admired so much as a youngster.

I entered the service at the New York State Reformatory at Elmira in October, 1906. The Superintendent was a fine gentleman and a genial soul, Colonel Joseph F. Scott. Uncle Joe the boys called him. The Elmira Reformatory was world famous. It had been well publicized. People from all over the world came to study its methods of operation and, where possible, to copy them. Visitors saw prisoners during the semiweekly dress parade. There was no striped uniform, no shaven heads, no lock-step, such as prevailed in adult prisons of that day. But there were things they didn't see. They did not sense the spirit of Zebulon R. Brockway hovering over that institution.

Prison administration owes The Prison Association of New York and Zebulon R. Brockway, the founder of the reformatory idea in America, a debt of gratitude for one far-reaching innovation. Both labored long and unceasingly for the adoption of the indeterminate sentence. To permit the prisoner to earn his early discharge by good conduct and diligent labor was in itself a worth-while objective. In outward physical aspects, Brockway adopted the traditional policies of established prisons. It must be remembered, however, that the Elmira Reformatory was established in 1876, at a time when repression and physical suppression were the last words in penal administration. Probably Brockway did not dare go too far. However that may have been, he brought with him into a Reformatory for youths many of the essential features of adult prisons. The ages of admission were from 16 to 30. As an English authority remarked later, the trouble with the American Reformatory idea was that it made youths out of adults and adults out of youths, subjecting both to all the odious and cruel oppressions that prevailed in prisons for men steeped in crime and viciousness.

The essentials of the Reformatory, as advocated by Brockway, included the following:

1. The indeterminate sentence.
2. A marking system and accounting with each prisoner, which should include wage-earning necessity.
3. Trades School, so that each prisoner-pupil shall learn and practice the occupation best suited for him to follow on his discharge.
4. School of letters, together with a supplemental lecture course.

5. Military organization, training and drill, embracing every inmate not disqualified.
6. Physical culture and gymnasium.
7. Manual training proper, with tool work, for use to aid recovery from discovered specific physical defects.
8. A well constructed library and religious instruction.

Mr. Brockway enumerated the principles of good reformatory administration:

A—Secure custody.
B—No outside influence or interference.
C—Resident executive officer with wide discretionary powers.
D—Subordinates responsible only to such executive.
E—Entire life of prisoner should be directed; all waking hours and activities, bodily and mental habits, also his emotional exercises.

This is, of course, an admirable program. I was familiar with it in theory before I joined the staff at Elmira. The difficulty was in its application. The atmosphere of the Reformatory had assumed too much of the dress parade. After a particularly strenuous military drill the company commander of an army unit permits a period of "at ease." It is physically and mentally impossible to drill continuously without that moment of relaxation. Brockway's principles permitted no "at ease" for the prisoners. You cannot straight-jacket good habits into men. Fear alone will never develop the desire for decent living. They had at Elmira the important elements that had to do with reform, but the setting was bad. Elmira was nominally a reformatory; actually it was a prison with more drastic rules of punishment and obedience. No encouragement was given to develop restraint born of honor and acknowledged responsibility. England adopted the Elmira Reformatory idea, but improved it with the Borstal plan which permits the prisoner a measure of self-development.

Brockway's iron-fisted administration led to many abuses which in time attracted public attention and popular criticism. The disclosures of brutality within the Reformatory were made the basis of a determined campaign by *The New York World* which finally forced his resignation in 1900. When I came to Elmira in 1906, Colonel Joseph F. Scott (Uncle Joe) was in charge. His administration was more liberal and understanding. Dr. Frank L. Christian, the present capable Superintendent, was then the head institutional physician.

That these repressive measures were not necessary is obvious from the report of the Reformatory in 1916, which explains that "talking at meals is now permitted, and in the shops, at the discretion of the officers in charge." "The old days of severe and repressive forms of punishment," it continues, "have passed, and for six years it has not been necessary to confine a prisoner in a dark cell or limit his diet." All this without disturbing the routine of the institution. From the date of its inception until Christmas of 1930, smoking, or the use of tobacco in any form, was prohibited by law. Yet the introduction of smoking and tobacco has not demoralized the organization or administration. It simply permitted legally what before was practiced clandestinely.

In those days I was a user of what was called rope tobacco. I kept it usually in my civilian clothes. On my arrival at the Reformatory, I would change into my uniform and leave my civilian clothes in my locker. Invariably in the evening my pockets would be picked clean. Every possible crumb of tobacco had been removed. A handful of tobacco was worth more to the boys than a handful of good old American currency.

The official staff at Elmira was, as a whole, honest and reliable. But sometimes the heart would get the better of a man's good judgment. I remember the case of the Jewish Rabbi, very popular and respected by both officers and prisoners. He was an eloquent preacher and his services were attended by men of all denominations. One day my chief clerk, a prisoner, was found in possession of a swig of rope chewing-tobacco. He was locked up and placed in the guard house. It was a serious offence. The important thing was to discover how he got it. We had the shock of our lives when we learned that our popular and gentlemanly Rabbi was the guilty party. There was no malicious intent. We realized that it was the victory of heart over mind. An act born of pity. No harm came of it.

Where force is the order of the day, men will resort to it frequently as the easiest way out. Strict disciplinary measures at the Reformatory at times led to physical encounters between officers and their men. I succumbed to the urge on several occasions. Once during the drilling of the "Awkward Squad" a prisoner was cautioned by his squad leader, another prisoner, about his appearance. It led to a fist fight. I stopped them and in order to properly impress the offender, I landed him one on the chin and knocked him out. We worked on him and he was as good as ever in a few moments. The fellow didn't resent my act. He took it for granted.

At the risk of telling tales out of school, I cannot help relating the story about the introduction of base-ball in the Reformatory. It was due directly to a violation of the rules by no less a person than Dr. Frank L. Christian, then Assistant "Super," and me, as Chief Guard. We were both quite young at the time and occasionally enjoyed a game of ball. We were thus employed one afternoon when several prisoners passed by and looked on with what, I felt, were longing eyes. We invited them to join us, and soon a regular game was on foot. Dr. Christian and I had a good time. The boys had a treat. The incident inspired all of us. A few days later the Assistant Superintendent and several of the officers got together and decided to organize several teams in the various shops. And thus was born a new spirit of outdoor recreation.

It was a violation of the rules but perfectly justifiable under the circumstances.

Publicists in penologic work are accustomed to point to the many reformatory "graduates" who find their way to prison in adult life. They are, it is claimed, the failures of the reformatory. In recent years we have been reminded rather forcibly of notorious criminals, as for instance, Gerald Chapman, and others who were all inmates of the Reformatory in my days. As I remember them they were all ordinary prisoners. They did not then display any particular viciousness. They became later in life the subjects of newspaper propaganda. Exaggerated accounts of their escapades turned them into headliners. They grew in their self-appraisement. They began to see themselves as others saw them in the large, black type of the sensational press. Notorious criminals are often the by-products of a sensational press that could hardly maintain itself without them.

Under the superintendency of Colonel Scott, the discipline of the Reformatory was liberalized to some extent. Dr. Frank L. Christian, the present Superintendent, does not permit corporal punishment of any kind. With the passing of Brockway, the iron rule was relaxed. Subsequent administrations have been doing their best with the material on hand to create a spirit of helpfulness between official and inmate. That they have not been able to accomplish as much as they desired, is due to faulty administrative powers and to inadequate and antiquated equipment. The tendency today is for wider discretion for administrators, with more intimate contact between the officials, staff and the prisoner population. I am firmly convinced that as this spirit of helpfulness and cooperation becomes more evident and is more widely invoked, we shall make our reformatories a more effective influence in shaping human behavior. They will then assume their proper places in the scheme of crime abatement.

I spent eight years at Elmira. They were happy years. But I was troubled in mind and struggled continuously to find the answer to the perplexing problems of Frenchy Menet, Old Chappleau and the groups of which they were outstanding types. Copper John's sneers bothered me. Was there a sensible, a human way of handling these men? Was there one method for Frenchy Menet and another for Old Chappleau? Or, having sinned against society, both equally guilty before the law, were they to continue on an equal footing, live alike, think alike, work alike—in fact, be subjected to exactly the same measure of punishment and reformation?

I had heard about the Marquis Becarria of Milan, the father of modern penology. I took him home and studied him diligently. He lived in the Eighteenth Century when men were men, criminals slaves, and prisons antechambers to the gallows. "We see the same crimes," he said of conditions in his day (a condition remarkably persistent through the ages), "punished in a different manner at different times in the same tribunals."

"The intent of punishment," I read, "is not to torment a sensible being, nor to undo a crime already committed . . . but . . . to prevent the criminal from doing further injury to society and to prevent others from committing the like offence." I had read of the researches of Lombroso who introduced something new in the penology of the Nineteenth Century. "If one walks through a prison," he said, "he will certainly see something common in most of the faces that is characteristic, however unable he may be to describe it." He approved, with emphasis, the old Tuscan proverb, "Be suspicious of him who laughs." Both these men were pioneers in the human sciences. Both were recognized authorities. Each had his disciples in the broadening field of penology. Yet I had already learned from experience that Beccaria's lesson went unheeded. For our prisons did not "prevent" the prisoner "from doing injury to society," and what was of greater moment, did not "prevent others from committing the like offence."

I did my best to follow Lombroso's thought. Some characteristic "common" to most prisoners? Assuredly

42

it was the look of distress, of hopelessness, of futility, of physical endurance, of repression and submergence of self. Prisons obeyed Lombroso literally. "Be suspicious of him who laughs," was a cardinal principle in all penal and reformatory institutions in the early years of my service. Mute communities. Silence. No wonder Copper John sneered.

In my browsings, I discovered John Howard who lived in the Eighteenth Century. Probably more than any other man, he influenced penal administrations in England, and later in America, toward betterment of physical conditions. He enunciated a new policy for improving prisons. "Make men diligent," he said, "and they will be honest." One cannot make men diligent en masse. Nor can honesty be impressed from without. John Howard and Elizabeth Frey called attention to prisoners' physical deterioration. My studies, supplemented by contact with prisoners, led me toward the school of progressive thought on penal affairs. I began to understand that each prisoner behind prison walls was a distinct problem. No two men were led to crime by exactly the same urge. So, also, no two criminals could be swayed from crime by exactly the same procedure. At the basis of all corrective influences was the sense of individual responsibility. The prisoner was a continuing social unit and must be impressed by society's continued interest.

I was ambitious, longed for an opportunity to put my theories to the test. But in those days no guard had ever risen to a wardenship or superintendency. Politics saw to that. I would have to find a more direct way. I decided to enlarge upon my studies.

In 1912, though married, with a family of two

children, I obtained a leave of absence from the Elmira Reformatory and enrolled as a student in the New York School of Social Work. I was soon confirmed in my ideals. Contact and study with enlightened men and women, such as Dr. Katherine B. Davis, Burdette G. Lewis, Dr. Orlando F. Lewis and others helped to a practical understanding of the policy of guiding rather than driving men to normal thinking and living. I returned to Elmira determined to find a niche for myself as a practical penologist. Through the recommendation of some of my teachers and associates, I received a tentative offer of the Wardenship of the Massachusetts State Prison at Charlestown. It was not confirmed. I was too young, I was informed. I later learned that I did not get the appointment because I was a carpet bagger from outside the State of Massachusetts and, naturally, without political backing. The best they could do for me was the deputy wardenship which I refused. I wanted a free hand. I continued on as Chief Guard at the Reformatory. I was never much of a politician, but I was satisfied that with advancing years and graying hairs, opportunity would somehow knock at my door. I wouldn't be caught napping.

My chance came on March 9, 1915, when the following telegram was delivered to me at Elmira:

"Can you come to New York immediately to discuss possibility of accepting position overseer of New York City Reformatory for male misdemeanants. Telegraph earliest possible date.

(Signed)   KATHERINE B. DAVIS,
*Commissioner of Correction
of the City of New York.*"

Within a week I was installed on Hart's Island where the New York City Reformatory was then located. There I met Mike the Rat Catcher, another lowly subject who helped to shape my thoughts and policies in penal administration.

If Mike the Rat Catcher hadn't started the riot at Hart's Island back in March, 1915, I would not have been invited by Dr. Katherine B. Davis, then Commissioner of Correction of the City of New York, to become the Superintendent of the New York City Reformatory. Whether I would have become the Warden of Sing Sing Prison later is something that only the gods can answer. The disturbance at Hart's Island was not a riot as measured by modern prison standards. There was no gun shooting, no knifings, no attempts to escape. All the boys did was to throw dishes at the keepers and yell. And Mike was the leader of the mob.

I arrived at the Reformatory in the midst of the excitement. Two things fixed themselves particularly on my mind as I reached the Island. On one side of the Reformatory was the Penitentiary where all kinds of drunks, narcotic addicts and hoodlums were housed, the very lowest in the social scale; on the other side was Potter's Field where whole boatloads of the City's unknown dead were buried daily. The Reformatory, where the boys were thought to be influenced for good, stood in the center. I remember thinking about that setting. Wondering how many boys were being trained for either or both of the neighboring institutions; with loss of identity for the living in one and obscurity for the dead in the other. I was not permitted to ponder long on the object lesson for conditions at the Reformatory were in bad shape and I had to face the practical problem of setting my new house in order. The first thing they showed me was the jail. You could call it either guard house, jail, cooler, detention or meditation room, depending upon the view one took of it or the nature of one's audience. I didn't care about the name; what I found there was more important. Twenty-seven young prisoners were locked up in seventeen cells, mostly two in a cell. And when the keys were turned on them their cell doors did not open again. These boys had apparently led the dish-throwing demonstration and were being punished. In those cells they ate and slept and performed their natural functions. Also their unnatural functions. Mike was among them. That night I inspected the dormitories. The population was divided into four division ratings according to age, about ninety in each dormitory.

The boys were marched into their dormitories at about five in the afternoon and sat on their beds until nine. All they were permitted to do was to sing hymns. If any one as much as turned his head or whispered to his neighbors the officer in charge compelled him to kneel down on the cold, concrete floor for two hours. He was supposed to spend his time in prayer. Whether he prayed or swore was something they never could find out.

My first thought was to bring order into the Institution, and restore peace among our youthful prisoners. I was told about Mike, looked him up and talked with him in the "cooler." I found the notorious "bad boy" to be a slim, narrow chested, wan looking youngster, of medium height. His eyes impressed me. They were bright and looked straight at you.

Mike began his career of delinquency at the age of

46

five. His father was French and his mother Italian. Both died while he was still an infant, and he was placed in an institution. He became institutionalized and drifted to the Protectory, then to the House of Refuge, and finally to the Reformatory where he became a leader because of his long record. His was a title of distinction. He had an uncanny faculty of catching rats without the aid of a trap. That made him a big shot with the gang. He always had three or four rats as his particular pets. Popular imagination invariably responds to eccentricity. With us, in these democratic United States, the eccentric often finds himself singled out for public homage. Mike's love for rats made him the hero of the Reformatory. With suitable advertisement he might, in later years, have landed in Congress or some other public office. There is often no accounting for the "people's" acclaim.

I had Mike examined and was advised that he was a mental defective and should be under permanent custodial care. Nevertheless, after a frank talk with the boy, I released him and his henchmen from the cooler and restored all privileges to them, first exacting their promise to behave and act like men. Instead of twiddling their fingers in the dormitories from five until nine, I permitted them to play games, read and otherwise enjoy themselves under the supervision of uniformed officers. I saw to it that their dishes were used for appetizing food rather than as missiles. I had no further trouble with Mike and his cohorts during the year that we stayed on the Island. My troubles were rather with my official staff who regarded me as a carpet bagger and did not take kindly to my appointment.

On a Sunday afternoon during a ball game, I was amazed and shocked to see a number of inmates drop to the ground as if struck by a bolt of lightning. We sent for our institutional physician and carried the stricken prisoners to the hospital. Our facilities were overtaxed, so that it became necessary to place them on the floor on mattresses. The doctor thought they should be sent to the Penitentiary hospital on Black-well's Island, but I regarded it as our problem and insisted that we assume the necessary responsibility.

Before all the boys could be taken to the hospital, representatives of the District Attorney's office were on the Island to investigate. Fortunately for me, on my second day in charge, I discovered that the drug room was accessible and insecure. I immediately removed all habit forming narcotics (cocaine, morphine, heroin) to a large steel safe in my private office, but poisons such as apo-morphine, belladonna, and the like were left.

We found that the drug room had been burglarized and almost ninety boys poisoned. Luckily the large doses they took acted as an emetic, which fact undoubtedly saved their lives. A grand jury investigation was instituted and I was called before them. On my way there, I met an ex-prisoner who had served time at Elmira Reformatory. He informed me that I was being "framed" by my own officers who resented an out-of-town man being in charge. Whether or not that was true, I am unable to state, but my respect for Grand Juries was strengthened by the helpful attitude of cooperation shown me. At the end of a year practically my entire official personnel was changed, mostly by transfer. Only two of the old officers remained.

Finally the New York City authorities agreed that

a Reformatory for boys should not have a pauper's graveyard and a home for derelicts as neighbors, and it was decided to remove the Institution to more satisfactory surroundings. Land had been purchased in Orange County for the erection of a new Reformatory. About a year after I became the Superintendent, we were ready to move our entire population to New Hampton where the new Institution was to be built partly with prison labor.

I shall never forget that trip to New Hampton. Five hundred and forty-seven boys and young men, all prisoners, tough lads from the East and West Sides of the great metropolis, accustomed to locks and keys and bars, were told to pack up their belongings and prepare for the journey. We had only our usual staff of officers, all unarmed and most of them newly appointed. The boys were in holiday mood as they boarded the City boat "Correction" that was to take them to the train in Jersey City. Some of the boys played their musical instruments; the Institution Band provided popular airs, and all our passengers joined in song. Someone improvised a special tune. The words were not entirely elegant. It ran something like this:

> "Where the old Correction flows,
> That's where all the tough guys goes;
> Where the tripping is great
> And you never come too late,
> But march right up in twos;
> And there's no returning
> To the hearts that's yearning;
> Where the old Correction flows."

"It was a disappointing trip," wrote a newspaper man who accompanied us, "for the reporter who had received advice of a 'human nature expert' before starting." The only genuine dramatics he observed were that "the nameless and restless dead of Potter's Field had no one to haunt last night. Hart's Island has been abandoned to them by the living." What he saw was a train load of happy boys, keenly anticipating the joys of life in the country and the fact that they were participating in the building of something new. All the boys had complete outfits and on the train there was one guard to every car—and he was unarmed. The route was through New Jersey. Had any of our prisoners escaped from the train we could not have taken them back legally. None of these prisoners had been convicted of a felony, and none, therefore, was subject to extradition. To get them back by force would have subjected us to a penalty, with a possible charge of kidnapping.

The point of debarkation was at New Hampton, New York. The train was emptied to the flare of the band. A poor country horse was scared by the noise. Perhaps he wasn't altogether pleased with the music and he started to bolt. "Funny," said one of our officers, "that a horse should be the only thing to start to run away."

We arrived in a sea of mud; some of the boys lost their boots in the soft, oozy soil. After hiking a mile to the camp the first thing we did was to set up canteens to feed the tired travelers. Those fellows were hungry and they surely did eat. There were no left-overs. All you could hear were remarks about the food. "Say, dat's sure some stew. And dat tea. W'y you can taste the tea in it. Whacher know about dat?"

That night all the prisoners slept in the makeshift

bunk houses. To most of them, brought up, "dragged up" is the better term, on the lower East Side and the Tenth Avenue district of the West Side, it was quite a lark. Not all of them realized that we were in for a lot of hard work. And though there were no bars, or walls, or cells, there were also no electric lights, water or drainage, or any of the other comforts to which they were accustomed. If they wanted to drink they had to haul barrels of water from a distance. They would have to build their bunks to sleep in, excavate and lay all kinds of plumbing and, in short, provide for their every necessity. The boys were put to work in gangs of twenty-five, thirty and thirty-five, with picks and shovels.

Some of our boys had never done a day's work in their lives. They wanted white collar jobs. One young man of about twenty-five and of decent appearance actually rebelled. "I never worked with a pick and shovel on the outside and I haven't the slightest intention of starting in jail. What are you going to do with me?" I had no punishment cell to put him in. I am not sure that I would have used it if one had been available. One of the dangers of prison administration is to surround the recalcitrant prisoner with an air of martyrdom. If you put a fellow under lock and key, with restricted diet—bread and water—he becomes so debilitated that he can sleep or doze twenty-two hours a day. He gets so that he can sleep most of the time and the close confinement does not bother him much. My object was not to create sympathy for the rebel. I might have returned the man to New York to spend the remainder of his term in the Penitentiary. In that case, perhaps 95 percent of my prisoners would ultimately have joined the rebellion so as to be returned to the City rather than continue work with pick and shovel.

I took Mr. Rebel to the temporary gate and directed him to stand there. "Can I walk up and down?" he asked. "Yes." "Can I sing?" "If you have a voice, sure." Thereupon he spent the morning strolling up and down the road humming to himself while the rest of the gang were reluctantly at work. He was happy enough on dry land, out in the open, until the mess hour arrived. An aroma of delicious stew filled the air. The men lined up and Mr. Rebel started toward the kitchen for his grub. I stopped him promptly. "Nothing doing," I said, "if you don't work you are not going to eat." The mess line marched by as he stood watching, his smile gone and a rather forlorn expression on his face. One fellow in line called out derisively: "What a Boob." "Good idea, boys," I called out. "That's the Boob Squad from now on." Each of the boys managed to save half of his dinner hoping to pass it on somehow to the Boob. Only our careful and alert watchfulness prevented that. Thereafter anyone who didn't come up to standard, who didn't fit in, was placed in that squad. "The Boob Squad" became the joke of the camp. The members of the Boob Squad didn't work and enjoyed no privileges. But the Boob Squad was always a small company. Men didn't relish the name or the inconvenience. Throughout the period of construction, that, with consequent loss of time, was the only punishment I employed. The "Boob" idea brought a laugh and saved the situation for me. Mr. Rebel capitulated before the week was over. But the Boob Squad remained.

On the second day at New Hampton Mike the Rat Catcher asked me for a job in the farm barn which was then about a mile from camp. I thought it over, expecting that Mike wanted to get away, "cop a mope" they termed it in those days. If anyone was going to escape I would just as soon have Mike go as any one else. I sent him over to the farm, but he went no further. He asked to take care of a team of horses and he took great care of them. The only thing we had to watch was that he did not steal the oats and hay from the other fellow's teams to give to his own. If we had appraised him properly we might have known that a fellow who tolerated rats would also have cared for horses and done well with them.

One day several months after our arrival at New Hampton, I was called to New York on business. Apparently the boys were at peace. A little past noon I was called to the telephone. "Better come back quick," one of the officers advised me, "the boys are up in arms about the stew, and it looks like trouble." The prisoners were living in wooden barracks at the time. Our staff wasn't very large and something serious might happen before I returned. I asked to talk to Mike the Rat Catcher. There was a nervous "Hello." I talked to him man to man fashion. "What's all the noise about?" He didn't know, he said. Had no part in it, but something was wrong, I wasn't quite sure of him. "Now, look here, Mike," I continued, "you fellows are taking advantage of my absence. You haven't got the nerve to start something when I'm around. I want you to round up the gang, whoever they are, and tell them to stop it. If they have anything to complain about, wait until I get back and we'll talk it over. But if you want me to be on the square with you and treat you like men, be on the level with me and don't wait until my back is turned to show how tough you are. Now you get busy quick." Mike stopped the riot. If ever I doubted a fellow's response to reason Mike's action dissipated that doubt. If ever I was convinced of the old adage about the good there is in the worst of us, I saw it then, when the fellow who had been pronounced irretrievably bad and who, in the judgment of the doctors, needed permanent custodial care, was the one man upon whom I could rely to check his fellow prisoners in their attempt to run amuck and cause irreparable damage to the institution and injury to my reputation as an administrator. Since that day I have never given up any man as wholly bad. That has been my theory of prison administration, both at New Hampton and later at Sing Sing. Looking back over my experiences in both institutions I feel certain that results, generally, have justified my conviction.

My family's first intimate contact with prison life began at the Reformatory at New Hampton. We were four. My two daughters were just growing out of infancy into childhood. Our house help were all prisoners. We were always in close association with the prisoners, among whom were incorrigibles who later became notorious gangsters and widely feared criminals. Yet no member of my family was ever molested or accorded anything but respect. The great majority of the population were entirely trustworthy in emergencies. I frequently drove to Goshen to catch the train for New York. Always my chauffeur was a prisoner. Always he returned alone to the Farms.

The men assigned to duty in my household were devoted to us. Hired civilian help could never have shown such attention and wholehearted interest in our welfare as did these men. I remember the first time the children were left alone in the care of prisoners. One young fellow was directed to look after them. We found him late that night lying on the floor at the foot of their bed, hard put to keep his eyes open, but patiently awaiting our return. Another prisoner would take the children for a ride to town or around the country. We never sent a guard along with them. We never doubted his trustworthiness. One day while walking through the farm one of the girls disappeared. She hid in the corn field and her companion could not find her. He called but there was no response. Soon he became exasperated. "If you don't come out right away," he yelled, "I'll— I'll escape!" He could think of no more effective threat. It worked. The girl came out at once. The men assigned to duty at my home generally slept in the cellar. They considered themselves part of the protective force of the household.

As soon as we were organized at New Hampton, I instituted the honor system. Not all of our prisoners were men of honor. They had to be watched. But like most others of their ilk no amount of watching would keep them in check. We were not running a Sunday School. So I wasn't altogether surprised one night when I awakened after midnight to the clatter of horses' hoofs. Very clear at first, they grew fainter and duller. They were already miles away, but sound travels far in the quietude of the early morning hours in the country. I decided to take a look at those night riders. Premonition, you'd say. Caution, I call it.

My home was somewhat removed from the guards'

house, and I didn't stop to sound the alarm. Nor did I wish to arouse the prisoners unduly. Those were flivver days. Mine was always close at hand, ready for emergencies; and I was soon racing down the road. I traveled over two miles before I overtook them. Two horses galloping at full speed, with their drivers whipping them, yelling and cursing, hoping to outdistance me. One was a burly negro and the other a ruddy faced youngster of eighteen. Somehow in the darkness they had managed to lead the horses out of the stable; had eluded the guards and were now hell-bent for New York. At my command they promptly dismounted and approached my car. In the negro's hand was a large calibre gun. My heart throb was only momentary for he held it by the muzzle with the handle towards me and he seemed anxious to get rid of it. "It ain't loaded," he grinned. "You sure got good ears, Boss." They were surprisingly docile. I directed them to tie the horses to a tree and crowded the prisoners beside me in the front seat. We were soon hurrying back to New Hampton and thus we arrived at the institution camp. I sent a guard for the horses and put the prisoners to bed. They were re-assigned to work and gave me no further trouble.

We arrived at New Hampton on Tuesday and on the following Saturday afternoon, a very rainy day, five men walked out on us. You will remember that we had only a makeshift organization, with only temporary wooden bunks built by the prisoners. No bars, no cells, no walls; we were without suitable lighting (kerosene lanterns only); no armed guards patrolled the grounds. Apparently these men had no hankering for their pick and shovel job. And they did not want

56

to join the "Boob Squad." So they decided to take French leave. They were missing at the evening count. All the prisoners were lined up and the count verified by calling each man's name and number. Every name was answered to and apparently every number accounted for. But the total still showed five short. We were puzzled for a time, until we discovered that the names and numbers of the missing prisoners were being called by their friends in the "know." A few hours later we captured four of the five men who escaped. Two of them have since become desperate criminals. One of them was recently the victim of a gang murder—a particularly vicious murder. He was actually the most intractable of all the prisoners and resisted the officers who attempted to return him to New Hampton. In the scrimmage that followed, he was somewhat manhandled. His friends on the outside took advantage of this and complained through the public press that one of our boys had been given a "bloody nose" by an officer of the Reformatory. There was considerable criticism at the time, even reaching the Board of Estimate. No one seemed to realize that the Reformatory was no place for Gaffney. He had a peculiar personality make-up that did not yield to orderly life.

In those days, however, we had no facilities for classification and segregation and no opportunity for psychiatric or psychological research. This Gaffney type of prisoner was almost negligible. But it was the group that gave us trouble and worry. Among them were three young prisoners. Marcus Basset, George Lepesque and a third known as Tiger. One night they, too, made their get-a-way. I was well rid of them. But my duty was clear. They had to be found and returned.

I quickly organized my force. All railroads and every State and dirt road were zoned. Converging points were numbered and posted by our staff. No officer was allowed to leave his post until relieved—a patrolling roundsman made his periodic check. All three were captured by our officers in Sussex, New Jersey.

The prisoners were "wise," and stood on their rights. They were only misdemeanants and as such were not extradictable from New Jersey to New York.

"You can't touch us," they insisted. "Better forget it."

Technically they were right. But we took our chances and bundled them into our automobiles and brought them back to New Hampton. It is possible that we were guilty of kidnapping. The tale can now be told for the statute of limitations now exempts us from possible prosecution.

The Commissioner of Correction, Mr. Burdette G. Lewis, happened to be at New Hampton at the time of this incident and witnessed our handling of the situation. I was gratified several days later to receive his letter of commendation.

"I wish to commend you and your staff generally for the effective work in the recapture of inmates Marcus Basset, George Lepesque and Ralph Tiger. I was present when the alarm was given and saw the speed with which the force responded. I appreciate more than ever the efficiency of the organization at New Hampton. It is as fine a thing as I have seen."

The majority of our prisoners were orderly, amenable to rules and regulations and generally obedient. We never experienced the slighest difficulty with our honor men on the Sunday afternoon hikes which became regular weekly features of the Reformatory routine. Headed by the Prison Band, the long line of boys marched for miles along the State road. At rest periods they were often allowed to pick berries. The neighbors, farmers by the country-side, enjoyed the spectacle as much as the boys did their hike. No one ever strayed from the line of march.

Our Institution Band developed into one of the best of its kind in the country. It participated in programs at Carnegie Hall, New York, at the Academy of Music in Brooklyn, and other places. Its official escort was never armed.

June 6, 1917, was registration day for the draft army in Orange County. All nearby towns joined in a tremendous patriotic demonstration. The Reformatory boys played a conspicuous part in the celebration at Middletown, New York. Fifty percent of our prisoners, with a mounted escort of about half of our official force, marched behind the prison band to the enthusiastic applause of the crowds on the side lines. I headed our contingent on horseback. It was a proud moment for me. Our prisoners and official family were gratified with a letter of appreciation from the Chamber of Commerce of Middletown, which read as follows:

"The Board of Directors of the Middletown Chamber of Commerce desires to express to you its sincere thanks for the splendid cooperation shown by your organization in the registration demonstration. The impressiveness of the entire program and the patriotic spirit manifested are bound to live long with the men of registration age. It is truly significant that your organization has aided so nobly in fostering the spirit."

Prisoners took the places of civilian employees who were enlisted or were drafted. Nearly half our prisoner population was soon in the army. Letters written by them from the front are among my prized mementos.

"I'm being paid," wrote one, "for every evil I ever committed, and then some."

"I don't think the Germans will last very long," another letter reads, "when we get over there."

The army experience was good training for most of them.

"I have learned," one of the boys commented, "during my service that 'yes' means 'yes' and 'no' means 'no'."

Despite the war and its attendant excitement the morale at New Hampton was not affected. Our 1918 farm crops—potatoes, onions and tomatoes, were the best in Orange County. We raised enough farm products for all our own needs and shipped many carloads of potatoes, onions, carrots, turnips, cabbages and canned tomatoes to other institutions in New York City. At that time the institution was still incomplete. The only fully equipped building was the piggery, called the "Pig Palace" by the boys.

Our prisoners were also busy at carpentry, plumbing, electricity, painting, tailoring, bricklaying and steamfitting.

I felt a sense of gratification with the results I had been able to achieve at New Hampton. Here was something new in the penology of those days. A prison without walls. Yet the great majority of the prisoners were orderly, trustworthy and well disciplined. I was further convinced of this in October of 1916 by an extraordinary experiment, the like of which, to my knowledge, has never been attempted in any other prison in the country.

I was riding one morning inspecting a section of our grounds along the Walkill River. I was on horseback. Two gentlemen were walking along the river side. They seemed to be interested in the scenery and greeted me cordially. I stopped to talk to them. "Do you own this property?" one of them asked. "No," I replied, "but I can get you in touch with the owners." They then introduced themselves as agents for a moving picture corporation, looking for a location to film a picture centering around the Rio Grande. The main feature was to be a battle on the "Mexican Border." "This river," they explained, "looks more like the Rio Grande than the Rio Grande itself."

I told them that I could arrange for them to use the grounds. "But where will you get the men?" They would need about one hundred and fifty men to impersonate the soldiers, and expected to find them in the adjoining towns and villages. I thought quickly. Why not our own boys? It would be worth considerable money to the moving picture company to have young men of good physique, picked for their especial purposes. I had hoped to be able to install a moving picture outfit in the Reformatory, but didn't dare to include it in the budget. Moving pictures for prisoners were not to be thought of in those days. That was in the nature of "coddling," and the Department would have invited severe criticism for even suggesting it. Here was a possibility and I chanced it. "I can also provide the men," I suggested and invited them to my home to talk it over.

I agreed to furnish one hundred and fifty men, fifty

for the cavalry and one hundred for the infantry. They were to send the horses and the outfits. I didn't realize at the time that soldiers would have to carry arms. One morning a large case was delivered at the Farms. On opening it, we found a little over a hundred Krag Jorgenson rifles and fifty .45 calibre Colt revolvers, and a large assortment of blank cartridges.

The great day finally arrived. The picture was the "Brand of Cowardice," starring Lionel Barrymore, Louis Wolheim and Grace Darling, who appeared at the Farm prepared to pitch in.

A holiday was declared. Nobody worked that day except the one hundred and fifty men picked for the film. The uniforms were distributed and in a little while one hundred men were assembled on the field resembling, in every detail, a unit of the United States Army. And in a few moments we heard the approach of a large company of horses, and fifty cavalrymen swept into view. Each one carried his regulation army rifle for the infantry and revolvers for the cavalrymen. Each was provided with blank shot.

I was proud of my men, but also somewhat nervous. None of us was armed. It was an open field, with absolutely no barrier between these prisoners and the outside world. Nothing except their honor. They were to engage in mock battle. There would be smoke and excitement. Horses would charge, and the infantrymen would run to attack and retreat. There was no way that we could have restrained the boys had any of them taken it into their heads to run off the grounds and away. Revolvers and rifles would have been handy in a scrimmage between them and the Reformatory staff. And though they had no real shot, the possession of a gun is generally enough to turn the head of any prisoner.

Just as the miniature army was assembled for their mock battle I was almost taken off my feet by the unexpected arrival of the Commissioner of Correction of the City of New York, Mr. Burdette G. Lewis. He was aghast at my temerity. He wouldn't stay. "I'm going back to New York," he said, "but if anything happens," he warned me, "you'll have to go further than New York."

Nothing happened. The picture was filmed. The boys had a rollicking good time. They fought like first class soldiers. The din of battle filled the whole neighborhood to the delight of the rest of the Reformatory population and the entertainment of the surrounding neighbors. And when it was over, every gun was accounted for and returned. Not a single item of equipment was missing. But the performance had its sequel. Another scene was to be filmed. The burning of the enemy's headquarters. The company waited for nightfall to achieve an effective setting. Long after sunset, in the pitch-dark of that autumn night, the deed was done. An especially constructed hut was set on fire. Prisoners stood around in the glare of the flames. A glorious time for all. While the movie operators cranked their machines, the boys reveled in the excitement of the incident. When, finally, the flames died down, the principals bade us good-bye, returned to their homes and the prisoner-actors went to their bunks to resume their routine.

We got our first class movie outfit. But more important was the fact that this incident did more to establish the morale of the institution than all the rules we could have evoked. The very fact that they, as ordinary prisoners, were trusted to that extent, gave my boys a sense of responsibility and led to other experiments which took our population out and away from the Institution on many occasions. I felt that I was helping my wards to attain a measure of self-respect and self-reliance that brought to them the earnest desire for better living.

A great many people applauded my efforts at New Hampton. Others questioned them. Especially the older men who had followed traditions and could not understand the new order. Zebulon R. Brockway was among the latter. I happened to be in Elmira one day. He was then ninety years old, a highly respected member of his community and Mayor of the City. He sent for me.

"I understand you have a Reformatory without walls," he said.

I nodded.

"Well, if you haven't any walls you must have something else. What is it?"

"We have morale, Mr. Brockway," I replied. "It's more effective than your strongest walls."

The old gentleman smiled. An unbelieving smile, I thought. He could not conceive a prison without walls.

The shadows are lengthening as the men begin their climb uphill toward the cell
...... the line of men it seems to be... *(Page 319)*

CHAPTER 3: MY INTRODUCTION TO THE BIG HOUSE

On December 5, 1919, the following telegram was handed to me at New Hampton:

> "Can you arrange to meet the Governor and me at the Biltmore Hotel on Tuesday, December 9th, at seven o'clock. Answer by letter or wire so I will receive it on Monday and can make a definite appointment with the Governor.
>
> (Signed)   C. F. RATTIGAN,
> *Superintendent of Prisons."*

It was my first intimation that I was being considered for the wardenship of Sing Sing. I was not particularly anxious for the job. Financially it was no preferment. The salary of the warden was no higher than the one I was receiving at New Hampton. Another consideration was that the civil service which covered New Hampton had not then been broadened to include the wardenship of Sing Sing. It was a political appointment, subject to the vagaries and fortunes of party politics.

Sing Sing Prison had received considerable notoriety. Wardens had come and gone. New theories of government and new policies were being tested. At times, scandal and ugly rumors seeped through the prison walls. "Few die and none resign in politics" applied to the wardenship of Sing Sing. One died in office. Most others left by request. One warden had

65

lasted three weeks. And so, though I felt complimented by the call for a conference with the Governor, I was not eager for the appointment; in fact, I was determined to decline it. I called on Governor Alfred E. Smith with the avowed intention of turning it down. He was his jovial and genial self.

"How about going up to Sing Sing and take charge?" was his greeting, "they need a man with experience."

I explained my position. He listened patiently. Then he looked up at me, with a twinkle in his eye. "Young fellow," he drawled, "it's all right with me. It's a tough spot. I don't blame you for being scared. It'll take a big man to go up there and stay." It was his challenge. And though I asked for a week to think it over, I knew then that I would be the new Warden of Sing Sing.

I had been in Sing Sing years before that, while I was Chief Guard at Elmira. My visit then was to check up the records of the prison to determine how many of our Reformatory "graduates" had filtered into the big prison. My recollection of it was not altogether satisfying. There was, at that time, little attempt at cleanliness. The yard was littered with debris. Companies of prisoners marched continuously through corridors and between shops. I left the prison that day with the shuffle of feet sounding in my ears. I decided to look it over again before I gave my final decision.

I arrived there late in December, 1919. Rumor had preceded me. Officers greeted me politely but with cool, questioning disdain. I knew, of course, what was passing through their minds. Another short timer. Another political protege. The prisoners were interested, but exhibited no special concern. So many wardens had come and gone that this impending change hardly impressed them. The shuffle was gone. Instead there was the slouch. The yard was as crowded with visitors as with prisoners. All mingled freely. In one respect the prison had retained something of its old atmosphere. There was the same accumulation of dirt and filth.

At a later date I made two other visits. One was to Mr. William (Bill) Ward, the veteran Republican leader of Westchester County. Up to this time the wardenship of Sing Sing had been the peculiar patronage of Westchester County. Apparently Mr. Ward had been fully advised of my prospective appointment. He was cordial about it. I explained that if I accepted the office it would not be a political job and that I intended to run it my own way. When I had finished, all he asked was, "Do you think you can run it?" "Yes," I answered. "Well," he replied with a slight smile, "don't let those reformers run it for you. I'll never interfere." He never did.

My next step was to see Mr. Michael (Mike) Walsh, the Democratic leader. Our interview was equally cordial and quite as agreeable.

The next day I dispatched my formal acceptance. I was to take office on the first of January, one week later.

It wasn't easy to leave New Hampton, where I had become identified with a definite penal policy and an institution that had been built upon a foundation of honor and trust. The majority of my wards at the Reformatory were minors, many of them mere boys. They were impressionable. They could be moulded and remoulded. At Sing Sing I would have to deal with men experienced if not hardened in crime. Many of them much older than myself. This was something different. My first thought was to get acquainted with my territory, to find out everything there was to know about Sing Sing. I delved into musty reports and records that had not been looked at in decades. It was hardly the librarian's fault that thick layers of dust had settled on those volumes. There were no customers.

No normal person ever reads prison reports. So-called reformers may, perhaps. They are prepared by wardens, inspectors or superintendents in conformity with the law or departmental rules. An occasional reference is made to them at Legislative hearings, or in conventions of social or penal agencies. A student of sociology will infrequently examine them to establish his thesis. For the ordinary citizen they do not exist. And yet, the pages of prison reports are replete with significant revelations of current social thought. They are of historic importance. Through them we can follow the variations and effectiveness of governmental policies, of inhibitions and latitude; we can witness the failure and weaknesses of public offices and officers. They are the mirrors in which are reflected the complexions of our social and political theories and practices. To the prison administrator they are more than that. They disclose to him the development of his institution. He can learn about errors of his predecessors and perhaps avoid pitfalls. I was anxious to know what had gone on in that cold looking and forbidding cell block that had housed over a hundred thousand men during the century of its existence.

It was an alluring study and bears the telling.

I discovered that Sing Sing was no lullaby, that its name was derived from the Indian words "Sint Sinks," a local tribe, a variation of an older term "Ossine Ossine," meaning stone upon stone. I found further that it was a mongrel. For while it was intended to replace the comparatively mild prison in New York City known as Newgate Prison, it was actually built and fashioned on the plan of the famous Auburn Prison, then the latest word in penal institutions in this State and country.

The Auburn system supplanted the old Pennsylvania system sponsored by the Society of Friends at Philadelphia in the last quarter of the 18th century, following the Revolutionary War. It was proposed as the first prison reform policy in America. The Friends stressed as the primary reformative feature in prison administration the absolute isolation of prisoners. They believed that association between criminals, with opportunity for daily if not constant contact must of necessity work for further corruption. The system of separate and solitary confinement therefore became the most important factor in governing prisoners. The cells or rooms were large and well ventilated but the prisoner saw no one but the warden, keeper, chaplain, physician or guard. Work was scarce and so the prisoner spent most of his time in idleness. Minds broke under the strain of idle, solitary confinement. The tremendous increase in insanity prompted the abandonment of the Pennsylvania system in favor of the Auburn prison plan of separate confinement at night, with conversation prohibited during the day under pain of severe corporal punishment. Prisons in most European countries are divided between the Pennsylvania and Auburn systems.

Newgate Prison was a prototype of the London

Prison of similar name. It stood on the shore of the Hudson River in what was then Greenwich Village and consisted of about four acres of ground, enclosed by massive walls. It contained fifty-four rooms, each 12 x 28, to accommodate eight persons in a room. Generally two prisoners slept in one bed. Only prisoners with sentences of three years or over were committed to Newgate Prison. The system of government provided for the payment of wages to every prisoner for his labor, from which was debited his keep, including clothes, board and lodging.

It was already realized in those early days that prisoners would have to be offered some inducement for diligent work and good conduct. The best work producer devised by our forbears was beer. And so every prisoner was provided with a daily ration of a pint of good, wholesome beer. In later years a brewery was built on the same site.

In the central part of Western New York the new theory of prison administration was put into practice. It was agreed that co-mingling of prisoners was not salutary. That herding of men in one room led to abuses and developed degeneracy. It was felt, too, that the mind of the man who had taken to crime was too agile. It needed a slowing down process. None better could be devised than solitude. Men were not allowed to talk to one another. They received no communications from the outside, nor were they permitted to send any. They were allowed no books or papers, and only sufficient food to keep them alive. Meditation was encouraged. The prisoner could brood and think. Not all could think. But every one could brood. When brooding becomes a habit it leads to disaster. In Auburn it

70

begot insanity and disease. Officials became panicky and sought to alleviate conditions by permitting men to labor. But silence was the order of the day. Prisoners were not allowed to laugh. They could not look up from their tables when at work, nor were they permitted to look at their officers. Always their eyes gazed downward. They worked in companies, within the shops. When their tasks were done the companies were marched back into their cells to spend the balance of the day in continued silence and the night in utter darkness.

By confining each prisoner in a separate cell the prison at Auburn could not accommodate the State's growing criminal population. Newgate, on the lower Hudson, was already filled to capacity. Apparently it served good beer to its prisoners and had become popular as a temporary shelter for the indigent. Also, it was too near New York. When riots occurred in Newgate Prison, as they did quite frequently, its officials were nervous about possible aid from prisoners' accomplices. And so it soon became evident that a new prison would have to be built. The site selected finally was at Mount Pleasant, near the village of Sing Sing on the east shore of the Hudson thirty miles north of New York City. It was an ideal choice. Stone quarries lay close by. The Hudson provided cheap transportation for prison products. The prisoners could be put to "hard labor," called for by their sentences. Furthermore, a goodly portion of the prison could be built from the material on hand.

The story of the construction of early Sing Sing is not new. Nor is it particularly interesting. In the spring of 1825, Captain Elam Lynds, the Warden of Auburn Prison, picked one hundred of his prisoners, hardy men all; transported them to the Erie Canal, seven miles distant, whence they were brought in two canal boats to the Hudson River and thence in freight steamers to Sing Sing, where they arrived on May fourteenth. Naturally the men were shackled during that long journey. As a matter of course each of the thirty guards who accompanied the company was well armed. This was not an honor camp in the sense of modern prison road or construction companies. These men had been picked because they had brawn and could hew stone and stand roughage.

At the moment of their arrival at Mount Pleasant the work began. The steep, rocky hillside had to be levelled for the prison site. On the first day a temporary barracks was erected, then a cook house, a blacksmith and carpenter shop. All work was done in sight of the muzzles of guns trained constantly on the men toiling in silence. Captain Lynds, then the foremost penologist of the day, was insistent, to the point of hysteria, on *silence* as the backbone of prison administration. "It is the duty of convicts to preserve an unbroken silence," was the first rule he laid down. "They are not to exchange a word with each other under any pretense whatever; not to communicate any intelligence to each other in writing. They are not to exchange looks, wink, laugh, or motion to each other. They must not sing, whistle, dance, run, jump, or do anything which has a tendency in the least degree to disturb the harmony or contravene to disturb the rules and regulations of the prison." And so, Sing Sing Prison, that was later to become world famous, rose from its rocky bed, amid a silence broken only by the sharp clang of steel on stone. The sea gulls in the

72

broad river, darting in large flocks here and there on the water, chirped raucously at these strange creatures sweating at their tasks in silence. Stone upon stone. An inner building. Again stone upon stone. An outer building. One enclosing the other. A Mausoleum with niches arranged in galleries. Every niche seven feet long, six feet high, and three feet six inches wide. A thickness of one foot of stone separated each compartment. And when it was done, with one thousand cells under the roof, men proudly surveyed this edifice. "It is a noble structure," was the verdict. "No better penitentiary prison was ever built at any time in this or any other country," was the report of the Prison Commissioners of those days.

Had the gentlemen who uttered those fine sentiments lived until 1904 they would have been rudely shocked. In no uncertain terms was this very structure denounced as a "disgrace" to the richest state in the Union. "The cells are small," the warden in 1904 wrote. "Too small for the purpose, and have been condemned for years as insufficient in their dimensions. They have poor ventilation, and their unsanitary condition is intensified by the necessary use of cell buckets, the most objectionable and injurious relics of the primitive prison system."

But in those early years, only one criticism was made of the construction of that cell block. A discerning eye discovered that the iron grated doors of the cells had been placed flush with the outer surface of the wall. Those doors were *only* three or four feet apart and there was grave danger of the prisoners maintaining a conversation from one cell to another, in a low tone of voice, by having the mouth of one and the ear of another applied to the apertures in the gratings of two contiguous doors. It was no answer that this arrangement provided the prisoner with at least six inches of additional walking space within that narrow cell. The prospect of the breach of discipline by possible whispered conversations was too dangerous. Despite the urgent recommendations of the prison inspectors, this arrangement was allowed to remain. It was for years the sore spot of Sing Sing's prison discipline.

Shortly after the completion of the first two floors of the prison, the entire prisoner population of Newgate in New York was transferred to the new prison —Mount Pleasant, as it was then called. No more wholesome beer for these men. They would have to labor without its invigorating influence. With the additional contingents from Auburn, every cell was soon occupied. In 1830 the population of the new prison numbered eight hundred.

Between the "proud structure" of 1830 and the "disgrace" of 1904, one senses the gradual evolution from the puritanical to the more enlightened social thought that began to take form early in the Twentieth Century. That is reflected in the story of prison discipline, as it swung from one extreme to the other, from severity to harshness, from harshness to mildness, from mildness to chaos, then back again to severity to make the round all over again.

The "cat" was the symbol of authority in Sing Sing. The "cat" in prison parlance was not a purring animal that approached one with soft tread and the desire for friendly contact. It was made of long strips of leather, attached to a stout wooden handle, and was not infrequently wired at the tips. The "cat" preferred its victim barebacked. It descended with deliberation and generally left its imprint—stripes and blood through broken skin. The "cat" seldom worked alone. Accompanying it was the salt water sponge that caressed the raw wound. Verily, the combination of the devil. But such was the eagerness (!) with which prisoners in those days acquiesced in this form of chastisement that, as the records show, one thousand lashes were inflicted within the space of three weeks. It is this system of prison discipline that the Governor of New York, in 1830, proudly described as one which "has already acquired, not only with our sister states, but in Europe," a reputation that "is a matter of just State Pride; and should stimulate us to further endeavors to aid the cause of humanity at large, by influence of our example."

It is apparent, however, as one turns the pages of these early reports, that the reign of the "cat" within the walls of Sing Sing was not as impressive as might have been expected. It is there in black and white. We find that labor was irksome to the prisoners who took no interest in their work. Escapes, or attempts to escape were weekly occurrences, inmates choosing to run the risk of being shot by the guards rather than remain to be killed by inches.

Administrators justified these harsh measures. Prisoners were described as "the most vicious and depraved of the human race, including some of the fiercest and most desperate spirits." That they were a hopeless lot of men without chance of amendment. Yet in 1840 a change occurred. There was a sudden rift in the clouds and a softening influence appeared. The newly appointed warden had different ideas. He locked

75

up the "cat"; stored it away. Punishment was less severe and less frequent. For the first time a Sunday School was inaugurated; prisoners were permitted to write an occasional letter; a small library was set up for the use of the prisoners, and limited visiting was allowed. What was more, the warden took personal interest in the prisoners. He made his rounds of the hospital wards to converse with the sick. Old time officers were aghast. "You are lowering your dignity," they exclaimed, "and destroying all discipline. In a month's time we shall have such a rebellion as no prison ever witnessed; we are afraid of our lives."

The rebellion never occurred. Instead, production improved and escapes became less frequent. But this regime was short lived. In 1843, a new political party came into power and a new prison administration was appointed. As political opponents of the former prison board, they made sure to annul everything suggested or introduced by their predecessors. The Sunday School was abolished, correspondence by prisoners vetoed, the library was destroyed, and all visiting prohibited. The old system was restored. It was the notorious "knock down and drag out" system. Crime rates took an upward trend. It was one of those periodic "crime waves." Prison officials were apologetic. "The vigor and perfection of prison government," they protested, "do not appear to be generally known."

The method of constant supervision in those days is impressive. Not for a moment was the prisoner permitted to stray from the vigilant eye of the guard or keeper. Every gesture was regulated. Every movement keenly watched. The "cat" hovered over the prison with hungry eyes, ready to descend at the least provocation. Prisoners were checked and rechecked, watched, warned, and punished for the slightest violation of the rules. Before 1845 tobacco was not allowed to prisoners. The report of a search of cells made during this period of rigid government of this multi-ruled institution reminded me forcibly of the well settled principle, "more law, more crime, more rules, more violations." Despite the vigilance of the keen eyed guards, the following articles were found in the prisoners' cells, all contraband and forbidden:

"Newspapers; story books; ornaments; bureau; pocket knife; pumps; alcohol; shoe hammer; cane; handkerchief; gloves; convict's account book; drill hammer; rags; Comic Almanac; Family Almanac; chest of drawers; songs; maps; account book; pictures; chalk; writing desk; box of rubbish; leather; shoe knife; bag of sewing implements complete; stone hammer; onions; thread; one piece of muslin; brad awl; scissors and silk; five quires of writing paper; dirt and vermin; bag of trash and dirt; lot of old bread; rags; tobacco; pipes; matches; lice and bed bugs; lead; rags; socks; dirt; bags; nails and spikes; yarn; looking glass; provisions enough to last a man a week; sock full of provisions; bone; slate and pencil; gauge; file; chisel; fancy box; convict's journal; paintings; box of trash such as meat, files, soap, nails, bread, etc.; box containing flint, steel, pipe, tobacco and matches; patch book; letters; songs; chisel; two hanks of yarn; a kit of tools; one paper of shoe nails; also the following books: Burglar's Companion; History of Buccaneers; Treatise on Surveying; Farmer's Instructor; The Murderer; French Grammar; Chronological Dictionary; Lady of Refinement; Lives of

Females; Latin Grammar; Latin Exercises; Ainsworth Dictionary; Assembly Report and Domestic Medicines."

How the "cat" must have relished the find! The reporter of this search naïvely informs us that "this involved the necessity of inflicting a good deal of punishment." That fellow with those miniature cooties. One wonders about him. The prisoners with the French Grammar; or the Latin exercises. How heinous were their offences! I can understand that Lives of Females might have been a bad influence for a prisoner expected to spend his hours in wakeful meditation, but the convict with the Treatise on Surveying—the "cat" must have snarled at him with gleeful rage.

Prison administrators felt hopeless. Prisoners had to be punished, of course. Else the morale of the institution would be destroyed. Yet there was no imagination among prison administrators of that era. "It is regarded as a standing rule of our system," the inspectors bewail, "that no offence of a convict in the prison shall go unpunished; the certainty of punishment being deemed of essential consequence in ensuring obedience. But no other mode of punishment seems to be contemplated than the lash. The prison is built entirely on that plan, and no provision is made for any other kind."

The lash made no discrimination. A violation of prison rules called for the application, regardless of the prisoner's mental condition. It was only when a prisoner by the name of Theodore P. Whiting died as the result of a series of lashings that the public fury was aroused. Whiting was punished for insubordination. It was admitted that he had shown signs of insanity, but officials decided that he was feigning and therefore repeated the lashings with each offence. The charge was made later that he was whipped to death. Prison officials denied the charge, but it left an impression on the public mind. The result was that a new system of government in prisons was adopted. It was thereafter reported that "the happiest results have attended the experiment," of limiting the use of the lash. In the female prison, the lash was never again used. Among the males the number of lashes diminished from 1,195 a month to about 200, while the number of offences against discipline decreased from 130 a month to 50; and in the female prison from 47 to 11.

In viewing the development of prison discipline as it is unfolded in the prison reports through the Nineteenth Century, one is struck with the fact that administrations were more deeply concerned with the offence against the majesty of the prison than with the individual guilty of malfeasance. Motivating forces, mentalities, emotional influences were all disregarded. Now and then, however, we read of an enlightened and progressive mind that saw through the fallacy of this method of administration. Governor William H. Seward was one of these. "While the punishment of offenders," he wrote in his message to the Legislature in 1840, "should always be enforced with firmness, the spirit of the age manifestly requires that discipline shall be tempered with kindness and that moral influences rather than severe corporal punishment should be employed to procure the submission and promote the reformation of the convict."

The attack against entrenched severity continued during the next several years. No impression was made, however, for the theory of the lash and the deprivation of all contact with the outside world were too deeply imbedded in the traditions of prison administration. Not until 1845 was there any sign of surrender. In November of that year a committee of public spirited citizens debated the advisability of allowing the use of tobacco to prisoners. After long discussion and learned debates they reported in favor of its allowance, and in February, 1846, the Warden of Sing Sing was directed to furnish tobacco to such of "the convicts as had been habituated to its use." It was a hard earned victory. "But," says the report of 1847, "the fact of its introduction upon the discipline was almost immediately manifest. It has diffused a measure of contentment over a large class of our inmates who had previously been a source of constant uneasiness and anxiety to the prison authorities and has, I am satisfied, contributed largely to the unusual respect given by convicts to the regulations and government of the prison."

This was followed by additional innovations. A definite policy was adopted permitting visits from relatives "as often as once in six months." "Several interviews of this kind take place daily," our informant tells us, "in the presence of an officer, and many of them *are of the most interesting character.*"

The administrators were cautious. They did not dare go too far. The right of individual keepers to inflict instant punishment was restricted. Reports of offences had to be made to the warden, who decided upon the punishment "most appropriate for the offence." The code of punishment describes the measures then adopted for disciplinary purposes:

"The following shall be the punishments to which the

80

convicts in the prison may render themselves liable for breach of prison discipline, and to no others, under any pretence whatever, except by order of the Board of Inspectors.

1. Privation of food.
2. Privation of bedding.
3. Privation of books.
4. Privation of tobacco.
5. Change of work.
6. Change of dress.
7. Solitary confinements, with or without light.
8. Change of rations.
9. Shower bath.
10. The lash.

"The withdrawal of a privilege granted as a reward or an encouragement to a convict shall not be esteemed a punishment within the meaning of this section."

A cautious lot, were those early administrators. They still retained the "cat" in the background for emergencies.

The dent, slight as it was, that was thus made in the traditional prison methods did not meet with universal approval. Not everyone condoned these "enlightened disciplinary rules." The prison inspectors for 1848 tell us something of their troubles. "We should hardly be excused, however, if we were to pass over in silence the fact, of which we could scarcely affect to be ignorant, that widely different views from these, of the character and results of the government which has prevailed here during the administration of the present Board of Inspectors, have been entertained by some and expressed by more, and that efforts have been made by ignorant and designing persons to prejudice the public mind, and especially the Legislature against every effort which has been made by this Board, as well as by philanthropists throughout the State, to meliorate the discipline of our prisons, and to subject it to the supremacy of the same intellectual and moral influences which are found most available in the government and training of the citizens."

It is interesting to note that during the period of harsh discipline for the prisoners the management of Sing Sing Prison suffered somewhat in efficiency. The vigor with which punishment was inflicted, the enthusiasm with which prisoners were watched, were not reflected in general administrative functions. Rumors of maladministration were rife and constant. Politics, of course, influenced appointments to office regardless of competency. It was even suggested that keepers were tempted by bribes and ill-gotten gains, to aid and abet unlawful and irregular transactions.

It seemed impossible to secure a true financial statement of the prison, or an accurate account of the prisoners. An inquiry was finally instituted. A professional accountant was employed. The clerk of the prison refused to permit him to discharge his duty, until and unless a member of the Board of Inspectors accompanied him. The report of this accountant is interesting indeed. Summarising it, in brief, it showed:

"The register of convicts which professed to be and ought to be a true account of all the prisoners received and discharged at the prison, differed materially from the number who were actually in confinement. In the Female Prison, by the register it appeared that there were in the prison 98 prisoners. There were four whose names were not on the books, but whose commitments were found, making the total of prisoners to be accounted for 102.

"The actual count in the prison turned up 82 prisoners. The deficiency of 20 prisoners in the women's prison could not be explained."

In the male prison the result was equally disconcerting. The register called for 795 prisoners. Actually there were 762. A deficiency of 33. How these missing prisoners had left the prison or when, could not be ascertained.

One especially interesting paragraph speaks of a prisoner who had been in Sing Sing five years. No authority could be found for his admission or retention. It was finally decided that he was a "volunteer" and he was discharged.

On another occasion we find that part of the prison property was sold for $34,233.34 and the proceeds placed to the credit of the prison authorities for use in improving prison buildings. Of this amount a record was found of $1,317.20. No mention was made in any report or books of the disposition of the balance of $32,916.14!

It was evident that these conditions were well known to prisoners. As exemplary influences they were no more effective in guiding prisoners' attitudes toward their keepers than all the stripes inflicted. It occurred to me, as I delved further into the story of early Sing Sing, that the lash was too partial to prisoners; that it invariably found the wrong victims. But it was an absorbing study and I continued on.

In 1848 came the definite recommendation that the "cat" as a form of punishment be entirely eliminated. There was to be a trial period of three years. Apparently this suggestion was adopted for thereafter we find little mention of that form of chastisement. The favorite punishment adopted was the cold water shower. Beginning with 1849 we find a constant flow of water on the heads of malfeasants, 203 cases in 1849. "The privilege of education, new books, the abolition of the 'cat' and the new table system of eating have a very good influence on the conduct of the prisoners," a report for 1850 tells us. Yet out of a population of 694, two hundred and thirty-four men were punished during that year, one hundred and twenty-four of them by the water cure.

Commencing with 1853 wardens and prison inspectors seem to have become convinced that something more than mere punishment was essential to effective prison management. They began to demand an improvement of the prisoners' physical surroundings. The first recommendation of this kind was for sufficient light for the cells at night to enable prisoners to read until at least nine o'clock. Like all other recommendations for the improvement of prisons this was not immediately adopted. And so punishments continued merrily on. Showers, dark cells, ball and chain, iron cap (a brand new invention), yokes. A combination of treatments that affected almost half the prisoner-population of Sing Sing for the next decade. For the next sixty years the administration of the prison floundered between two divergent theories of government. Severe punishment, minus the "cat," on the one hand, and more humane indulgence, warily bestowed on the other. Four hundred and sixty-one punishments were listed in 1855 on a population of 1,026. One drastic punishment was inflicted. A prisoner was shot to death. "The difficulty that occurred in November of that year, which resulted in the shooting of one convict, in consequence of his insubordination, his menacing attitude and for the morale of other prisoners." Killing a prisoner in order to impress others!

In 1856, though punishments of shower, ball and chain, yoke and dark cells were imposed in 501 cases out of a population of 963, we find also that additional light was introduced to permit prisoners to read easily; steam heat was installed in the chapel, mess rooms, hospital and main prison.

In 1857, 794 punishments were meted out on a population of 983. We read that Sing Sing Prison "was in some degree affected by the spirit of insubordination." For the first time in the history of New York State Prisons we find a reference to the "great drawback on discipline in the constant changes in the appointment of officers, subject as they are, to the varying political parties that are in power."

The inspectors for that year inaugurated the campaign for rewarding well behaved prisoners by the shortening of their sentences. Thus "time-compensation" for good behavior became a new objective of understanding prison administrators.

Physical chastisement still held sway. Reforms come slowly within prison walls. Water continued to drench the heads of prisoners. Eight hundred and fifty punishments were accorded to 1,072 prisoners in 1858. Severe as these measures were, they apparently did not check the constant influx of prisoners. So that in the following year, 1859, Sing Sing was overcrowded with a population of 1,228 and cell capacity of 1,072. For the first time in the history of Sing Sing it became necessary to place two men in a cell. More than two hundred of the narrow cells, three and one-half feet wide housed two prisoners. That did not contribute to prison morale.

The year 1861 witnessed 706 punishments to a population of 1,280. Again water treatment played its major part, but there were also the dark cells, the yoke, ball and chain, iron caps. Evidently the futility of all this was recognized. We read in the report for this year the call for real reform. "Let one of the prisons be set apart or, if need be, a fourth one built for prisoners of lighter offences. Take away the degrading stripe, banish the lockstep, let good behavior be rewarded by shortening of sentences. Let the main object be reformation, not paying expenses."

The call went unheeded. Nothing happened except that prisoners were henceforth allowed one visit every three months instead of one in six months as theretofore.

Still, physical force held sway. In 1863, 1,213 punishments were meted out to a population of 890. In addition, protection against disorders within had to be provided from the outside. The Governor was called upon and did send one hundred soldiers, fifty policemen and thirty extra guards to help maintain order and discipline. Punishments continued to climb. In 1864, the population was 796. Out of these 613 men actually received some form of physical chastisement, and the number of punishments handed out was 1,403. One prisoner was punished twenty-two times. Steel yokes, iron caps, showers, ball and chain, dark cells, everything was employed.

Prison officials complained about a "libelous article"

that appeared in a New York newspaper charging the officers of Sing Sing Prison with a series of cruelties inflicted upon a convict named Evans, from the results of which, it was alleged, Evans died. The explanation given was that this prisoner had attempted to take the life of one of the officers and was punished accordingly, by the proper officers.

During all these years, every report tells of fires, epidemics that resulted in many deaths. Dysentery, scurvy, Asiatic cholera, smallpox—all took their overwhelming tolls. Prisoners' diet was barely enough to keep body and soul together. Two eggs a year for each man, the records show. Famished prisoners timidly entered the mess kitchen to beg for more food but were driven away, probably lashed for their temerity. Judged from this distance, Sing Sing Prison seemed to have been actually a devil's workshop. Fire and water played their important parts. Officers fought against some invisible curse that pervaded the prison atmosphere. Prisoners struggled to avoid and overcome despair and despondency.

Finally the State Legislature at Albany took a hand in the situation and abolished all forms of punishment in Sing Sing except the dark cell. And we hear from the administrator of the day, in 1871, that "the general discipline of the several prisons is as good, if not better than might be expected under existing conditions." Contrary to frequently expressed theories of pseudo-penologists about the relation of mild prison discipline and the increase of crime, we find for the first time in several years that "there is a population small enough to permit only one man to a cell."

"A man may be down," a prisoner of that by-gone

era remarked, "but he is never out until his time expires." The routine of the prison saw to it that he was down during his sojourn within the walls. By the time the day of his discharge approached, he was "out" in more ways than one. He found himself outside of the walls literally a broken down, helpless hulk, unfit for normal life or occupation. A prisoner with a faculty for the comics described it aptly in the following colloquy:

Pat—"Some men live on hope, Moike."
Mike—"How much is it a package?"
Pat—"It doesn't come in packages."
Mike—"Well it doesn't matter, it's not down on the lisht av things they are lettin' in here just now."

Such was the Sing Sing of the Nineteenth Century. A hopeless, oppressive, barren spot. Escapes were frequent, attempts at escape almost daily occurrences. Suicides were common. Prisoners were considered a tough and dangerous lot of men. The kneading process of the prison made them still more dangerous and tougher. The whole theory of the prison was to inure the prisoner to hardship and suffering.

The prison warden is primarily a custodian. His function under the law is to keep his men within the confines of his prison. They are his stock in trade. His stock must always be properly accounted for. And so wardens looked with some degree of misgiving at the many escapes and the frequent attempts to leave their bailiwick. Naturally, the first thing that occurred to them was security. The institution must be made foolproof. Sing Sing needed a wall. Wardens for twenty years advocated the building of a stone wall around

88

the prison grounds. Every annual report prayed for this relief. Finally in 1877, the wall was completed, the one that now surrounds the old prison. Twenty feet high, punctuated here and there with guard posts from which armed keepers could view the prison grounds and buildings. But life within the prison continued along traditional lines. The warden now was sure that his subjects could not escape him. They would be there to receive their dues. And so the shower drenched its unending victims; the ball and chain restrained rebellious spirits; men continued to languish in weary abandon within the dark recesses of inaccessible dungeons. All this despite the legislative prohibition of 1870 against corporal punishment.

Is this picture overdrawn? Is it a fact that these harsh measures hardened prisoners and officers alike? Let me lay aside for a moment the prison volumes which, for the first time, are now seeing the light of day. A prisoner by the name of George Appo found himself in Sing Sing in 1874. Appo had served three prison terms between 1874 and 1883. He had been a witness before the Lexow Investigating Committee. John W. Goff and Frank Moss became interested in the discharged prisoner and obtained honest employment for him. Sixteen years after his last prison term he wrote the story of his prison experiences. It is a voluminous document but has never been published. We find therein a vivid picture of prison life and discipline of that period.

Those were the days of contract labor. Contractors bought labor. The income went to the State. The prisoner got nothing. Appo tells of his experiences.

"I was at work only three days when the paid instructor of the contractor put a dozen shirts on my table. 'You will have to do these shirts today,' he said, 'and see that you do them perfect or I'll know the reason why.'

"I told him I would do my best. I finished two shirts, but unfortunately while on the third shirt, I had to go and get a hot iron. Before using it I dipped it in water to cool off. Then I started to iron the sleeve of the shirt and accidentally scorched it. I reported the accident to the citizen instructor. He went to the keeper and told him I willfully burned the shirt. The keeper said to me: 'Get your hat and coat.' I did so. He and the instructor took me to the guard room to the Principal Keeper and reported me to him as deliberately burning shirts.

" 'What have you to say about that?' the Principal Keeper asked. 'It was an accident and I couldn't help it,' I said.

" 'Accident, hey! Couldn't help it, hey! Well, we'll make you be more careful after this. Take off your clothes,' he shouted.

" 'Take off your clothes,' he again demanded and when I did not respond quickly enough he shouted, 'Seize him.' Two big six-foot keepers grasped me by the throat, tore off my coat and pants, knocked out my front teeth by shoving me violently over the paddle board, pulled my hands behind my back, handcuffed me and pulled them up behind my back, as I lay across the paddle board, by a small tackle attached to a frame work on sides of the paddle board. After securing me, the six-foot keeper took a board shaped just like a canoe paddle with small holes in the blade and swung it over his shoulders and brought it down with all his

90

might on my bare back and spine. I counted nine blows before I became insensible. When I came to, I was lying on the floor. I heard the Doctor say, 'he's all right now.' The Principal Keeper said to me: 'Do you think you can go back and do your work all right now? If you don't, we have a way to make you.' I replied, 'You punished me for nothing and the next time I am brought here, you will punish me for something.' 'No insolence; take him back to the shop.'

"When I got back to the shop, with my teeth knocked out and my body black and bruised from the paddle, I took the shirts that were on my table to iron across the shop to the stove, kicked open the stove door, put the shirts into the fire and slammed the door shut again.

"I was again brought over to the guard room and asked why I did it. I would not answer. The Principal Keeper said, 'Put him in again.' But the Doctor objected. 'No, lock him up in the dungeon.' So they took me to the dark cell.

"I lay there for fourteen days on two ounces of bread and a gill of water every twenty-four hours. When I was taken from the dark cell, I was carried to the hospital injured for life. When I was released from Sing Sing I had to go to St. Luke's Hospital to be operated on by Professors Otis and Peters, and after nearly three months under good medical treatment, I left the Hospital and as I had no means or way to obtain the necessities of life, I naturally went back to stealing for a living."

Appo tells of another incident that sheds light on the prison government of the day.

"The keeper of the shop was a French Canadian

named Edward Gay. His name belied his disposition for he was too free with his heavy stick. For the least thing, such as turning one's head around from work and other such trivial mishaps, he would come from behind and push the stick into one's back or neck violently, with the threat to take one over to the guard room and that, of course, meant punishment. One day he pushed his stick into the back of a convict named Brun, who had a twenty-year sentence to serve. After doing so, he told Brun the next time he would take him to the guard room. Then he started to walk away. Suddenly Brun grabbed an iron lever from my machine and ran up behind the keeper and struck him a blow on the back. Had I not tripped him up, the blow would have caught the keeper on the head. Brun again swung the iron lever at the keeper when a convict named Campbell grasped Brun by the throat, took the iron lever away from him and held him until the keeper got up. Two other keepers came and took Brun to the guard room for punishment."

Appo was discharged, but his resumption of stealing soon returned him to Sing Sing. "On my arrival at Sing Sing Prison," he tells us, "I found a new Warden in charge, but the discipline was just as severe and brutal and the food and everything in general unfit for the lowest animal life. In fact, there was a general epidemic among the prisoners caused by rotten and filthy meat and other foodstuffs they had to eat, and during the whole course of my first two terms, I never saw or knew of a place to bathe after a hard day's work in the Stove Foundry."

I found in Appo's story an incident that brings out in a forceful manner the nature and extent of the silent system, as it then prevailed at Sing Sing. A system that was for almost a century the "Pride" of American penal administration.

"In this shop (the plumbing shop) was a convict by the nickname of 'Ginger.' He was there under the name of Thompson, with a five year sentence to serve. This convict had occasion to speak to the convict who worked next to him on the work bench. One was instructing the other how to finish a piece of work. The keeper, one Tierney, saw Ginger talking to his neighbor and rushed over with his big stick and poked Ginger in the neck. 'Stop your talking.' Ginger, who happened to have his working hammer in his hand, was taken by surprise. He jumped from his bench with the hammer in his hand, tried to explain that he had to instruct the other man, but Tierney, with another jab of his stick, told Ginger to 'shut up,' put his hammer down and not give him any back talk. Ginger jumped back, and the keeper pulled out his gun and shot him dead. Afterward Tierney claimed that he shot poor Thompson in self-defence. Nothing was said or done to Keeper Tierney. Thompson had no relatives or even a good friend in the outside world to take an interest in the case. He was only twenty-seven years of age at the time and was raised up from boyhood down in the fourth ward. The prison authorities nailed his body in a pine box and buried him up on the hill, or as the graveyard is called by convicts, '25 gallery,' without even a prayer from the so-called Chaplain."

What a forbidding picture was the Sin   of the
Nineteenth Century! Conceived along
Dante's imaginative Inferno. A proce
Sensitive souls were hardened. Strong

weak and helpless. As an "example" it failed miserably of its purpose. Crime continued. As a deterrent, it was futile. New laws created new crimes. In 1902, the number of laws violated had risen to forty-eight. By 1926 they totalled sixty. Sing Sing's population continued to grow.

It was then hardly realized that the prison was only a link in the scheme of crime prevention. Origins, sources, motivating forces did not concern the administrator, prosecuting or judicial agencies. Nor was a consideration given to the fact that prisoners were a continuing social problem. When, finally, administrators timidly called for modifications in prison routine, it was with the apologetic suggestion that they would make their own task easier. Brutalizing prisoners worked havoc with their keepers. It was then a case of brute against brute. Why not tame the animal?

The first thought in the taming process was toward dissipating the darkness of the cells. "There seems to be no sufficient reason," is the mild suggestion, "for confining seven hundred men in almost total darkness, and consequently in idleness for so great a portion of the time as at present. It is difficult to see what good can be accomplished by it, while it is quite easy to conceive that much evil must be consequent upon this unenlightened policy."

This recommendation was adopted. The result was gratifying. The Chaplain of the period comments on it.

"A light has been furnished at the cell door to those who were to be taught, on a given evening, and continued for about two hours. The teacher then passed from cell to cell, and gave such instruction as was

94

needed. To enjoy a light is esteemed a privilege by the convict and, hence, should he become negligent, it has only been necessary to inform him that he would be deprived of his light to secure his continued attention. We can clearly perceive that much good has been the result not only to the convict himself, but to the general discipline of the prison. Solitary confinement during the long winter evening with nothing to occupy the mind but their own evil thoughts becomes exceedingly irksome, and there is a strong tendency to endeavor to while away these long hours and dissipate gloomy feelings by an attempt at mirth and noise. The night watch, whose duty it is to notice and report all indecorums of this kind, states that he had never been obliged to report those who are furnished with lights."

Yet these lights were sparingly furnished. It would not do to indulge these prisoners too liberally. All this happened in 1850. Many more years elapsed before every cell was lighted so as to permit every prisoner to spend "those long winter nights" in reading or writing instead of in complete idleness.

In 1859, prison administrators began to advocate a new plan of reward for good conduct within the walls. "An important and salutary reform could be effected by giving to convicts an opportunity of gaining a portion of time, for which they have been convicted, by reason of good behavior. It needs no argument to show the good effect such a provision would produce in preserving order and obedience among the unfortunate prisoners. It would be an incentive for good conduct, which few of them would fail to keep in mind and comparatively few disregard.

"We earnestly request the Legislature to make provision by law to enable us to inaugurate these or similar reforms. We feel confident that most of the punishments now necessary to the preservation of discipline in the prison would be done away with."

The Law-Makers at Albany deliberated four years on this recommendation. Finally it was adopted. That its results were as satisfying as had been anticipated can be gleaned from the report for 1863, which states that "the hope of commutation of their sentences, for faithful observance of all rules and regulations of the prison, has done much to correct the discipline and maintain order throughout the prison."

Politics was of course, still the bane of all prison government. Within fifteen years preceding 1873, Sing Sing's administration changed ten times. The result of this constant change in personnel was the instability of all forms of improvement and the neglect of the physical portion of the prison. In 1873, the newly appointed warden who had served in the same capacity ten years before, was led to remark: "Ten years ago I was warden of this prison; I then considered it a failure, and yet, compared with it now, it was a model of perfection. The system of labor has degenerated, the convicts have grown saucy and lazy, officers and convicts mingle on a complete social basis, buildings are in a terrible condition of decay, some having been torn down for supplies."

During this year 364 punishments were inflicted on an average population of 1163. Ninety-four men were capped, 98 were placed in dark cells, and 72 were strung up by the thumbs in a dark cell and left standing there with their toes barely touching the floor.

The years from 1874 to 1883 were the period that George Appo so vividly described in his unpublished manuscript. Not every prison official agreed with the punishments then in vogue. Thus we find the prison physician protesting that "the dark cells are entirely unfit to confine convicts for punishment." A criticism that was gratuitous. But it did not go unheeded, for in 1879 a building, containing ten cells for solitary confinement, was completed. It was situated in the yard separate from the other structures, one story high. It was well ventilated, with a supply of water and closets for each cell. These ten cells seem to have been the forerunners of the modern prison cell in the New Sing Sing on the hill.

Conditions apparently improved with the years, for in 1884, out of a population of 1522, only eight men were locked in their cells for any refractory dispositions. This is the more remarkable in view of the vicious practice of doubling men in their cells. A practice that in the words of the then Prison Physician, "was in all respects objectionable, unwholesome and demoralizing."

During all these years prison administrations struggled with what was known as contract labor. There is very little good that can be said for that system. The prisoner was actually hired out to the contractor who regulated the kind of work to be done and the manner of its accomplishment. It kept the prisoner occupied, but gave too much power to the employer who cared nothing about the health or condition of the prisoner in his anxiety to have his contracts fulfilled. For years labor unions waged war against this system. Not out of sympathy for the prisoner but because of the alleged effect on the labor market. The system was bad, but its sudden abolition still worse. Nothing was substituted in its place. Contract labor was abolished in 1888, and as the result over one thousand men were kept in idleness, locked in their cells with nothing to do. "The last prison year," said the warden in 1889, "was the most unsatisfactory and most unfortunate that has been experienced in our State. The causes of this condition did not exist in the prisons, but were outside of them. By the provisions of Chapter 586, Laws of 1888, the pursuit of usual industrial operations in the state prisons was almost wholly suspended and the increased population of the prisons was doomed to idleness."

It had been suggested, as a further means of prison regulation, that convicts receive a portion of their pay. "Nothing has been done," remarks this warden, "toward a plan to pay the convicts a part of their earnings for the good reason that there have as yet been no earnings to divide." A plausible explanation, indeed.

In 1891, we find a significant reference to the indeterminate sentence law. After a long period of agitation the Legislature finally passed the indeterminate sentence law of 1889. It was to be a reformatory influence on prisoners and of great aid in prison management. Judges and prosecutors were timid about it and refused to take advantage of the law. In 1891, the Warden of Sing Sing writes that "not one convict received at this prison has been so sentenced." Traditional procedure is difficult to overcome. Nothing proves that more than the pages of the prison reports. Officialdom held on with all its power to old theories of government and administration.

98

We hear a great deal in these advanced days about classification of prisoners. It is really not a new theory. It was tried in 1897 at Sing Sing and at other New York State Prisons. Prisoners were, in that year, divided into three groups.

Group A consisted of prisoners serving their first term for a felony.

Group B for prisoners serving their second term for a felony.

Group C for prisoners serving their third or subsequent term. The plan was that all first offenders were to be retained at the prison to which they were originally committed. Second offenders received at Sing Sing and Clinton were transferred to Auburn. Members of Group C received at Sing Sing were to be transferred to Clinton Prison.

The plan was not successful because prisoners were classified, not according to personality or mentality, but according to the number of crimes committed. It was soon abandoned.

With the turning of the Twentieth Century a new light dawned in the old cell block at Sing Sing. For the first time in its history a ray of sunshine was allowed to penetrate within that damp and dark interior. For seventy-five years it had been lighted by a great number of little windows approximately ten inches wide by twenty-four inches high, mere slits in the thick walls. The interior of the hall was always gloomy and depressing and in the summer quite damp. In 1901 at the recommendation of C. V. Collins, Superintendent of Prisons, the Legislature provided for the installation of large windows in the walls of the cell house, and during 1902 twenty of them were put in place. The effect of those windows, 31 feet high, and 5½ feet wide, exceeded "all expectations." The report of the prison inspectors reflect the enthusiasm occasioned by this change. "The place is now flooded with light and sunshine and the hall, thus transformed is one of the most cheerful in the prison. The improvement is one of the most effective and satisfactory that has been made in the prison buildings in many years."

But the "red letter" day in the history of Sing Sing was August 9, 1900. On that day the hateful and degrading lock-step was discarded by order of Superintendent Collins. A custom that had become traditional. It had imbedded itself in the life of the prison. The lock-step not only affected the prisoner as he marched to and from his various tasks, but more than any other rule, gave the prisoner that sluggish, shuffling gait that affected his mentality and his views on life. Its abolition put new spirit into the hearts of prisoners. They could walk like men. Probably, later on they would be able to talk like men, and what is still more important to think like men.

Things moved fast in those early years of the Twentieth Century. Nineteen hundred and four witnessed the abolition of the prison stripe. Of this the then administrator remarks: "We expected good results from the change, but the effect reaches far beyond our expectations. The men are cheerful and appreciative. The very tone of the institution has changed, and we are confident that the atmosphere thus produced will prove to be an active and powerful reformatory agent."

Every one of these physical improvements had been frowned upon by many legislators and not a few prison officials.

We find now among progressive penologists and socially minded people a definite desire for a plan of prison government that will help to reform, not only the institution, but also the men confined therein. Just as important as was the improvement of the physical surroundings of prisoners was the reshaping of their mental outlook, the remoulding of men's minds. A Committee of the Legislature of the State of New York reported in appreciation of this objective. The report was not unanimous. A minority on the committee voiced its protest:

"The cardinal object of all penal discipline is supposed to be the reformation of offenders. To this doctrine the minority cannot subscribe. If the doctrine of the majority is to prevail (that of teaching the prisoner in the ways of normal life) the most vile and hardened in our prisons will be placed on a footing with the honest but unfortunate inmates of our almshouses, and poverty will henceforth take its position in the catalogue of crime, equal in rank with manslaughter, arson, burglary, and highway robbery."

"The undersigned believe," the minority go on to say, "that punishment is a necessary and proper attribute in prison discipline.

"Let prisons cease to be a terror to the depraved and a warning to others who may be disposed to wander from the highway where travel the good and the virtuous—let a frenzied sympathy excite the passions and swell the bosom of the community in soothing the imaginary wrongs of criminals, and misguided philanthropy seek to mitigate the ills of mankind in converting our penitentiaries into schools for the instruction alone of its inmates—let the principle that punishment is no part of our prison system, and moral suasion and reformation obtain the ascendency over calm and judicious observance of an 'enlightened policy'—a policy that would be a terror to the depraved and evil doers, and terrify the youthful rogue, and prevent a continual drain upon the treasury for the support of those who the taxpayers are under no obligation to support, and then the period will arrive when insurrection, incendiarism, robbery, and all the evils most fatal to society and detrimental to law and order, will reign supreme." This minority protested against the discarding of all the traditional methods of prison management. The silent system, the "cat," the cage, the paddle, the dark cell, ball and chain, bread and water diet, the pulley, all were part of what they termed "a beautiful system which has heretofore been applauded by almost every state and civilized nation, as a pattern of prison discipline."

This minority dictum is an interesting sidelight on a penal philosophy which disregarded entirely the fact that imprisonment alone is, in a large measure, a most effective punishment; actually, the most salutary punishment yet devised by man. They disregarded entirely the now well established theory that the criminal is concerned mainly with avoiding detection and imprisonment. That though it might be impossible, in many cases, to change human nature, the prison can do much in at least trying to understand it.

This school of thought did not realize that the elimination of brutality was only a beginning toward a new order which emphasized morale based upon individual responsibility instead of physical fear. A responsibility that can be trained to respond volun-

102

tarily to a directing influence more readily than the body can be made to yield to blind force. The possibility of individual responsibility is latent in every person. Properly appealed to, it can invariably bring out what is best in him to the advantage of society and his own reconstruction.

Warden Clancy in 1913 made a novel if not daring experiment. It had never before been attempted. Prisoners' every move had been supervised, regulated and checked. When not at their tasks, they were in their cells with plenty of time to brood. The longest period of confinement was over the week end. From Saturday noon until the following Monday morning the men never left their cells. Did they spend their time in repentance? Did they emerge on Monday morning chastened in spirit? The prison records show otherwise. Monday morning in Sing Sing was invariably "blue." Prisoners were irritable, resentful, difficult to handle. Instead of keeping the men locked up for thirty-six hours, Warden Clancy permitted them to remain out in the open air on Sunday morning. They were not permitted to roam about but stood or sat at ease in companies, each with their keepers. It was only a gesture. And a very timid one at that. But it worked. "This reform," reads Warden Clancy's report, "has proved to be highly beneficial and is much appreciated by the inmates; it is, I believe, conducive to better discipline." Mr. Clancy went one step further. Columbus Day in 1912 marked the beginning of a new era in the administration of Sing Sing Prison. It was the very first time that prisoners were permitted to remain out of their cells for a whole day and, as Mr. Clancy put it, "allowed the freedom of the prison." Men were put on their honor. The Warden did not dare to repeat the experiment. Officialdom was not quite prepared for it. And so it was passed by as a novelty in prison administration. Its success, however, encouraged Mr. Clancy's successor to broaden its scope.

Warden McCormick's administration is important as the first which succeeded in "opening up Sing Sing."

Mr. McCormick's administration was short lived; not over a few months. But it was an effective administration from an institutional point of view. He proceeded on the theory that confinement within the walls of the prison was punishment. That the law never intended to confine prisoners within the prison. From a moral point of view, it was putting the prisoner in double jeopardy. Actually it was a double punishment. Mr. McCormick introduced the system of regulated leisure. Prisoners were allowed the freedom of the Prison Yard Saturday afternoon and all day Sunday.

Officers and prisoners still remember the first "free Sunday." Men roamed around the prison courtyard timidly, as if fearful of their steps, like children just learning to walk. Administrators and officials had expressed dire forebodings. The prisoners had no responsibility, no honor. The prison would be terrorized. Prisoners and their guards eyed one another furtively, hardly knowing what to expect of each other. Men breathed deeply of the free outdoors. Authority and subjects moved closer together understandingly. Blue Monday was outmoded; it became a myth. Prisoners started their week's tasks with renewed energy. But what was more important was the feeling among the prisoners of Sing Sing that they were on their honor. It was during this administration that baseball was

introduced on the recreation field. To Warden Mc-
Cormick belongs the credit of organizing the first inmate organization for self-government. It was known
as the Golden Rule Brotherhood, the forerunner of
the Mutual Welfare League.

McCormick's innovations did not meet with unanimous approval and he was succeeded by a gentleman
outstanding among prison administrators as the man
who aroused popular interest in prisons and penal affairs, Thomas Mott Osborne.

Of all the array of incoming and outgoing wardens
in the century of Sing Sing's history, his name stands
out in bold relief. To him must be given the credit for
a more enlightened policy that, while not entirely complete, pointed the way toward the new penology. In
the swift flowing currents of human emotions, the warden of a prison must be able to guide his institution on
a straight and unvarying course. He is like the pilot at
the helm of his ship. Unusually strong waves will hammer him off his course. Now the tug will be in one
direction, then in an opposite direction. The pilot must
have a steady hand, a clear vision and know his com-
pass. This man knew his objective. His thought was to
arouse in the prisoner the spirit of self-responsibility
without force. He recognized clearly the principle that
corruption cannot be sweated out. He mapped out his
course. He was headed for port. He had the right idea.
After a while the ship began to flounder. It could not
be kept on an even course, and before long it found
itself entirely off the beaten lane. That is the story of
Sing Sing Prison during the seven years from 1913
to 1920.

Mr. Osborne introduced the prison to the public.

He made it a subject of free and popular discussion in the press and on the platform. He was the sincere reformer and advocate, whose deep and abiding faith in his cause encouraged his successors to develop prison government along sane, human, practical and effective lines.

"Life, liberty and the pursuit of happiness," form the cardinal principle of American government. They constitute the heritage of every citizen. The only one of these vouchsafed to the man in prison was life. A precarious life, at best, but there was the pious insistence upon its preservation. It was Osborne's objective to accord the prisoner, while doing time, the other two essentials so as to make his life within the walls as normal as possible. He firmly believed that it was possible to have liberty within the walls accompanied, naturally, by the right to pursue individual happiness, each in his own peculiar way. What Mr. Osborne did not see clearly was that prisoners are, actually, people who have quarreled with the law. That regardless of motivating forces or underlying causes prisons are communities of nonconformists. In communities where the law has become ineffective, constituted government calls for martial law. It is an extraordinary measure, seldom invoked. But prisons are extraordinary institutions. They house men who have broken with good government, with law and order, with society. Prison administrations are in the nature of emergency governments. All prison administration savors of the nature of a despotism. The successful administrator will be the benevolent despot as well as the understanding leader.

Peoples and civilizations have flourished happily and

successfully for centuries under benevolent despots. There is a school of political thought that questions the permanence of government founded on democracy. However that may be, the fact is that there can be no pure democracy within prison walls. Nor can anything even faintly resembling a republican form of government long prevail. It is now an almost generally accepted fact that prisons must permit their inmates to engage in useful occupation. Also, that prisoners should be encouraged to spend their leisure in healthful recreation. I believe, further, that prisoners should be allowed a measure of self-expression, a voice in the kind and character of their social and recreational activities. These, however, must at all times be subject to administrative supervision and censorship. The defect of Mr. Osborne's administration was in the overlapping of prisoner self-government with the warden's responsibility as an administrator. His intense desire to raise the prisoner to a normal plane led him to surrender his prerogatives. He became an advisor instead of a leader and ruler. The swing of the pendulum from severity to liberality was too wide. It resulted in chaos. Mr. Osborne was not given the opportunity to correct this fault. His term of office ended too soon. Dean George W. Kirchway took the helm from Mr. Osborne. He contributed greatly to the prison's educational facilities, and continued the self-government idea among prisoners. Subsequent administrations tightened the reins. They were either too short or too ineffective.

* * * *

I turned the last pages of the prison reports, convinced that I had a man-sized job ahead of me. I would have to straighten out the ship's course. The benevolent despotism would have to be reestablished without curtailing the normal activities of my wards. The quest for normal life, liberty and happiness was theirs by right, as it must be that of every human being. Before they could succeed, they would have to attain a full measure of self-respect, self-restraint and self-reliance. That was the Warden's real job. With that objective I entered upon my duties as the Warden of Sing Sing Prison.

Courtesy Fox Movietone News.

. . . at six-thirty o'clock, when the first bell is sounded for dressing and making beds. . . . *(Page 160)*

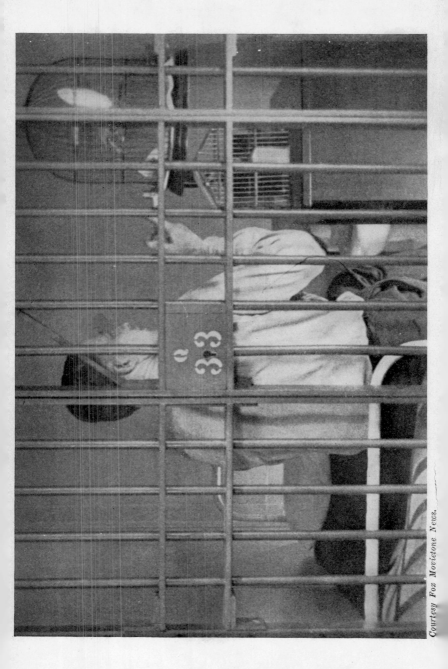

CHAPTER 4: NEW TRAILS FOR OLD

"THE quickest way to get out of Sing Sing is to come in as warden," was a popular joke of the day in 1920. It was more than a joke. For a period of twenty years the average term of service had been little over eleven months. I have entered the thirteenth year of service.

The inaugural ceremonies were simple. I arrived on the first of January, 1920, and met the prisoner population for the first time, as a group, in the old mess hall at the noon hour. The then Superintendent of Prisons introduced me to the men. I was invited to address them from an improvised platform in the center of the hall. I refused. "I'd rather talk to you men on the level," I told them, "I hope to stay here."

I explained to my audience that though I was willing to meet them half way and give them all the breaks they were entitled to on their records, there would be no "you be a good boy and I'll be a good warden" policy. What they would get in the line of privileges they would have to earn. On the other hand, if their conduct justified it, they would get as much leeway as was consistent with their status as prisoners in a State Prison. That has been my theory and practice during the twelve years of my wardenship. I have never had occasion to regret the theory nor to seriously modify the practice.

Advice and admonition poured in on me from every side. In the main the volunteers were divided into two factions. One cautioned, "Treat 'em rough." The other said, "Don't treat 'em rough." There did not seem to be any middle course advocates.

Gossip was rife and virulent during those early days. Everybody had something to say about everybody else. My predecessor had been in office only six weeks. There had apparently been some friction between him and one of his subordinates. The story came to me later about the wager these two men made that hinged on my decision. Said the warden to his clerk, "If Lawes declines it, you go." And the clerk replied, "But if Lawes accepts, you can just bet your last dollar that I'll stay."

The relations between them had been strained to the breaking point. I had met the warden casually, but was not at all acquainted with the clerk who occupied a confidential post in the prison.

On the morning when my decision was due, both men sat in the office waiting. Both were well on in years, gray-haired and determined. They did not talk to or with each other. But at every ring of the telephone both would jerk up nervously from their seats. "Not yet," the clerk at the switchboard would announce. The two elderly gentlemen sat back in their chairs and glared at each other.

Then towards noon the telephone rang once more. "It's the Governor," the clerk called. The warden, with a venomous look toward his enemy, grasped the receiver, listened to the message, then slowly hung up. "You win, you old codger," was all he said. That old clerk was a good gambler. He stayed on. He is still at his old desk, one of my trusted employees and friends.

The warden whom my immediate predecessor suc-

110

ceeded had lasted six months. It must have been a strenuous six months. It was said that he reduced forty pounds in weight during his incumbency. Whether it was because the prisoners, or officialdom, had led him a merry chase, or whether the mental strain was too tense, I could never find out. The fact was, however, that I had no desire to lose weight on this or any other job. It became quickly apparent to me that under conditions as they were, the prison warden, to be effective, would have to constitute himself not as an instrument of punishment but a firm, frank friend in need. He would have to stretch humanitarianism to the limits of the law, with a stiff punch always in reserve. I have been charged, since my incumbency, with being too kind. I wish I could plead guilty to the accusation, but my sense of duty will not permit it. My job is to hold my men and, as far as possible, to win them over to sane, social thinking. And I judge the effectiveness of that job not so much by obedience to rule, for rules can be enforced, but by the humor of the general prison population.

When I came to Sing Sing its population was slightly over one thousand. The administrative officers were the Principal Keeper, Assistant Principal Keeper, one Sergeant, and also the Captain of the Night Watch.

The Bertillon Department was manned by inmates except for a competent civilian with one eye, who at times also acted as receiving officer. The prison had no cook, only a kitchen keeper. There was no civilian painter or plumber. The school had only one civilian school teacher. There was no pathologist, no psychiatrist, no psychologist, and only two doctors in attendance. The comptroller's clerk and assistant clerk were political appointees. Generally their sole qualifications were outside the field of finance. An ex-motorman would do. Sometimes an ex-fishdealer. The enclosed prison grounds then consisted of about fourteen and a half acres, with one cell block and a large dormitory. Shacks and huts for personal use filled the prison yard. Rabbit holes were all over. The Mutual Welfare League was part and parcel of the administration, and its officers were permitted out of their cells long after midnight and had free access to the visiting room.

A clever prisoner aptly described the workings of the League at that time. "It may be truly said," he wrote, "in the light of events, that at the very period of its inception the 'League' failed to fully fulfill its appointed mission. The moment it was put into the exclusive control of 'cliques,' 'gangs,' etc., it perforce lost its mutual features. It was to their individual benefit to maintain this control, with the result that the lowbrow contingency has always maintained its ascendancy through inspired fear and intimidation. If one was willing to sacrifice his personal self-respect and worship at the shrine of the Chief Gorilla of the Harlem Goofers, he was persona grata and welcomed to the inner circles of the 'exclusive and limited association' which has long masqueraded under false colors as the Mutual Welfare League.

"I myself have formed the opinion that if they will only consult the best interests of the institution and permit you to put into operation your plans and ideas, a new Sing Sing will be the order of the day and the very ones who may criticise you now will be the first ones to praise you in the end. It invariably works out that way.

"For myself, I renew my pledge, as an inmate, to do all in my power to lend support while here to your administration. I have no interest other than to show thereby that I applaud the executive ability which you have manifested. Yours is indeed the task of a Hercules —you have an Augean Stable to clean of the putrid accumulation of years, but I, and quite a number of others in here, are confident that you are capable of tackling the job."

Beyond all doubt, the Mutual Welfare League was a worth-while organization, but it was badly administered. Any remedy, either for physical or spiritual ills, when badly administered, can become mortally dangerous. Self-government in prisons must not be allowed to descend to the level of ward politics. If self-government is to accustom the prisoner to self-restraint, if it is to become a basis for character building, it cannot be permitted to encourage campaigns among the prisoner population that will arouse passionate partisanship with all the evils and intrigues of practical politics.

I found the League membership divided into two party camps. The energies of both parties were concentrated toward corralling sufficient votes for election purposes. Eloquence alone did not suffice. As the result, the better element among the prisoners held themselves aloof from the League, and it gradually became the plaything of the less desirable class of men. Prison officials looked forward to elections with considerable apprehension. The first-aid clinic was very busy on that day. Often prison surgeons were called upon to perform hurried operations. Here was the old-time ward politics with all its traditional fury and vehemence. The stakes were probably worth fighting for.

Visiting through the institution was popular in those days. "Sing Sing, the prison in New York State," wrote a special writer of those days, "is more famous perhaps than the Statue of Liberty in New York Harbor. Visitors from out of town seeking 'to do the prison' are so numerous."

The League officials had full charge of all visiting and invariably guided visiting parties around the prison. There were gratuities, of course. Prison officials never interfered with a visiting party in charge of a League member.

The League had full charge and control of the store. It made its own purchases, banked its money, and disbursed its funds. Little supervision, if any, was given to this department.

The Executive Board of the League designated its Sergeant-at-Arms, who in turn appointed his staff of deputy sergeants. They had full charge of the recreation field, the chapel, and all entertainments and athletic events. They also functioned as monitors in the mess hall. It was their right and duty to report any prisoner for violation of rules or for delinquencies. Reports were made to the League Court which consisted of seven judges before whom the accuser and accused presented the facts. The judges, sad to relate, were not always of the highest calibre. They were, it was whispered around, hand-picked and did not examine facts with impersonal impartiality. Often the prisoner would be placed in double jeopardy. He would be punished by the Warden's Court and thereafter had to answer, as well, to the League Court for the same offence.

Officials of the League were assigned to the visiting room. They had unrestricted contact with visitors and strangers. There was little, if any, supervision over possible contraband that might thus find its way within the walls. Through its Director of Entertainment it was its own censor of what was decent and presentable to the general prisoner population. I remember my first experience with the Director. He showed me a play which was to be produced at the Annual Show. I suggested several deletions. He protested vigorously. "That line is in the book," he said, "and went big on Broadway."

"There's a lot goes on Broadway," I replied, "that won't get over in Sing Sing."

There were also a number of things that went over big in many political wards that could not go over in Sing Sing. There were a great many things in Sing Sing that would have to be stopped for the good of the general population and the morale of the institution. "The fact is," one of the prisoners said to me, "that the intellectual part of the inmate population has never, to any appreciable extent, been represented in the conduct of the League's affairs. It is not in control now by a very noticeable majority, but there is a feeling prevalent (it's in the air, as it were) that with you at the helm there's going to be a radical departure which will bring the League back to the functions for which it was ostensibly created."

I had a talk with the officers of the League. I wanted to get acquainted. What was their idea of prisons and prisoners? What was their philosophy of life? We sat in my office and talked things over. One of them turned to me and said, "Warden, there are only two classes of people in the world."

"What do you mean?" I asked.

He laughed. "Those who are in jail and those who ought to be."

The crowd roared. I explained as carefully as I could that they were wrong. There were three classes of people. Those who were in jail, those who were on the way, and the third who will never get there.

But what impressed me was the attitude of these men, the leaders of the prison population and, apparently, its accredited representatives, toward authority and law and order. I doubted if this was the judgment of the population of the prison. Surely, however, this was not the type of men whom I would want to speak for Sing Sing's prisoners.

I had always maintained that the collective judgment of a group is generally good. Where the group is disintegrated into sects and parties there can, of course, be no unanimity of purpose, no cooperation. Even within the walls of a prison there must be a singleness of purpose among the inmates as well as among the official family. Self-government among prisoners, to be successful and worth while, cannot work at cross purposes with the administration. The important problem that faced me was to clarify the responsibilities and obligations and relationship of each group of men within the walls of the prison. On the one side there were the officers who had their responsibility of maintaining discipline and order. On the other hand were the prisoners whom we had to treat as subjects, but in whom we desired to inspire the spirit of self-confidence

116

and the desire for right living which naturally is based upon the power of restraint. I explained my attitude at a meeting of the Executive Board of the Mutual Welfare League.

"Most of the inmates of this institution are decent individuals and I am going to do my duty toward them as I see it, without partiality. But I want a fifty-fifty break and I shall hold each man accountable for his full share of responsibility."

That all was not right with the personnel of the League was apparent from a report that appeared in the prison paper, "The Star Bulletin," at that time, about an incident that had to do with the League Court.

"There was the deuce to pay when the Executive Board notified Judge Schott that his term had expired and that another man had been appointed to succeed him. Immediately the Judiciary Board got together and resigned in a body. They drew up a letter that contained some acrimonious accusations and sent it along with their resignations. This called for an immediate session of the Executive Board. The judges were sent for and asked to substantiate their charges of graft and political favoritism. Some said they couldn't, and the others said they wouldn't. Three withdrew their resignations and two stood pat. Schott was reinstated and so were the others, except Vaght and Lanyon. Potruch and Schott were elected in their places. Charlie Kennedy was promoted from clerk to Judge to fill a vacancy caused by the departure of 'Doc' Stapler. George Liljewall, a newcomer, was appointed clerk and general stenographer to the League."

Incidents such as these might be all right on the

outside. People are more or less accustomed to sharp political practices. In prison they are out of place. The purpose of a prison is to correct irregular conduct and motivation. Subterfuge and chicanery within the walls lead to grosser excesses outside. I took a long step and abolished the League's Court. I went still further. I abolished party politics. Most of the "big shots" belonged to the majority party. It was rumored about the prison that their tactics were not always ethical. They were expected to hand out "plums." During election periods large posters hung conspicuously throughout the prison yard and in shops and offices. "Vote for" signs were in evidence. The excitement of the campaign was a disturbing element in prison morale. In normal life the emotionalism of a political campaign dies with the counting of the votes. Victors and vanquished seek peace and restfulness in the quiet of their firesides, in clubs, and in places of amusement. Within the congestion of a prison, with its lack of emotional outlets, antagonisms loom large and are not easily quenched. Intense partisanship continued among the men long after election day. Nor could either party offer inducements or make promises that the other could not fulfill as long as they were not inconsistent with the policy of the institution. I did away with party politics and placed the choice for delegates on a purely personal basis.

"Self-government" in prison is a much abused and greatly misconstrued term. A group of men who have quarrelled with the law cannot be expected to set up a government patterned after the one they antagonized and suddenly become conformists. Prisoner self-government has no relation with politics. It means exactly what the term implies. The government of self.

I defined clearly the sphere of influence of the League in its relation to the prison administration. Its primary obligation was to regulate the leisure hours of the prisoners. It would have charge of all recreation, on the field and in the chapel. Subject always to the censorship of the warden, it would be permitted to provide musical entertainments, arrange the schedule of moving pictures, engage in whatever social welfare work that was called to its attention by prisoners on behalf of their dependents; in fact, all extra-administrative demands of a community such as the prisoner population represented.

A Board of Delegates working, not walking, was to be elected, one from each shop, or company. Where there was more than one candidate, the one with the highest number of votes would naturally be the winner. It was to be a matter of person rather than party.

These delegates in turn selected an Executive Board, who had actual control of the affairs of the League. They selected a secretary and a sergeant-at-arms. The former was to be the spokesman of the League with the administration. The latter, with his deputy sergeants, appointed by him, would be responsible for the orderly conduct of all athletic events, and at pictures in the chapel. They would regulate the lineup at mess and supervise the marching to the mess hall.

In the large population of Sing Sing it was physically impossible for the warden to hold interviews daily with all the men who wanted advice, or needed help, or felt a hurt. All prisoners who sought the warden's help about their intimate problems or troubles could present their difficulties to the League Secretary who would convey them to the warden during one of his two daily interviews. If the matter could be settled between them, the warden would decide upon the matter at issue immediately. If further investigation was necessary, the prisoner was sent for by the warden for more intimate discussion. It was made clear, however, that breaches of discipline would be handled only by the administration through its Warden's Court. The League was to be a moral force. If it could not maintain itself in that capacity it was futile and should be eliminated. If prisoners really intended to reconstruct their lives and regain the respect of their fellows, they would have to be swayed by moral influence rather than by force. That was all that I was willing to concede to the League. That is all I have ever accorded it. In the main it has succeeded.

With the disappearance of partisanship, more dominant men came to the fore. They exerted a good influence on the general population. I had very little trouble with either the delegates or officials of the League in the ensuing years. Generally, the secretaries were willing and anxious to aid in maintaining a helpful attitude throughout the prison. The membership and officers of the League were, naturally, transient. The material that supplied the leadership varied. Each secretary had his own peculiar method of approach. Four of these stand out above their fellows in personality and method.

There was the doctor. Ex-doctor, rather. For his name was marked off the roster. He had performed an illegal operation which had resulted in the death of the patient. He was convicted of manslaughter and

120

sent to Sing Sing. A man of fine education and a very clever fellow, about fifty, I should say. He did not belong to any particular group within the walls. He was regarded as a silk stocking, a sort of intellectual. But his outstanding ability soon found him recognition, and in the turnover at one of the League elections he was pressed into service by the better element and designated as the League secretary. I was pleased with the designation. After all, it is much more satisfactory to deal with a man of sense and worldly knowledge than with one who knows nothing of mob psychology or human nature.

Doctor took to his job like a veteran. He was a radical by nature. He was also reputed to be a very wealthy man. But in all the years of his imprisonment he never wore anything else than prison clothing. Even his shoes were from the State Shop, although prisoners are generally permitted to order them from the outside.

He was more than a radical. He was a Russian and a Bolshevist. An intellectual communist who adored his Lenin and sought every provocation to talk about him.

Doctor would come into my office in the morning with a sheaf of papers. Letters from Grade "B" men whose correspondence privileges had been curtailed. They were allowed one letter a week. All extra letters had to be approved by the warden. Among his papers were requests for restoration of privileges, commissary, visiting and others. Probably he would have a request from a prisoner to visit his dying parent, or to attend the funeral of a deceased relative. There might be a request for permission to have the Comptroller draw a check on the prisoner's account to send to a wife or parent, or a request from the Director of Entertainment for a special picture. All these the "Doctor" would lay on my desk in a heap. At my nod he would sit down.

One could hardly resist listening to his discourse on Russia and the problems of Lenin's government. He never criticised America, nor the capitalist system.

"It's an experiment, Warden," he would say. "A lesson in self-control. Can the proletariat measure up to it? Time will tell. It may be all wrong but it's worth the try."

And then after he had expounded on the under-dog and his lack of perspective and opportunity, he would hand me the batch of papers. "All under-dogs, Warden. They didn't know any better. Grade 'B's.' Give them a chance. Maybe that will help, too."

He would argue for the lowliest of his fellow prisoners. Never missed a trick. But he would never present a request that was objectionable. He argued it out with the dissatisfied prisoner before he came to me. The respect which he commanded among the prisoners helped to weed out petty and unreasonable demands and complaints.

"Doc" left us some years ago. It is rumored that he now holds a responsible and confidential position with the Russian Government. Rumor has it also that he has amassed another fortune. Possibly he still wears flannels and the attire of the "common people" which he so steadfastly adhered to in Sing Sing.

Pitney was an entirely different kind of personality. He never refused to accept a request from a prisoner. "I am just your messenger boy, fellows," he would say to them. "Pile them up and I'll take 'em to the Boss. It's O. K. with me, if he'll stand for it." It is some years ago since he left Sing Sing, but I remember well his first visit to my office in his official capacity. He was a practical man, had been a banker. And he did not go in for much argument or discussion.

"Warden," he said, after a few words of greeting, "you know the story of the customer who had just been shaved in a barber shop. The barber stood in front of him with a comb in one hand and a brush in the other and he said: 'Wet or dry?' The customer answered, 'Comb my hair. I don't want to start no argument.'

"That's me, Warden. You're the Boss. Just mark these 'yes' or 'no.' I'll tell the boys."

And when I had gone over his papers and marked them he would pick them up and, with a courtly bow, retire from the room.

Another secretary was the prisoner doing a sentence of twenty years to life. He was a husky young fellow. He was never backward in expressing his opinion. Hardly an intellectual, he was more inclined toward the rough and ready kind. It was rumored that he had taken the "rap" for another member of his family, but apparently that had not soured his disposition. He was a "square shooter" but inclined somewhat toward the so-called "big shot" element. He retained the respect of the men in the yard by brawn rather than brain. And he had a good command of prison slang which he used to perfection.

A denial of any request that he thought fair and reasonable and plausible was met with the demand for an explanation. He was never disrespectful, but would not hesitate to "have it out."

"Aw, Warden, have a heart," he would persist. "Give the boys a break."

Sometimes he won; often he didn't. But he surely did fight for his men.

Harry was an ingratiating personality. He was an efficient secretary. And he retained a fairly good control over the men in the prison. He took his office seriously. In his desire to impress the officials of the League he confidently promised the Warden's "O. K." before he brought the matter to my attention. He often got himself in hot water because of his over-confidence. Then he would appeal to me for aid. "It's my mistake, Warden. Won't you back me up this once?"

He did that once too often and as the result his entire executive board resigned in protest. I had to take a hand to straighten the matter out. But that did not seem to dim his self-confidence, for he repeated his tactics again and again.

Harry was an intelligent sort of fellow. He had a flair for big words with which he impressed his fellow prisoners who seldom understood what he was talking about. He accomplished a great deal for them, but one had to be careful in dealing with him. It would never do to give him a verbal order. It was sure to be distorted far beyond its meaning. In the morning he would come in with a constructive suggestion. "For the good of the administration," was the way he put it. But he would ask for something in return. Something that was not so good "for the good of the administration." A denial of the latter would leave him sulking. But in his next interview he would return with the same request. He had a dozen plausible explanations for irregularities of which he was accused. In trying to

124

work both ends against the middle he made enemies among the prisoners and eventually had to retire from office.

All this happened over a period of years. I found on my assumption of the wardenship that my official force was just as disorganized as the prisoners. Guards had become resentful of the latitude allowed to the prisoners. They hoped that the incoming administration would tighten down. On the other hand there were officers who had established very liberal and intimate relationship with the men. They were fearful of any change.

I soon discovered that prisoners had been playing the horses; that with the help of inmate operators telephone calls were being made by prisoners to their friends on the outside; that permission to wear small items of personal wearing apparel had been abused, to the extent that silk shirts of all hues and grades were common in the prison yard. In the visiting room, through contact by members of the League and promiscuous visitors, contraband was being brought in. It was rumored, also, that booze and dope were not strangers to certain cliques who profited by these contacts.

I discovered gross carelessness in the business management of the prison. Assignments of prisoners to important clerical jobs were haphazard and led to many abuses. In the shipping room it was the custom, so to speak, to toss up a penny as to whether the goods should be sent by express or freight, regardless of classification rates and other considerations looking toward reduction of traffic expense in connection with deliveries of merchandise. "You never miss a slice off a cut loaf," an officer explained to me when I asked for an explanation. The prison was common property. Why worry? That seemed to be the general attitude of the prison officials.

During my first year of office the prison personnel changed rapidly. The principal keeper retired. His successor resigned after five weeks of service. The assistant principal keeper retired after twenty-seven years of service in Sing Sing. The yard master retired. In addition scores of keepers were retired or resigned. The result was that I was holding down a new job, with a new staff and a brand new policy of administration.

Running a prison was never designed to be a pleasant job. And running Sing Sing, as I early discovered, was no pink tea affair. Because of its proximity to New York, Sing Sing is always more or less in the public eye. Hardly anything escapes the alert newspapermen. That is as it should be, for prisons are public institutions and not the private estates of wardens or prison officials. But when, as a sanitary precaution, I ordered all rabbit nests removed and the rabbits banished from the prison, and several emotional editors took a fling at me for my "unfeeling" attitude toward the prisoners and their pets, I resented it as undue interference. It is perhaps interesting to observe that some of these very same newspapers later condemned me for being too lenient.

Suggestion and advice came from all quarters. On the morning before he left the prison the assistant principal keeper who had been in the service for twenty-seven years left me his impressions of how to run a prison.

"I started twenty-seven years ago," he said, "as a keeper, and the old principal keeper instructed me to keep a sharp watch over the men and not permit any infractions of the rules.

"On my first night in the old cell block I discovered a prisoner conversing with another prisoner through the ventilators between their cells. This was, at that time, strictly against the regulations and I told them to cut it out or I would report them. One of the fellows hopped down from his bunk and came to the grating of his cell door.

" 'Say, are you a new man around here?' he asked.

"I admitted it.

" 'Well, young fellow,' the prisoner continued, 'let an old-timer give you a bit of advice. You may be here a long time and some day you may be promoted to assistant principal keeper, or maybe principal keeper. Just take a tip from one who has spent most of his life in prison and don't see too damn much.' "

Administrators are unanimous in the logic of this advice. Trivial infractions of rules are often overlooked. But there is always the danger that the things that seem trivial and of no account are fraught with the greatest danger and the most serious consequences. Such an incident led me to offer my resignation to Governor Alfred E. Smith during the first year of my administration. It was the result of too much attention to trivialities on the part of one of my superiors in the department.

The Sing Sing Bulletin was then flourishing as the prison paper and had achieved fame of a sort in the world at large as a well-edited sheet. It had always been run under the supervision and censorship of the warden. The then Superintendent of Prisons suddenly decided that he would be the censor and ordered that nothing be printed in the prison paper without his approval and sanction.

Standing alone it was a harmless order. Under ordinary circumstances I would have welcomed it because it relieved me from "just another job." And there were many more important jobs within the walls of Sing Sing at that time. I did, however, object to it in principle. I had understood that I was to have a free hand; that I was to run the prison in the light of my own conscience and judgment. This order might lead to others and ultimately I would be the man with the keys of the prison whose job was merely to lock and unlock doors, deprived of every opportunity to develop a definite and positive policy. I expressed my resentment and not getting any satisfaction from the official who issued the order, determined to take my appeal to the Governor. I met him by appointment at the Biltmore Hotel in New York.

I stepped off the elevator on the floor of his suite and was amazed to find myself suddenly in the midst of a score of fashionably attired women. They were separated in groups of three and five, all engaged in vociferous talk. I was about to withdraw, certain that I was on the wrong floor, when an attendant espied me. He approached me and whispered, "Warden Lawes?" I nodded. "Come with me. The Governor will see you first. These dames can wait. It's some welfare crowd and they want to be photographed with the Governor. They'll wait till the cows come home and then some."

The hubbub died down somewhat as we passed

through the corridor. They had no idea of my identity and thought, probably, that I was a lowly friend of Al Smith's, or one of the chieftains of Tammany Hall. I was escorted into the Governor's suite and ushered into a large room, with an informal "Here's the Warden, Governor."

It was an altogether different sight that met my eyes in that room. A contrast that spoke well for the spirit of America. Outside, waiting impatiently, were those fashionable ladies, social register names and all that. They represented, no doubt, some of the most prominent families in New York. All anxious to be in the picture with the Governor. At the table before me sat the object of their quest, in shirt sleeves, his striped suspenders loudly proclaiming the informality of the man. And as I entered he was biting into an ear of corn with all the vigor of his indomitable personality. After a word of greeting, he resumed his munching. "What's up, Warden?" he asked, between bites. "I thought you could run that place. Are the boys too much for you? Pulling your leg, so to speak?"

I told him the story and reminded him of his promise to let me run the prison in my own way. "If that is not to be continued, you can have my resignation at once." He was at his second ear of corn when I had finished. I remember to this day how he slowly buttered it, salted and peppered it thoughtfully. Then he looked up at me and said, "Now, Warden, you go back and tell that crowd that you're to run that prison as I said you should. Without any interference. We've got to get this thing on a sensible basis. I won't let politics interfere with our prisons any longer. Now, you go back and tell 'em that, will you, like a good fellow?"

"My resignation stands, Governor, unless that word comes from you directly to them," I answered.

He looked at me quizzically. "All right," he said, impatiently. "I'll tell 'em. You go back home and it will all come out fine."

And thus the incident was closed. The delegation of ladies in waiting breathed a sigh of relief at my exit. Several days later the Governor showed up handsomely in a newspaper photogravure, surrounded by a charming group of women. I wondered about those bright suspenders that might have shocked their esthetic senses.

I had no more trouble about the prison paper. It was finally discontinued because of an opinion handed down by the then Attorney General of the state, which forbade paid subscriptions for any prison publication. This was our main financial support. Without it, we could not carry on.

Not seeing "too damn much" on the part of some of our officers almost cost me my job several years later. That happened while Brindell, of labor fame, was a prisoner at Sing Sing. Brindell had been the labor czar in the building trade. It was rumored that no construction job could go on without the payment of tribute to Brindell. As the result of the notoriety he achieved and peremptory methods pursued by him, he was convicted and sentenced to Sing Sing. He came to us during the period when the first cell block on the hill was under construction.

Brindell was a good prisoner. He was well liked by officers and men. Mingled democratically in the yard and took an interest in deserving cases. Many destitute families of prisoners received through his efforts anonymous contributions with which they paid their rent or bought sustenance. He was, also, a willing worker. He was assigned where he would be most useful, on the construction job. It was outside the walls of the prison, just overlooking the old cell block and is today enclosed in the new wall which surrounds the entire prison property. There was, of course, no danger of Brindell's making any attempt to escape. He was hardly that kind of a prisoner. But he had been a "czar" in his own right. He knew what he wanted and how to get it. Prison rules and prison uniforms did not awe him in the least. And so, because some of our officers did not "see too much," he was to be permitted to receive a visit from his wife in a shack on the hill. I got wind of it in short order.

The "tip" was that Brindell was to have his visit on a certain afternoon and I promptly prepared for it. A high-powered limousine drew up alongside his shack. A woman stepped out, apparently Mrs. Brindell, and passed quickly through the door. I stepped in a moment later with an officer.

Brindell was apologetic. "I never did this before, Warden," was his excuse. I might have overlooked the offence or passed it over with the usual punishment of prohibiting all his further visits. But the brazenness of it outraged me and Brindell had to leave for another prison upstate, where he spent the remainder of his term. Not "seeing" things in this instance resulted in the guard's dismissal from the service.

Not everything connected with prison administration can be learned in school or taught by rote. Every officer in the ranks and higher up must learn more or less by feeling his way.

The prison officer, regardless of post, is a responsible official with positive duties—not only to maintain order and secure obedience to rules. He deals with human beings, not machinery. Prisoners must be guarded—and guided. The latter is generally the greater and heavier responsibility. The officer who can influence his charges in mental and social outlook will have little difficulty with the mechanics of his job.

A gentleman of some psychologic sense with a flair for the penologic which he probably acquired in the quiet of his well-furnished studio, held forth not long ago that wardens cannot see further than their prison walls. However that may be, the fact is that what they see within those walls is probably clearer and more definite than the long distance examination made by professional enthusiasts.

The warden knows that fifty per cent of his wards are not really criminally minded. That half as many more are the products of circumstance and environment. That of the remaining twenty-five per cent only a possible half are aggressively anti-social and dangerous to the community.

The warden understands that by surrounding the prisoner, regardless of his mentality and training, with nothing but institutional inhibitions, the prisoner is put on his defensive. Repression, among normal people, is responsible for many ills. It is also the cause of many of our failures in corrective and penal institutions.

On the other hand, a too liberal atmosphere lends itself to dissipation of energies. It defeats its own purpose. One is as bad as the other. It has been difficult for the American people to find a medium. In a moment of reflection, and a warden does have his moments, I thought of Old Glory, the American flag with its stars and stripes. Was it really an indication of the American mind? The wide swing of the pendulum? Heaven or hell? Are we to reach high into the stars and if we fail, are there only stripes? But then the good souls who fashioned that emblem hallowed it with the symbol of mercy. Those stripes of white tempered the severity, of the red.

My thoughts carried to the days of the lash and its counterpart, the leash. Both were made of the same material. Yet one was used for torture, and the other for guidance. In the hands of brute and unseeing force, the one became the symbol of fear; in the hands of the teacher of men, it became the instrument of sympathy and the vehicle for right thinking.

On his last visit to America, Premier MacDonald spoke of the risks of peace. Every statesman realizes the importance of such risks. But they are worth-while risks and gladly assumed by all right thinking men. The warden of a prison, though far removed from national leadership, must also take his risks. Severity has always defeated its own ends. The chances he takes are those that have to do with inspiring trust and self-restraint. I have taken such chances. At times the risks were seemingly hazardous. Compared with the successes attained, the percentages of failure were negligible.

I took a long risk when I curtailed the almost unlimited privileges of the Mutual Welfare League and thus disappointed a number of prisoners who had thereby acquired soft berths, which they were desirous of retaining.

I took a chance when I cleaned up the prison yard

and demolished hidden nooks and corners that were being used for nefarious purposes by so-called "big shots."

It was a risk, I knew, to permit the prisoners to present their annual theatrical performance to the public.

A number of my officers thought it a serious risk to open up the ball field to the public, even though visitors were entirely segregated from the prisoner population.

I was advised against the removal of cook stoves installed in various parts of the prison for use by distinct and favored groups, and also against the installation of a cook house for the use of anyone who had his special things to prepare.

There had been considerable talk about abandoning Sing Sing Prison for another site. A modern institution was to be erected first at Bear Mountain, across the Hudson from Ossining and somewhat to the north. A company of Sing Sing prisoners traveled on the ferry across the river to clear the ground in contemplation of actual construction work. The Bear Mountain site was abandoned when the entire section of that country was included in the State Park—a much more satisfactory undertaking for the comfort and enjoyment of the general public.

The next site selected was at Wingdale, in Dutchess County. It was rather low ground, but the Commission appointed to find the location reported unanimously in its favor. Prisoners from Sing Sing were drafted to the new site, and they were soon busily occupied in clearing the ground. Considerable work was done before it was discovered that the choice of location for the new prison was not a fortunate one. A cell block had been completed, the power house almost entirely equipped, and several additional buildings either finished or well on the way toward completion, when it was suddenly decided that it was wiser not to move the prison at all and any new additions and buildings should be erected at Sing Sing on the hill.

The old prison wall encircled fourteen and one-half acres of ground. The new and old prison covered a combined area of forty-seven and one-half acres. And so, in October, 1920, the corner stone for the new Sing Sing on the hill overlooking the old prison was laid by Governor Alfred E. Smith. Many public officials, including the Superintendent of Prisons, were there. The prison band furnished the music, prisoners acted as ushers, the men who had worked on the excavation and foundation work were permitted to leave the walls of the old prison, one thousand years of them, to witness the ceremony. The laying of that cornerstone marked the longest progressive stride in prison reform in the State of New York, and, perhaps, in the entire country.

It was my second experience with cornerstone ceremonies. Years before I had participated in a similar event at New Hampton, where the then Mayor of the City of New York, John Purroy Mitchel, was the central figure. The man of the hour at the Sing Sing event was Governor Smith.

"The time is coming," the Governor said in part, "when the prisoner will be made to feel that he is put in prison for the protection of society until such time as the State has impressed upon him that he cannot take his place in society until he appreciates and respects the laws of the State."

It was a call for the absolute indeterminate sentence

which would measure a man's possibilities of reform by personality traits instead of inflexible codes that disregarded the individual and measured the criminal act by the length of prison term provided for it.

My own thought was expressed on that occasion. "Institutions of learning are judged by their successes. Prison reform is judged by its failures." That is as true today as it was then.

I pointed to the prisoners in the prison courtyard below us, close to the river front in the old prison. "It may surprise some of you people here today to see those men down there playing ball and having a good time in the sunshine. But it doesn't surprise me. That is the kind of treatment they deserve and are going to get as long as they merit it."

That sentiment has been my mainstay during all the years of my prison service. Merit should play as great a part in prison as in the commercial world outside. I am always willing to take a chance on the fellow who shows a willingness to work and abide by the rules of the institution. No matter how hard-boiled a prisoner may appear to be, give him a job with a semblance of responsibility, and he will invariably respond. I proved that theory to my own satisfaction in March, 1920.

The Warden of Clinton Prison at Dannemora had died. With Mr. James L. Long, Superintendent of Prisons, and Mons. William E. Cashin, then our efficient and capable prison chaplain, I visited the prison still known at that time as the "Siberia" of America. We found there twenty-four men in solitary confinement. Several had been locked up for long periods. All were undergoing punishment for breaches of discipline, some for attempting to escape. We talked with them and found that practically all were penitent and ready to pledge themselves to conform with prison regulations if they were put back to work with the other prisoners.

"If I take some of you back to Sing Sing with me and put you to work in the shops and give you all the freedom and privileges that our men enjoy, will you give me a square deal in return and behave yourselves like decent men?" I asked.

Would they? Every man responded eagerly in the affirmative.

The Acting-Warden of the prison was favorably impressed with the idea. We immediately conferred with the Superintendent of Prisons and obtained his approval. Action followed quickly. Every man in solitary confinement was released. I brought some of them with me to Sing Sing, others were transferred to Auburn, the balance were put to work in the shops at Clinton.

I do not know how the others fared, but the men that came to Sing Sing kept their word with me. Several of them later became my most valuable men in their particular lines of work. A few of them are still in Sing Sing finishing up their long prison terms. They could have been discharged years ago without danger of returning to crime.

It is often difficult to determine upon the vital spark that will warm the heart of the cynical prisoner and make him meet you half-way. The man with a long criminal record is especially hard to reach. He has encased himself in a sheathing of surliness and cynicism that is often hard to pierce. He has prepared himself, through years of constant vigilance against the forces of law and order, for guerrilla warfare. Merely questioning the men will seldom bring satisfactory results. He generally knows the answer that will cover up his emotions, if he has any. We intercepted a letter from a prisoner that clearly illustrated this type of mind.

"You know when I get started," the prisoner wrote to his brother, "I can make the average liar look like George Washington, so I had no trouble in answering questions. Then I was led to the 'croaker' to have my lamps examined. He asked me if I ever wore 'cheaters.' Next we visited the knowledge factory and when the head teacher asked me if I had ever attended school I told him that I had been sent but that generally I got 'flagged' by a fire or a ball game.

"I next visited the 'Sky Pilot.' Say, Ben, he's a regular fellow. He said: 'Dinnie, me boy, what brought you here?' I spun him a bunch of lies and, Ben, he knew all the time I was lying and I knew he knew it, but he never let on and he said, off-hand like, 'Well, Dinnie, any time anything goes wrong with you come in and see me. If you want any good books to read, you will find plenty of them in the library.' When I left him he wished me good luck. I figure he was wishing me luck so I wouldn't forget any of my lies before I hit the next station of my rounds."

These men will not be preached to. They seldom understand the language of prayer. But they will listen to "straight" talk. There was a fine response to the short message delivered one day by His Grace, Arch-Bishop, now Cardinal Hayes, of New York, while visiting the prison. There was a great turnout to hear the famous clergyman. Many came out of curiosity. Others because of their religious affiliations. But every prisoner was impressed with the words of the great man.

"We have all quit," he said in the course of his talk, "at some time in our lives, but if we have been quitters that does not say that we must remain quitters. Do not look backward, men, but if you have quit, get up and go on again for you will find happiness awaits the man if he can carry on, even after he has quit. So don't be a quitter and stay a quitter." The boys liked that kind of a message.

No gesture of friendliness and sympathy to prisoners has ever equalled that of the late David Belasco, "the genius of the American theatre." He was told about Sing Sing and its first annual show and how badly in need the prisoners were of suitable equipment. He came up with a number of his assistants to study conditions. He found out what he could do to help. A short time thereafter he decided to build a portable stage and equip it with the necessary lighting apparatus and essential properties. The cost was estimated at about eight thousand dollars. He presented it to the Mutual Welfare League as his Christmas gift to all the men.

Understanding hearts and sympathetic vision are not given to all men. I frequently entertain visitors at my home within the walls of the old prison, where I have lived with my family during all the years of my wardenship at Sing Sing. Not all of them agree with my policy of administration. They try to be at ease, but one can detect their nervousness when they see themselves surrounded by men in gray. My household is fairly representative of all nationalities. Probably the most cosmopolitan retinue in any home in the world. The dominant races of mankind are represented in my white butler, my Mongolian chef, my black-skinned porter. Catholic, Protestant, Jew, Buddhist are among the great religions. Murder, manslaughter, kidnapping, robbery, burglary, pick-pocketing, arson, forgery, larceny are among the crimes for which the men who are assigned to the warden's house are doing time.

Not long ago an Assistant District Attorney was having lunch at my home. He had accompanied the Grand Jury of his county on a tour of inspection through the prison. The butler on duty was a gentlemanly fellow who did his work quietly and efficiently. But my guest was a voluble official who aimed to impress his audience. He called to the butler, a Japanese at that time, a thoroughly intelligent young man with a fine education. "Tell me, my man," he addressed the butler who had answered his summons, "have you learned your lesson? Will you go straight when you get out of here?"

The prisoner was rather taken aback for the moment. He looked around the table at all those men who stared fixedly at his flushed face. Then he laughed. "Me? Nothing doing. You don't suppose anything can ever reform me!" And he walked away.

"You see," the Assistant District Attorney exclaimed to his fellow guests. "That's the type. Nothing can ever change them." And the other gentlemen at the table nodded thoughtfully.

That group of men might be surprised to hear that the object of their solicitude is now a free man, having been discharged from prison on the termination of his sentence, and engaged in honest toil in a respectable household.

Equally fearful was the gentleman who visited the prison and remained over night. He had heard a great deal about prisons and prisoners and did not intend to take any chances. Before retiring for the night he secreted his available cash for safe-keeping. The next morning I was awakened by a loud knock at my door. My visitor stood before me in his pajamas, flushed and excited.

"Say, Warden," he whispered hoarsely, "I've been robbed. You had better have all the boys searched before it is too late. My money is gone."

Such a thing had never before happened in my household. I accompanied him back to his room, thinking all the while of the dire punishment I would mete out to the man guilty of such lack of hospitality. I searched every nook and corner of his room. There was no sign of any money, nor as far as I could see any evidence of pilfering. In the meantime my visitor was dressing hurriedly. He was putting on his left shoe when he suddenly looked up at me and crimsoned. "Look here, Warden," he said sheepishly, "it's my error. I forgot all about it. Here is the money just as I put it away last night. In the tip of my shoe."

It is surprising how many men of the world, of large and varied experiences in life, still adhere to tradition as it affects prisons. The prisoner to them is always the man with a physical peculiarity or deformity. He must not have regular features, or be able to speak the English language as it should be spoken, or be familiar with problems or affairs that occupy normal men on the outside. Such was the attitude of a gentleman who visited me some years ago. No less a personage than an associate editor of one of our leading magazines. I was occupied at the moment and he waited in an adjoining office where several clerks were busy at their typewriters. He soon found himself in conversation with one of them. They talked about international politics and a number of other matters of current interest. Suddenly the gentleman pointed to a company of prisoners marching along the road in front of my office.

"It must be pretty tough on those men," he mused, "sleeping in those narrow cells in the old cell block. Especially the first few nights. Did you ever ask them how they feel about it? It would be interesting to find out."

The clerk looked at his questioner and laughed. "No, I don't ask them. I don't have to. I know."

The associate editor was amazed. "You don't tell me you're a ———!" he exclaimed.

"Yes, I am. A prisoner. Just like any of them, and I surely do know how those first few nights feel."

A liberal-minded gentleman was this visitor of mine. But tradition had him in its throes. A prisoner should look like a desperate criminal. And a desperate criminal must look his part. Otherwise the whole thing was shorn of its glamor.

As we talked later in my own office, my youngest daughter, Joan Marie (we all call her Cherie), interrupted us as children will. She is the only child ever born within the walls of Sing Sing and is now a bit of a girl of ten. In her infancy her nurse was a coal black negro who was more careful of her than he would have been of his own child. She bent over to whisper in my ear. I nodded and she left us with a smile and a childish skip. I noticed the look of curiosity on the face of my visitor.

"She asked my permission to go to the picture show," I explained.

142

"What, alone?" the editor asked.

"It's the only place I would ever let her go alone. The prison show in the chapel," I answered.

"Remarkable," was all he could say.

And yet it is not so very remarkable that any member of my family can pass through the prison yard, or in any shop, or corridor, without an escort to clear the way or for safe-keeping. We have done it for over twelve years and have yet to experience any discourtesy or disrespect. We realize, of course, that there are many dangerous men among our prisoners. Men who bear watching. I have found, however, that the gesture of trust will bring its return in honor and faith. I had occasion to emphasize that some years ago. Among our prisoners was a long termer and an old timer. He was considered one of the real bad men of the prison. He had spent many years behind the walls, the best years of his life. His institutional record was bad. Escapes and violations of rules filled every inch of his card. He was, in popular estimation, as also among prison officials, a typical bad man. We were very careful with him. And rightly so.

One day word came of the death of his mother. Under the rules he could be sent down to the funeral, if, in the judgment of the warden, it was safe to do so. The prisoner was anxious to go. I was willing to let him go but hesitated to take a chance with that type of prisoner. I sent for him and frankly explained the situation.

"Warden," he said when I had finished, "you have my word that nothing will happen. I will not make any trouble for you. Do this for me and you won't regret it."

I did not give him a definite answer, but told him that I would let him know in the morning.

Early the next day I sent him to the State Shop to be dressed. He came out looking very much the man of affairs. An officer had him in tow.

"All right, officer," I told the guard, "leave him with me."

Just then a member of my household, a woman, came in. "I'm ready, if you are," she smiled to the prisoner, the bad man. "Let's go, the car is waiting."

The prisoner looked at me, then at her. He seemed dazed and unable to move. I motioned to him to go and he left my office as docile a man as I had ever seen. His right arm hung limply. Its wrist was familiar with the pinch of handcuffs. They were not in evidence, nor was any prison official. None but the civilian chauffeur.

Late that afternoon the prisoner and his woman guard returned. He said nothing. But I am sure that his day's experience influenced that prisoner's outlook on life. Not long thereafter he was recommended by the assignment board for a responsible job which he has held and filled to our every satisfaction.

Old-timers among the prisoners have little faith in any new ideas of crime regulation. When psychiatry was introduced in Sing Sing they regarded it with disfavor. "I can't understand it at all," one elderly prisoner said to me once. "I am called to the doctor's office. They place dominoes upside down on the table and if I can't play the game they say I'm subnormal."

"If they want to psyche me, they can go ahead and do it," another prisoner remarked. "I only wish them luck."

The importance of psychiatry in prison administration will be discussed later in this volume. The fact remains that prisoners do not take to it kindly. They resent the doctor's probe into their intimate histories. And, as that other prisoner wrote to his brother, they do not always tell the truth. Prisoners seldom do in formal tests. Thomas Meighan, of screen fame, told me of an incident that happened to him while filming his picture, "The Man Who Found Himself," in Sing Sing. An old prisoner, a trusty, who worked around the yard, joked with "Tom" between shots. "Too bad to see a likely-looking young fellow like you in here," the old-timer grinned, "how did it happen?"

The Paramount Star shook his head in mock regret. "The movies put me here, brother," he said sadly. "But in this case the law got the wrong man. I'm innocent."

The old lifer laughed gleefully. "So's every one else in here, to hear them tell it," he chuckled.

But when you get the prisoner off his guard he will talk. Occasionally you will hear some fine philosophic comment. I enjoyed particularly my talk with "Bill" who was one of the old timers. As a matter of fact, I found him in Sing Sing when I became the warden. He had acquired an education in prison, had grayed considerably, and was looking forward to the completion of his term. He was in my office one day and was telling me of his plans for the future.

"Sure you're through, Bill?" I asked him.

"Through's the word, Warden. You know, past the danger age. Can't afford to take any chances. No, I won't come back. I'll look up my wife and kids and settle down at home, if they'll have me."

"Bill," I asked him, "now as you look back, can you

figure out what put you on the wrong track? How did you happen to stray off the straight and narrow?"

Bill looked at me musingly. I motioned to him to sit down. He crossed his legs, hunched his shoulders, clasped his hands with his elbows on the arms of the chair, and talked.

"Warden," he asked, "you're human. Did you ever want to be bad? Not go to church of a Sunday? Did you ever want to run away from business for a day for just no reason at all? Or come home late for dinner, so's to have it out with the wife?"

Bill paused. I did not dare to interrupt him.

"Did you ever, in the privacy of your chamber, alone with your conscience, confess to your secret self the desire to do the unconventional? Something different? Away from the beaten path? And then, when you've about made up your mind to take the plunge, and cast precaution to the winds, something clicks within you and it remains undone."

Bill paused again. I felt that his thoughts were far away. I waited patiently for him to go on.

"That was me, Warden. I had the urge, only I didn't hear that click. And when I found myself plunging no brakes could hold me. That's all there is to it.

"You've been with us fellows a long time, Warden," he continued. "Have you ever found a man who really wants to be bad? Unconventional, yes. Contrary, perhaps. Maybe the fellow's stupid or selfish. But no one starts on this kind of life by wanting to be merely bad. You know how old Shakespeare puts it. 'There is nothing good or bad, but thinking makes it so.' And when the public makes up its mind that a fellow is bad, he

146

will become bad, even if he had no ambitions along that way originally."

No formal test in the mental clinic could have "psyched" Bill as successfully as he did himself.

Bill is home now, successfully operating a small haberdashery, and probably watching for those "clicks" in his children's lives. But I had occasion to remember his words later, "When the public makes up its mind that a fellow is bad, he will become bad." And what is more, he stays bad.

Roy Sloane was that kind of a fellow, the product of sensational journalism. He was not happy or contented unless engaged in subterfuge and deceit. An egoist, he gloried in the notoriety that came to him. The press built him up as a super-intellectual criminal, and he played his part. Actually he was a super-failure. But he was shrewd—smart is the better term, a college graduate, of good parentage. His intelligent and educated mother had high hopes for her only son. In legitimate enterprise Roy Sloane would have been successful.

Like scores of other notorious criminals, he was the natural product of glorified crime. The publicity given him on the several occasions when his name appeared in print, turned his head. If there had previously been any chance for a change of heart that undoubtedly stifled it. He was pictured as the ambitious prisoner so set on achieving his freedom that he pored over law books in his cell and worked his typewriter assiduously as he pounded out voluminous legal documents to present to Appellate Courts. As a matter of fact, Sloane seldom opened a law book, for there were few to be had within the prison. Nor did he ever type his papers. They were prepared by other prisoners. Citations were provided by outside attorneys and the actual work was done by convict-lawyers. Any prisoner of average intelligence can defend himself in court without the aid of counsel. Most prisoners are familiar with criminal court rules. Points of law, recent decisions and court procedure are always important topics for discussion in the prison courtyard. But Sloane had the sense of theatrics.

He assumed the pose of a law student and a persistent defender of his "rights." He became good "copy" for special feature writers. A gullible public and an impressionable jury helped him get away with it. And so, a prisoner of more than average intelligence became a "prodigy" who, in popular imagination, fought with his back to the wall against the power of the State of New York.

Sloane was not a good mixer, although I was led to believe that many of our so-called prisoner "big-shots" would go to him for advice and counsel. He had a few close friends, and to them, during recreation hours, he would discourse on philosophy, history, psychology and the mechanics. He was given a high "I. Q." and an excellent mental rating. In intelligence he was rated 112, superior, with a mental age of 18—one of the best we have had in Sing Sing.

But I knew my man. He had a peculiar mental twist that decried all authority and resented orderly routine. I suspected him of many irregularities, some of which could be traced directly to him; others he was shrewd enough to cover up. Of one I was sure. And so I felt it my duty to prosecute him for attempting to escape and for possessing dangerous weapons which he had secreted in his cell.

148

The public at that time generally agreed that he was a dangerous man. Its sympathy was aroused later when he acted as his own attorney before a jury in White Plains, at the retrial of his case ordered by the higher courts. He was acquitted of a crime which officials knew definitely he had committed.

Yet public sympathy followed him back into prison, where he was still held on another charge. Later the Court of Appeals decreed his release, basing its decision on the acquittal he had won in White Plains. Privately, on the day of his discharge, I expressed my opinion of Sloane. I had no confidence in his much heralded intention to go straight. He would play to his public which got its thrill out of Sloane, the bad man.

Shortly after his discharge he was arrested again and indicted for robbery. He had been identified as one of a gang of men who staged a daring hold-up of a mid-town jewelry store. While out on bail on this indictment, he was "put on the spot" in the usual gangster style. While in a speakeasy with some friends he was called outside on a pretext. At the curb an automobile was waiting, machine guns tattooed, and Sloane fell to the ground mortally wounded. Had he been able to read the glaring headlines that announced his death and told of his finale, he would have been happy.

Several days after Sloane's death, I received the following letter from Hon. John S. Kennedy of the State Correction Commission:

"I would be interested to have your answer to the question, 'Why Roy Sloane?' Many of us know the answer to Crowley, but Sloane is another problem. I recall distinctly your prophecy at the time he left Sing Sing Prison. It has been fulfilled completely."

The public enjoyed Sloane's badness. It liked the show. That type of prisoner becomes a warden's major worry. He is the "big shot" whom lesser lights would ape. These are some of the things that are not apparent to the visitor during an occasional inspection of the prison grounds.

It is not often that visitors or observers see prisoners from an objective point of view. By watching them as they work in the shops, or march to mess to the tune of the prison band, or on the ball field, or even at religious services in the chapel, one cannot detect the strain and stress of human emotions that fill those ranks. That is the warden's peculiar province, and in the course of his daily experiences he faces problems that are sometimes ludicrous and often tragic.

A prominent prison administrator from a western European country looked us over about a year ago. He toured the prison shops and the grounds, and seemed to be impressed. It was late in the afternoon when he had completed his inspection and, at my invitation, remained over until the next day. "You do things differently over here," he remarked to me at dinner, "the warden is more democratic. Our wardens wouldn't think of going into so many individual problems as you do. Don't you think it tends to weaken your power over your prisoners? Seems to me you're too approachable."

I explained to him that the warden of a prison is really the arbiter of his men's lives. He is not only a jailer. His job is to know his prisoners; to study their problems and help in their solution. The understanding administrator will realize that prisoners must be continuing social problems. The prison gate does not mark the beginning or the end of society's

150

responsibility toward its wards. It is the warden's province to appraise each individual problem, to correct perspectives, rectify distortions and help in the removal of obstructions to clear vision and sane thought. He does not always succeed. Some men may have been so hardened by inexorable forces and influences as to be utterly beyond correction. The warden must assure himself of these types, as well. Otherwise their contaminating influences will endanger the morale of his domain. To accomplish this purpose there must be close and intimate observation of prisoners by the administrative authority. It is not always possible in large prisons. With our average population topping the 2500 mark, it is as difficult as in other large and overcrowded prisons to maintain the necessary contact with prisoners. As the guiding head and motivating force of a community of several thousand men, the scope of the warden's duties becomes widely varied.

"The only reformation possible," wrote a well-known prison authority some years ago, "is the influence of a dominant personality upon the inmate." That, of course, is axiomatic. Prisoners who are surrounded every moment of the day by keepers and guards who are ignorant, if not utterly illiterate, may be cowed into submission, but they will have little respect for authority. They will sharpen their wits to circumvent their jailers and will continue dodging on their discharge. Cunning becomes a habit. Men who handle prisoners should be trained for their jobs. In the very nature of things prison guards must be able to handle arms. But they should know, as well, the handling of men.

One of our old-timers, a prisoner of seventy doing a

life sentence, and who has spent nearly half of his adult life in prisons throughout the country, was telling of his early prison experiences. One cold, wet day in the late fall, he found himself with worn shoes. He approached the principal keeper. "May I have an order for a pair of new shoes?" he asked.

The officer looked down at the prisoner's shoes. "What's the trouble with the old pair?"

"Water is coming in through a hole in the side. They're quite worn, sir," the prisoner explained.

"Is that all?" the principal keeper laughed. "You can fix that easy enough. Make a hole in the other side and the water will run out again."

The old-fashioned, traditional, blustering prison official has no place in a scheme of social planning that looks for restoration to decent living and the respect for order.

Intimate association between prisoners and guards is not undesirable, if that association is helpful. A word of encouragement in moments of distress, friendly advice in trying moments, are salutary influences. Prison officials, from the warden down, cannot afford to be sloppily sentimental. No prison can be run without discipline and obedience. But it should be the discipline and obedience born of respect and understanding.

My visitor from western Europe would have been surprised one morning, several months ago, to find a prisoner in my office, a man about fifty years of age, asking for my advice on an intimate matter. He was a Hebrew of the old school, and the father of grown-up children. In the general classification of prisoners he might well be placed in the group of "accidental" or "occasional" criminals. He stood before me with tears in his eyes. "Please, Warden, help me," he pleaded in his broken English.

I had some difficulty in getting the story from him. The gist of it was that he wanted me to persuade his son not to get married. It was a peculiar request.

"Do you object to the girl?" I asked him.

"No, Warden," he protested. "She is a fine girl and comes of a nice family."

"Well, then, what is the trouble? Why not let the boy marry and settle down?"

"You see, Warden," he explained. "I am an old man and with us Jewish people our greatest joy is to be present at our children's weddings. Now I ask you, Warden, how can I allow my son to marry while I am in prison? That's what we live for. Don't you understand?"

Elopements were, apparently, unknown or abhorrent to his sensibility. The man was thoroughly unhappy. This was hardly within the scope of a warden's duties. And yet, after an intimate discussion of his affairs and prospects the prisoner left my office determined to write to his son, give his consent to the marriage, and send the young couple his blessing.

It is a long step between listening to the troubles of my middle-aged Jewish prisoner and the practical problems in administering a three million dollar corporation. For that is exactly what Sing Sing is today. A big business with a turnover of $3,000,000 annually. The warden is its guiding head and motivating force. His is the deciding voice in practical problems of production. He initiates building construction and co-operates with the Commissioner of Correction and the State Architect in carrying it to completion. He must personally approve every order for the government of the prisoner population and for the administrative force consisting of uniformed guards and civilian employees.

He hears charges of misconduct and neglect against prison officials, and there is no appeal, except to the courts, from his judgment of acquittal or conviction, followed by suspension without pay or dismissal from the service. All are major problems of administration.

But above all these responsibilities and burdens of practical business and government is the warden's privilege of shaping human lives. To do this effectively he must be patient with intimate problems of his wards. Some of them may appear trivial to the average man. To the prisoner doing time, they are important. The warden must see them through the eyes of the prisoner.

Such a problem came to me recently for decision. A prisoner in Grade "B," who had been reduced from Grade "A" for an infraction of some rule, had written his Sunday letter, the only weekly letter allowed to men of his grade. He wrote another letter which was rejected by the correspondence department. The denial was justified under the rules. The matter was appealed to me.

I read the first few lines of the letter. A father was writing to his married daughter. "I am glad it's a boy. My best wishes and love to both of you." The prisoner's first grandchild. Rule or no rule, that letter went out. The wheels of progress may have stopped for a moment while I read that letter; a problem in administration might have been kept waiting while I weighed its merits. The incident was probably insignificant. But it brought a measure of happiness to a man to whom the

154

event was vibrant and soul-filling. Is it not a warden's duty to help in the safeguarding of that bit of happiness for his wards, even at the risk of staying the problems of State?

CHAPTER 5: A PRISON DAY

JOE, an ex-farm hand, is a natural lifer. After his commutation from the chair by Governor Nathan L. Miller, Joe was put in charge of Sing Sing's three and only cows that furnished milk for our household. Joe loved his cows. But, like Joe who has turned fifty, they were getting on in years and ailing. Joe is a Pole and speaks only a few words of English, though he has spent ten years in prison. One of those helpless cases that will not respond to schooling. He is deeply religious and spends hours on his knees praying. He never eats meat. His diet during those ten years has been only bread and an occasional cup of tea.

Joe was told of my order to have the cows slaughtered, and the following morning he was waiting at my door, his cap in hand.

"Warden, please, good morning," he smiled.

I returned his greeting.

"Warden, please," and he fumbled for words.

Something was on his mind. I suspected what it was.

"What is it, Joe? Can I do anything for you?" I asked.

"Warden," he said, "you kill my cows. Why?"

I explained the situation to him so that he would understand. But Joe shook his head. "Good cows, Warden. No kill," he insisted.

It was useless to tell him that the animals were sick and under the law we had to get rid of them. They were his pets and he would have them live.

"Well, Joe, see me this afternoon and I'll see what can be done." The operation was scheduled for later in the day when the butcher would be at leisure.

After the noon mess Joe was standing in my waiting room with a wistful look on his face. I motioned to him to come in. That was Thursday. Three condemned men were to go to the chair that night. I expected word from the Governor's office about a respite, pending developments about newly discovered evidence.

As Joe entered my office the telephone bell rang. Albany was calling. The Governor's counsel informed me that the respite had been granted—the men were given two weeks in which to restate their cases. I announced the news to my staff. Joe heard it and his face lit up with hope. He approached my desk with eager steps.

"Warden, please. Boys no die, cows no die. Please." There were tears in his eyes. What could one do but grant his request? His pets were reprieved. Ultimately those condemned men went to their deaths. Joe's charges suffered a like fate. He made no further plea.

A warden cannot afford to be emotional. Yet he is often hard put to avoid it in the face of the intense emotionalism of his prisoners, always one of the most difficult of all prison problems. They are easily aroused. Unless firmly handled the results may be disastrous.

We had one such incident on the sixteenth day of May, 1927. That was the day when two notorious murderers were admitted to the prison. One of them was a woman. Somehow the prison population had little sympathy for the man, but, unlike the outside community, there was considerable feeling for the woman. The prisoners felt, rightly or wrongly, that she should not have been sent to the death house. The excitement outside the walls, with airplanes flying overhead to take pictures of the death house for tabloid newspapers, intensified the atmosphere within the walls.

Now, prison fare is not, or rather in those days was not all that could be desired. Prisoners, however, do not often complain about food unless it is utterly unpalatable. The day the condemned woman came in the menu was pork and beans. Beans are beans at all times. All housewives know that sometimes they are overdone, often underdone. Prisoners were accustomed to both kinds of cooking. They seldom complained. If the men were hungry, the beans disappeared regardless of their quality. If the prisoners were not particularly famished the beans were left over and that was all there was to it. But that day the men were under a nervous tension. A woman in the death house! And all because a man talked too freely. Their peculiar sense of chivalry was touched. It did not need much to arouse them. The beans did the trick. As luck would have it, the beans were overdone and hard as marbles. The men not only refused to eat them but commented freely in protest. And what was more, on their return to the shops from the mess hall they continued their agitation and, under the urgings of a few ringleaders, refused to work.

Reporters were hovering around the prison gate and in my office, trying to get a line on the condemned woman prisoner. I could not ignore them. Inside the walls the men were to all intents and purposes on strike, keyed up with emotionalism about something that had no direct relation to their real cause for complaint. I made a tour of the shops. No officer was permitted to carry arms or blackjacks. I simply allowed the men in the shops to remain idle for the rest of the day.

As I passed through one of the buildings a voice called an uncomplimentary remark. The silence that followed was eloquent. I stopped in the center of the shop. "If the man who said that has any guts, he'll step up and repeat that to my face," I said. "I won't deal with him as the Warden but man to man fashion."

No one stirred. Late that afternoon a committee of the prisoners asked for an interview. We had it out. I explained that their complaint was a just one, but they had taken the wrong method of calling it to my attention. The beans were bad, but the prisoners' attitude was worse. The men were locked up that night without disorder and the next morning the entire population marched to breakfast in usual routine and then to their shops where they started the day off with hilarious recitals of the famous bean rebellion. The incident was closed by my writing the Chef a lengthy and pointed letter with instructions on how to prepare food—and beans in particular.

It is not often, however, that prisoners' emotions find articulate expression. Generally they are repressed as on that Fourth of July in 1927. The Fourth is always an important holiday in Sing Sing as it is on the outside. There are athletic events, a double-header baseball game and other special features. Not least important is the chicken dinner. Chicken is a delicacy within the walls. It is permitted only twice a year. Fourth of July and Christmas. Not a single prisoner misses those chicken dinners. Yet, on this occasion many of the prisoners at Sing Sing sat at their mess tables and passed up the delicacy that was being served to them. I cannot say that they were altogether to blame for their loss of appetite. That morning, in full sight of the prisoners, as they marched down the hill to the prison courtyard along the river front, two men were drowned in midstream in the Hudson, and though hundreds begged to be allowed to swim to their rescue the gates were not opened and the guard on post threatened to shoot anyone who dared climb the spiked fence that faced the water. I was not told of the incident until it was too late to do anything.

The guard felt he was doing his full duty in restraining those men from leaving the prison grounds. He remembered a similar occurrence some time before when a boat in the river appeared to be in difficulties not far from the shore and cries for help were plainly heard. This turned out, however, to be a well planned plot to get a certain group of men outside the prison walls on the pretext of swimming to a rescue. Whether the guard was right or wrong this time, the fact was that the latter incident so wrought up the entire prison population as to spoil their holiday. Passing up their special dinner was their way of giving vent to their feelings.

"Humor in prison bursts like a bomb," was the sentiment of a noted publicist. If humor is a bomb, emotions are dynamite. When prisoners are swept by emotion there is no telling where it may lead. The casual observer sees nothing of that feature of prison life or government. To him it is all a very simple matter of adhering to routine. The schedule is not complicated.

The day begins at six-thirty o'clock, when the first bell is sounded for dressing and making beds. The night watch has already made its count. All prisoners accounted for by the night force are re-checked by the incoming morning shift. Nothing has happened during the night to disturb the peace of the prison or the equanimity of the officers.

At seven o'clock the second gong signals to the officers on the tiers to open the brake that controls all the cell doors on each gallery. The prisoners step out of their cells and march to breakfast. It is Monday morning. The menu today is plain but wholesome. Cornmeal with fresh milk, granulated sugar, bread and coffee. The cereal is served hot, cafeteria style. The men line up holding their plates or bowls and the food is ladled out as they pass. On the long mess tables are pitchers of steaming coffee; a cup for each man. The rule is that each man may have as much as he wants and needs, but waste is strictly forbidden.

Breakfast over, the men rise from their places, drop their utensils in waiting baskets at the door of the mess hall, and march down hill into the old prison for a half hour's recreation before the eight o'clock whistle calls them to their appointed shops and tasks.

Prisoners who work in shops must then hurry to their respective shop buildings where they line up for the count. Outside companies, assigned to construction or sanitation, line up in the yard. Heads are checked, the count balances and the wheels begin to turn. Sing Sing is now an active, busy community.

Sing Sing's industries manufacture about seventy articles for sale to State, County and City institutions and departments. The State of New York has not yet rounded out its problem of prison labor. Its laws confine the sale of prison products to public institutions which are not actually compelled to purchase or give preference to such products.

161

Despite this handicap, Sing Sing's sales for the fiscal year, ending June 30, 1931, totalled $801,000, which showed a profit of over $200,000. Over seven hundred men are engaged in the various industries, about one-third of Sing Sing's average population. The following is a complete list of articles manufactured:

Brush and Mattress Shop

Mattresses
Pillows
Covers
Brooms
Brushes
Pads

Print Shop

Letterheads
Forms
Envelopes
Cards and Tags
Books

Knit Shop

Hose
Shirts and Vests
Drawers and Pants
Gowns
Bathrobes
Straight Jackets
Canvas Covers
Petticoats
Pajama Coats
Pajama Pants
Spreads
Pads

Night Shirts
Night Gowns
Pillow Cases
Sheets
Aprons
Red Danger Flags
Money Bags
Wool Flags
Cotton Flags
Doctor's Gowns
Mittens

Twenty-five additional items are manufactured in smaller quantities.

Shoe Shop

Boys' Shoes
Men's Shoes
Women's Shoes
Men's Slippers
Women's Slippers

Sheet Metal Shop

Cans
Can Carrier
Scrapers
Street Broom Scrapers
Can Covers
Bottoms

Great strides have been made in recent years in the industrial department of the prison. The two, three story, concreted structures you see in the old prison near the river edge have been completed within the past two years. They are fireproof structures. One of these buildings is already occupied by the Shoe Shop and the Sheet Metal Shop. Both shops are equipped with modern machinery. In style and quality of production, both industries can now compete with any outside manufactory.

Our Knit Shop, Brush and Mattress Shop and Print Shop are still housed in the old building which has been long condemned. Most of the machinery and equipment in these shops are antiquated. These industries have been carried on under difficulties, but our second fireproof shop building is now ready for occupancy. We are equipping two floors with up-to-date machinery for the Knit Shop and one floor for the Brush and Mattress Shop. The appropriation for a third shop building is now available. With these improvements the quality and quantity of our merchandise will measure up to par, and we shall be able to increase production and improve quality to an extent never before equalled at Sing Sing.

The visitor at the prison, viewing any of these shops in operation, will see a normal factory at work. The atmosphere is that of a busy industry with rules no harsher than those which prevail in outside factories. Smoking during working hours is not permitted. Men must pay strict attention to their tasks. There is no loafing. Yet there is an air of informality that speaks well for the normal human being and the utter absence of oppression or slave driving. One sees an officer in

163

uniform. He is there to preserve the peace. But he does not seem to be busy. The telephone rings. One of the prisoners is being called to another department on some special errand, or for a visit. The officer makes out a pass for the man, which permits him to leave his work and gives him the courtesy of the yard to do his errand or go through the Key Room for his visit in the new Administration Building at the entrance of the prison.

The directing force of each shop is the civilian superintendent. He is a civil service employee and usually well equipped in the use of machinery or the details of his tasks. He regulates the quantity and quality of production and is answerable directly to the Superintendent of Industries whose office is in the Central Office Building where, with his Assistant and a staff of twenty-six prisoner clerks, he keeps accurate account of production, sales and daily requirements of the prison industries.

The men in the shops appear to be ordinary workers, hardly to be distinguished from employees in any similar industries on the outside. It is the visitor who is prison conscious. He is curious about these men doing time. What were their crimes? How much time are they doing? Where do they come from? Are they vicious and dangerous? If so, how are they curbed? And how are they picked for particular assignments?

If it is Monday, we can take our visitor to the meeting of the Assignment Board. We find there the Assistant Principal Keeper who presides at meetings of this board and is also the disciplinarian officer. With him we find the Psychiatrist, Assistant Physician, the Head School Teacher, the Superintendent of Industries. Every newly admitted prisoner appears before the Assignment Board immediately after his Reception period of fourteen days, during which he makes the rounds of all the departments that have to do with health, psychiatry, education and religion. His personal history and qualifications, physical and mental, have already preceded him and are before the members of the Board while he is examined orally for placement purposes.

A long line of men are waiting their turn. It is a slow process. Each man is given thorough consideration. There is no haphazard decision. The prisoner with weak eyes cannot be placed in the Knit Shop where threading needles and the ability to discriminate between hues and shades of colors is an essential qualification. The Sheet Metal Shop calls for men with brawn and a knowledge of mechanics. Clerks are needed in various offices, men who can use the typewriter and have a fair knowledge of the English language. Construction companies who do all the grading and road building need men with muscle and strong physique. Consideration must also be given to the length of sentence. Thus the man who will be with us fifty years or during his natural life, must prove his reliability before he will be allowed to work with a company that has demonstrated its responsibility to such an extent as to entitle it to medium or minimum of custodial care and supervision.

Our visitor sits in with the Board for a while. A gray haired prisoner is ushered in. George is turned seventy. He has spent most of his adult life in prisons. He has been a forger, a "con" merchant of by-gone days; he has sold gold bricks and "green goods." He claims to have sold shares in the Brooklyn Bridge and lots in City Hall Park of lower Manhattan. "I got $10,000 a lot," be boasts. I ask him how he bamboozled his customers and whether they did not go to the police when they discovered the fraud. And George sighs. "Ah, Warden, them were the days. The coppers were our friends." George is here, doing life as a "fourth offender," for forging a check for $135. His only living relative is a sister who never visits him. He stands before the Assignment Board and gazes in perplexity at the gentlemen who sit before him. This is something new in his experiences. He has been psyched and tested and examined. Incidents long forgotten had been resurrected from his early life. He stands before these men stripped of all his glamor. A willful boy had grown up and developed into an irresponsible man. Here he is just a foolish-looking old man. The physician looks at his card. "This man is a cardiac case. A very bad heart. I would not advise any work that requires physical labor." That is all George has to show for a lifetime of crime. George is given an assignment. He will join the squad of prisoners who keep the prison courtyard free of accumulation of scraps of paper. A long pick with a wooden handle will be his tool. It is the end of the trail for him. A home for the aged and infirm might have been a more reasonable abode for him. He accepts his assignment with a shrug of his rounded shoulders and shuffles out of the room to make way for the next.

A young man swaggers in. Thin faced, slim figure, sallow complexion, with an air of confidence and assurance. His gray prison coat hangs loosely on his shoulders. "Back again, Mike," one of the Board remarks. Mike grins sheepishly. "Just a violation, Boss. Just a violation," he explains apologetically. "They tried to

166

frame me, but didn't get away with it. I had my alibi all sewed up. You know how it is," he continues, "the bulls don't give a fellow a chance. The Board gave me a year." He looks around the room. It is a familiar sight to him. He smiles at the group. "I'd like to have my old job back again."

Mike had been discharged on parole six months ago, after doing six years out of a seven and a half year sentence. He was a poor risk, but the Parole Board had no alternative. His was a definite sentence as a second offender and the law decreed his release. Five months later he was picked up with another fellow on a charge of robbery. Failure of positive identification followed by a "foolproof" alibi, led to his acquittal. But the Parole Board exercised its discretion and brought him back for violation. As an old timer Mike had gradually advanced himself in the prison service and at the time of his discharge was a runner for one of the shops. It was a position of some trust and Mike had always lived up to his job. Now, he would like to return to it.

"Sorry," said the Assistant Principal Keeper, "you'll have to start all over again. You'll do well in the Brush Shop. They're short of men there just now." Mike makes his reluctant exit. He would like to argue the matter out. But a keeper already has him in tow and is taking him to the shop where he will operate a machine and stuff mattresses for the use of inmates of other public institutions.

The line moves rapidly. A portly fellow, apparently in the late thirties, with hair graying at the temples, and a worried expression, enters. He comes forward with hesitating steps. The spokesman for the Board looks up at him. "A lawyer?" he asks. "Was," the prisoner answers shortly. "What work can you do?" the officer questions. "I am not particular. Almost anything, I guess," the prisoner replies. "Can you type?" "Two fingers. That's about all." The Head Teacher is heard. "I can use a man in the school just now." One of his teachers has gone home. The assignment is made. The former attorney will teach English to foreigners.

"I'd like to go to the mess hall," the next prisoner volunteers. He is a young fellow, not over seventeen. A likely-looking lad, who appears much younger than his given age. Robbery was the charge and fifteen to thirty the sentence. His is an innocent expression as he asks to be assigned to the job of his preference.

"Why?" the officer wants to know. "Know anybody there?"

"Yes, sir. A friend I used to know on the outside."

The crime in which he was implicated was a group affair. Not exactly a gang, but one of those countless cliques that dart here and there of a night and prey upon small delicatessen shops and lunch rooms. They are youngsters for the most part. And they carry arms. Drink and infrequent use of dope bolster them up and in a moment of fear and nervousness their guns pop. The shots go wild. It is their lucky break. Had this boy's hand been steadier he might now be in the death house awaiting execution and not before the Assignment Board.

"A friend, eh?" the officer repeated. "You'd better keep away from those friends. The Knit Shop is a better place for you. You'll have plenty of time to meet your friends later on."

And so the Assignment Board continues its labors. Doing its best to meet every situation. They have to consider mentalities, brain, brawn, education, emotions, group affiliations, personal feuds among prisoners, everything that might tend to disturb the peace of the institution. They make mistakes. The results may be tragic as in the case of two bitter enemies who were assigned to the same company. Not many months later one of them was brought into the first aid clinic mortally wounded, the sequel to a feud that started long before their arrival in prison. Often they are ludicrous, as was the case of the prisoner who was placed in the invalid company. He was blind, the doctors said. The reports that came with his commitment papers disclosed his ailment. Tests made in our hospital confirmed it. Another prisoner was assigned to lead him to and from the mess hall. The blind prisoner seemed well satisfied and contented with his lot. Everyone pitied the poor fellow but admired his grit. The keeper in the mess hall went out of his way to make things easier for him. One day he placed a large platter of roast beef on the table where the blind prisoner sat. The latter pushed his fork toward the plate, but did not take the first piece of meat he touched. He dug in for a more likely looking portion underneath the top layer. The keeper was interested. The next day, he experimented with the blind prisoner. Two bowls were placed before him. One was empty, the other filled. The blind man did not hesitate a moment but went right for the full bowl. That afternoon the invalid company was reduced by one, and the "blind" prisoner was given a job where he could improve his eyesight by constant and diligent use.

It is getting well on towards noon and we can make another stop before the call for mess. We climb two flights of stairs to the top floor of the old hospital building. We stop on the way to inspect the library. Fifteen thousand volumes are arranged on the steel shelves, all catalogued and indexed. On one side is the fiction library where books are loaned out to prisoners for two week periods. On the other side of the large room is the reference library. Here books can be used in the library and are not to be taken from the room. The circulation of books and magazines for the last fiscal year reached the total of 24,452. A proud figure for a community with an average population of twenty-five hundred men.

We meet here the civilian librarian who is also one of the supervisory school teachers. With his staff of prisoner assistants he looks after the order and cleanliness of the book shelves. Each volume has its place. No well regulated library on the outside can boast of better or more thorough records. Prisoners may come for their books during recreation hours, or Saturday afternoons and Sundays.

We stop in for a moment at the office of the Supervisor of the Extension Courses, a civilian employee who is also an assistant school teacher. He tells us that 877 men were enrolled for courses during the last fiscal year, and completed 8,492 lessons aggregating 499 courses. He shows us a list of these courses. They are interesting as a sidelight of what men are trying to accomplish behind the walls.

Everyday Arithmetic
Plain English
English for New Americans
Business Arithmetic
Applied Mathematics

Business Administration or Management
Drawing—all classes
Elementary and Intermediate Arithmetic

170

Elementary English and Rhetoric
Elementary Spanish
Elementary French
Accounting
Bookkeeping
Business English
Industrial Organization
Blue Print and Plan Reading
Algebra
Commercial Correspondence

Short Story Writing
English Composition
Penmanship
Business Geography
Salesmanship
Personnel Management
Slide Rule
Gasoline Motors
Punctuating and Paragraphing
Economics
Newspaper Writing

Toward the far end of the same floor we find the prison school. Five classes are in session; they change every hour. Eighteen inmate teachers conduct these classes under the supervision of two civilian instructors. They average about thirty pupils for each hour of instruction.

The Head School Teacher tells us something about his work. A total of 1,111 men attended his school during the last year. The average daily attendance was 471. Of the prisoner students 578 were native born, the balance were all foreign born and represented a large and varied aggregation of nationalities. Italian, Russian, West Indian, South and Central American, Greek, German, Austrian, British, Polish, Irish, Spanish, Finnish, Chinese, Japanese, French. All these were instructed in elementary English, reading and writing.

Quite frequently prisoners come to the school office for special information. The quest for knowledge leads them far afield. "Professor," one asked the Head School Teacher one day, "will you please settle a bet? We decided to leave it to you. Can you tell us just when

Genesis was born?" I do not know how the Professor dealt with that question. Had I been the referee, I should have referred it to the Chaplain.

The gentleman in charge of the Correspondence Courses was plainly doubtful about the prisoner of middle age who was anxious to enroll in a course in "Eugenics." He was patient with the ambitious applicant and was able to ascertain, after considerable questioning, that it was "Economics" the prisoner had in mind. But then Eugenics and Economics are more closely related than that prisoner imagined.

The call to school takes precedence over all work assignments. Regardless of the importance of the particular task of the moment, the prisoner must leave it and hurry to his lessons. Attendance is strictly enforced. Absence without cause is severely dealt with.

Not all prisoners are required to join the school. Our regular school curriculum is equivalent to a fifth grade grammar school education. Those of our prisoners who are further advanced are not required to attend classes. For them the special correspondence courses are available.

We hear a steam whistle. It is 11:50 and the prisoners are being called to the noon mess. We hurry down into the courtyard of the old prison. The shops have emptied and every company is lined up in its accustomed place waiting for the blare of the prison band which guides the prisoners' march to the mess hall on the hill. Few officers are in the yard. They are posted along the line of march. Each company stands at attention in pairs. Deputy Sergeants, prisoners designated by the Mutual Welfare League, direct the order of precedence which is changed daily. The music begins and the first column steps forward. It marches the length of the courtyard, around the death house and behind it through the old south gate and then climbs up hill to a height of one hundred and thirty-seven feet. It passes through the entrance to the chapel building and winds its way through corridors to the mess halls.

The menu is well assorted. Roast veal with mashed potatoes, turnips and brown gravy. Bread and cocoa. For dessert there is cornstarch pudding.

Our visitor wends his way through and along mess tables. There is an air of homeliness. Men talk. You hear laughter. Not suppressed and afraid, but open and free. It helps digestion, our doctors say. It is an aid, also, to morale and clears away the fog of hopelessness. No finger language here. If a man needs and wants an extra helping he asks for it. "Take as much as you need, but no waste," is the general order.

We stop for a moment to talk with the Sergeant of the Guard who has general charge and supervision of the mess hall and the buildings on the hill. He is an old timer. Has been in the service over twenty years, yet he has not lost his good natured smile and occasional chuckle. "Things are different today," he explains. "In the olden days it was hash every day of the week. A prisoner with a sense of humor made a drawing and hung it up at the door of the mess hall. It showed a plate of steaming hash. Underneath were the words, 'You may go, but this will bring you back.'" He laughed. "To judge by the returns, that hash did bring them back."

I wonder, as I listen to that officer, whether it was the hash or its after effects. Was it the unvarying diet or the unending monotony of prison life that wore down souls and hearts and minds to send out into the world mere human husks that "wandered to and fro, not knowing how or where to go" and found themselves ultimately back within the familiar haunts of the prison walls.

The men are leaving their tables to return down hill to the prison courtyard where they will spend a half hour in the open air. There is no time for extended play. Here and there on the recreation field, two prisoners may engage in a brief "catch" of baseball. In the main yard, men are walking around the flower beds. Stragglers at first, others soon join them, and in a little while there is an endless line of marchers treading unending circles around the flower beds and the large fountain. The distance is small. It takes many circlings to make a worth-while walking distance. But there they are, two by two, walking, turning corners, stopping to greet others who stand aside. Our visitor, if he is observant, is interested in the spectacle.

It is a mid-summer day and the sun is strong. The men are more or less in informal dress. All wear the regulation trousers in gray. Shirts vary in style and color. White or gray cotton is the rule, with collar attached. Such a thing as a collar button is unknown among the prisoners. Probably just as outmoded as in the world outside. It is not fashion, however, that governs the dress of Sing Sing. It is simplicity. The fastidious dresser in prison is easily detected. He wears a black tie. The man who takes the trouble to wear a tie in prison is the one who takes time from his recreation hours to keep his trousers pressed and creased, his white shirt in an almost perpetual state of cleanliness, and his shoes well polished.

174

Look at this procession closely. You will see the prisoners at close range. As variegated, many hued and motley an assortment of men as there is to be found in our most cosmopolitan of cities. White, black, yellow, copper colored faces pass you in review. Each major color has its peculiar shades. One needs be an expert and a well practiced linguist to be able to distinguish nationalities in that Babelic confusion of tongues. Yet it is not what you hear that is important. It is rather what the eye beholds.

That old gentleman, gray haired, soft eyed, with his benevolent smile and deliberate stride and neat appearance. You would hardly believe that he was, in his prime, the man who presided over the destinies of the greatest and most powerful aggregation of banks in the world and thus, indirectly, an important figure in international finance. For years he sat with the mighty. I am not concerned at the moment with his guilt or innocence. I marvel at the fact that he answers with an indulgent smile and a ready ear when the lowliest among his fellow prisoners greets him by his Christian name. Is this man doing penance? Is he paying his debt to society? One cannot peer into his mind to ascertain his reactions to confinement. I remember the voice that was raised in loud protest that this sixty year old prisoner was assigned to a "soft berth" in the prison library where he daily guides lesser intellects in their reading and study. I wonder if that vociferous critic, well meaning though he may be, would have assigned a thick-fingered and slow thinking, untutored hod-carrier to the library and this cultured old gentleman to the rock pile.

Other prisoners catch your eye. Two of them pass

you by. One a broad shouldered, hard faced fellow of about thirty, walking with a youngster of seventeen. The older man is doing all the talking and the boy is drinking in every word with eager attention. One is an old timer. His record card is filled with arrests and prison terms in almost every section of the country. The other is doing his first "bit." Of the older man's fifty-one arrests only two resulted in felony convictions. The others were reduced by expert bargaining to misdemeanors and "turns" in workhouses and penitentiaries. He is an expert "can opener" known to police heads of every large city. He is doing a flat sentence of ten years. The younger prisoner is a novice. Bungled his first attempt at hold-up and was given a sentence of fifteen to thirty years and sent to Sing Sing. Here he is with the "big shots." We know that these associations are bad for the youngsters. That he is learning things and absorbing influences which his impressionable mind will fertilize.

Classification and segregation of prisoners have been preached for over a hundred years. Officialdom has turned a deaf ear to both projects. We have arrived at last at a classification stage. Some of our commonwealths, particularly the State of New York, under the able and liberal prompting of its Governor, Franklin D. Roosevelt, are hard at work to provide an early method of segregation. But who can guess at the numberless lives that have been shattered and the bodies that have been wrecked by the neglect and indifference of a hundred year old penal policy?

I point out to our visitor one of the marchers. Ill kempt, with a chin that has been unshaven for several days, a shirt with several buttons missing at the neck, trousers baggy. Looks like an habitué of one of our metropolitan slums. He is surprised to learn that the prisoner was once a fastidious gentleman and a well known figure in the fast and gay life of Broadway. Prison has done something to that man. The corners of his mouth droop. He walks with a slovenly stride. His face is careworn and his forehead creased. And he walks alone.

Two men are passing by. Probably in their early thirties. They are laughing good-naturedly. One is holding a paper. I am curious and stop them. "What's the joke, boys?" I ask, for the benefit of our visitor. "Nothing much, Warden," he answers, with a chuckle, "only a letter from the wife. She tells me we'll have to be patient about that commute. The Governor is sick. He's got the writer's cramp." Yes, he will need patience. Probably ten years of it. His was a notorious case. He will have to prove himself to the prison authorities and the Parole Board before he will get his break. Let him live in hopes. He will be the better for it and the years will be brighter for his expectations.

I guide my visitor to a secluded spot, somewhat apart from the main courtyard. Men are lying in the sun, with upper clothing removed. I explain that these prisoners are "getting short." They are rapidly approaching their day of discharge. Each is ambitious to tan his face and chest, and present himself to his unknowing neighbors as a returning vacationist. Miami and the Riviera have nothing on this bit of sun-baked ground. These prisoners spend every moment of recreation in the open. As winter merges into spring, the urge for tan and bronze becomes desperate. Every possible vantage point is utilized for the sun bath. Isolated corners are crowded with hatless, shirtless men.

Daily one can notice the deepening tinge. Pale, pallid skin gives way to healthy tan and is gradually toasted to a rich bronze. Toward the end of the summer a goodly portion of the population is deep-hued.

"I shall always look with a measure of suspicion at my neighbors who return with a deep tan after a protracted absence," my visitor remarks. "For all I know they will have just returned from a sojourn at your hotel."

We hear a prolonged whistle. It is 12:50 and the prisoners are being called back to their shops and their work. There is a sudden movement in the yard. Everyone must be prompt for the count. Before the routine can be resumed, every man must be checked. Every officer assures himself that his entire company is present or accounted for. He sends his report to the office of the Principal Keeper and the wheels of industry grind on.

It is the hour when new prisoners are due to arrive. We shall stroll toward the Administration Building where we can witness the procedure of initiation. We leave the old office building and walk up the road toward the main gate. On our way we pass several companies of prisoners at work on the hillside. Men of brawn are these. Working with pick and shovel. We hear a warning whistle. The men stop their labors and step away. A muffled detonation and a roar. A rock gives way up there near the crest of the embankment. "Blasting down the hillside," I explain to our visitor. "We have been doing that for ten years or more."

The steam shovel begins its work. A busy location

178

that. Thousands of prisoners have attacked that rocky height. At the present time we have over seven hundred men in our eleven construction companies.

Since 1920, when I took office, eight million dollars have been expended for new buildings at Sing Sing. Additional and final construction work is now being pushed to completion. Four new cell blocks have been built, with a cell capacity for 1,752 men. Also a new hospital and clinic, a chapel, mess hall, kitchen, bakery and a new Administration Building. Nearing completion is the new building overlooking the Administration Building, which will house the laundry, clothing shop, bath house and barber shop, with provisions for lockers. Work has actually been started on a segregation building (for non-conformists) and a new power house to be located outside the walls to the north of the old prison.

At the same time the topography of the prison is being revised. New sewers and water lines are being laid. Concrete roads have to be mapped out so as to connect the old prison with the new. There must be easy access to all the prison buildings on the hill. They must be solid roads, for Sing Sing's thirty trucks are heavy and seldom idle. The three steam shovels keep them scurrying and well laden. Our hills have given up hundreds of thousands of tons of sand and rock, some of which we used in our unending construction work, the balance we hauled down to the river edge to push back the persistent tide of the Hudson. Many acres have thus been added to the prison property.

All this work is not yet done. In one respect the Legislative Commission of 1821 chose wisely when it selected Sing Sing as the site for the new prison. They could not have known that its population would in the course of time climb to 2,500 and that in 1932 we would be hard put to find work for all these men. The rock pile is not an illusion in Sing Sing. It is there in obstinate persistency. For years it has been attacked with steam shovel, compressed air, dynamite and pick. It will be several years more before that work will be done. After that, when Sing Sing will have been renovated, its surface cleaned and smoothened, roads all constructed, barren spots landscaped and freshened up, we may have difficulty in finding work for all our prisoners. At present, however, we fare well. Our most relentless critics may rest easy and be happy. Sing Sing has its rock pile.

I guide my visitor to the rear entrance of the Administration Building, up one flight of stairs to the Bertillon Department. We find there the Chief Clerk, who is also the receiving officer and the civilian in charge of the fingerprinting, Bertillon measurements and photographing. Fourteen new arrivals. Only three prisoners were discharged that morning. The count for the day will be increased by eleven. Thus the totals grow higher daily. Who knows where it will end? Or when? Probably only when we shall have discovered its source. But that is another matter. We are interested in these newcomers. They are lined up against the wall. As bedraggled a gang of men as our visitor ever saw. Most of them are wan, worried looking and nervous. The Chief Clerk shows me the commitments that accompanied these men. Three counties represented. New York, Kings and Queens. The Bronx and Nassau and possibly Richmond will be up the next day.

The crimes represented in this group of new admis-

180

sions range from murder in the second degree, with a sentence of twenty years to life, and forgery for which, the papers show, the prisoner was sentenced to natural life as a fourth offender under the Baumes Laws, to attempted grand larceny in the second degree with a sentence of one to two years. Robbery is included, of course. Every incoming group of prisoners includes its quota of robbery cases. Mostly youngsters under twenty. All these men have spent considerable time in city jails awaiting trials and sentences. During those weeks and months of waiting they were never permitted out of their cells, except for a short period of indoor walking in the corridor of the jail. They come to us unkempt, languid and sluggish.

The Chief Clerk is taking their pedigrees. One or two greet him familiarly. They have been here before. They know the ropes. "Do I get a new number?" one of them asks. Yes, he does. He is doing a new "bit" and no matter how many times he returns he is always given a new number, except in the case of a parole violator who is returned to serve out the balance of his old sentence.

The youngest of the group is a boy of sixteen. He looks younger. Our visitor agrees that he is hardly over fifteen. I question him. "How old are you? The truth, now."

"Sixteen, sir," he answers quickly.

"Sure?" I ask again. "If you're under sixteen, we can send you back for resentence and perhaps you will be sent to a Reformatory with a much shorter sentence," I advise him. "Don't you want me to look into this matter?"

"No, sir. I'll stay here."

That boy has ambitions. He is to mingle with "big

shots" in a State Prison. He has heard of notorious names in Sing Sing. He'll be one of the mob and expects to graduate with honors. It will take him four or five years to wake up. Then one day he will get tired of prison life; possibly when on the threshold of manhood he will realize the futility of it all, or a dominant personality will influence him toward better living. He will sue out writs of habeas corpus to test the validity of his sentence and claim that he was under sixteen when indicted and tried for his crime. The Court will demand positive and fool-proof evidence which, after the lapse of years, will be hard to procure. His many writs will be dismissed and he will return to Sing Sing bewailing the injustice done him and the prejudice of the judge.

The men answer the Chief Clerk's questions rapidly. It is a simple routine. Parents' names and nativity, their own nativity, religion, occupation, education, and such other information that may be important for identification and future study of environment and personality. "What made you do this?" asks the clerk. "What was the cause of your crime?" It is a routine question that must be answered. The experienced prisoner knows the answer. "Bad associations," he grins. The others take their cue. "Bad association" it is for all of them. It is not within the province of the receiving officer to inquire further. My visitor whispers to me. "I am wondering what made those associations bad?" He has hit upon the backbone of the problem of delinquency.

"How much money have you with you?" is the final question of the receiving officer. "You've got to turn over everything of value and money and it will be kept for you until you are discharged." Each prisoner turns

The parting good wish from Cherie... (Page 219)

his pockets inside out. The sixteen year old prisoner has nothing. No money, no property. Others lay all their cash on the table. One has twenty cents. He is the fellow with the natural life sentence. The officer looks at his ring. "What's that worth?" he asks. The man hesitates. "Nothing to anybody else, sir," he replies. "But it means much to me. It's an old fraternity ring." "Better leave it with me," the clerk suggests, "we'll hold it for you in the safe. Something might happen to it inside. When you go home it will be returned to you."

The life prisoner looks longingly at the ring as he hands it over. He has travelled at headlong pace since that day in the dim past when he placed it on his finger. The ground rolled beneath him and with each surge he was brought nearer to the final plunge. Now he is at the bottom of the pit. Though facing a life sentence in prison, there is always the hope that he may be able to climb his way up and back again. He might, in time, earn a commutation of sentence or the law be amended so as to permit his discharge after a lapse of years. If he has the strength and courage to reach the upper level where life is real and normal, that ring, the symbol of what is left of his respectability will be returned to him. If he fails—well, we have a large accumulation of similar tokens and symbols. It is getting to be quite a problem. There are no claimants.

"How much in money?" I ask the admitting officer. "Twenty dollars," he tells me. My visitor looks at me in amazement. Two hundred and fifty odd years of prison service and one natural lifer, with an aggregate of twenty dollars for their trouble. He looks wonderingly at me, then at the men. "Where is the glamor of it all?" he asks. "Wait," I tell him, "there is more to see. This isn't the worst of it."

Things move rapidly in the Bertillon Department. Fingerprints are taken; histories compared; prisoners sit for their photographs with their consecutive numbers attached to their coats. They are ready for the trip to the State Shop. There all clothing is removed; they are given a shower bath, are handed prison clothes. Heads are not shaven, only the sides are trimmed slightly. There is no real reason for this, except possibly a tradition handed down from the old days when heads were shaved clean and bare.

It is past the lunch hour, but the newly admitted prisoners are escorted to the mess hall for their late meal, marched to the bucket rack where they pick up their portable plumbing, still in use because of Sing Sing's congestion, and are marched to their cells to join the Reception Company on the first tier of the old cell block. They will remain in this Company for a period of fourteen days. During this period they are practically in isolation. The general prisoner population is not permitted to have any contact with them, either personally or in writing. They may write one letter a week, the Sunday letter, at the expense of the State. "Smokes" are handed to them the same afternoon by a representative of the Mutual Welfare League. They are provided with reading matter. Except for meals and routine visits to the various departments they are not allowed to leave their cells.

Sick calls are answered by a civilian nurse. If taken suddenly ill a doctor attends them. In case of serious illness they are admitted to the Hospital.

A representative of the mental clinic makes the

rounds daily among the prisoners in the Reception Company, to make certain that there are no mental cases in need of immediate attention. During their two weeks of practical isolation these newcomers will be taken to the Hospital for a thorough medical examination. All physical deformities will be carefully checked. Cases that need surgical attention will be noted. A record will be made of organic diseases. Blood tests will be taken to detect venereal disease.

The Chaplain will interview them to establish more definitely their religious affiliations and for such spiritual advice and encouragement as may be required.

They will be called to the Correspondence Department where they will be instructed how to write their letters; the restrictions on general correspondence; how to order their newspapers and magazines and books. The penalties attached to "kiting" letters out of the prison through irregular channels are explained in detail.

The Psychiatrist will examine them orally and give them the mental test. They will be asked to give as much of their personal history as is essential to a thorough understanding of their mentalities and outlook on life.

They will appear before the Classification Board where all departmental records are available and where, in the presence of the heads of the various departments, they will be questioned by a representative of the Department of Correction who will then place each prisoner in one of the following classes:

(A) Colony—Choice 1 or 2, indicating minimum security prisoners available for prison camps and so-called cottage plan prisons as contemplated under the recent recommendations of the New York State Commission to Investigate Prison Administration and Construction.

(B) Temporary restricted group for medium security prisons, available for short term prisoners.

(C) Restricted prolonged tractable group—which include well behaved prisoners with long terms.

(D) Restricted prolonged intractable group—comprising troublesome prisoners regardless of length of prison terms.

(E) Hospital groups—consisting of (1) acutely ill (2) infirm (3) tubercular.

(F) Psychiatric groups—composed of (1) hospital cases (2) observation (3) ambulatory.

Finally they will appear before the Assignment Board for designation to a particular shop or company.

Sometime during their period of isolation a representative of the Mutual Welfare League, usually an old time prisoner, will address the Reception Company in the office of the League. He will explain to them that prisoners have only two legal rights. One is to attend whichever religious worship is in accord with their beliefs and conscience. The other is the right to a specific food allowance. All other activities and interests are special privileges, granted through the courtesy of the Warden.

Recreation in the yard after working hours is a privilege.

The visiting room without screens is a privilege.

Motion pictures, baseball and football games and all other forms of amusements are privileges.

Purchasing supplies from the Commissary is a privilege.

Receiving packages of food and clothing from relatives and friends is a privilege.

Writing and receiving letters is a privilege.

Receiving newspapers and magazines is a privilege.

Wearing any articles of apparel not supplied by the State is a privilege.

Smoking in the yard and in the cells is a privilege.

The Warden may confer these privileges or he can revoke any or all of them, whenever he thinks it necessary to maintain the discipline or for the general welfare of his administration.

All men are placed in Grade "A" on their admission, except parole violators who are automatically reduced to Grade "B." Violation of any rule of the prison is punishable by reduction in grade with consequent withdrawal of privileges and loss of good time allowance.

This Reception period is probably the most irksome of the entire prison term to the newcomer, especially the first offender who must thus acclimate himself to his new surroundings. Some find it difficult to overcome their emotions. Depression sometimes leads them to attempts at suicide. Every precaution is taken to guard against such incidents. Yet occasionally the prisoner determined on suicide will succeed. One prisoner facing a twenty-five year term was found strangled by his leather belt. He lay on his cot, to all appearances asleep. He was not disturbed until the evening count was taken when all prisoners must stand at their cell doors to be checked. The keeper called to the figure on the cot. There was no response. Investigation disclosed that he was dead. There was silence in the corridor that night. Suddenly the quiet was disturbed by a loud yell in one of the adjoining cells. "Tell that to those who invented these long sentences. They would like to hear about it."

But we must not forget our visitor who is waiting to see more. He is apparently in no great hurry. I ask him to stay for dinner. He accepts with alacrity. Meantime he is seated in my office, an interested onlooker. Four gentlemen are waiting for their daily conferences. The Superintendent of Industries, the Principal Keeper, the Assistant Principal Keeper, who is also the disciplinary officer, and the secretary of the Mutual Welfare League.

"I've got the blue prints for the new power house," the Superintendent of Industries tells me. "You know since the cut in the appropriation we have had to change our plans considerably." We go over them together. Decide on suggestions and recommendations to be made to the State Architect who must make the final plans upon which contracts are to be awarded. It is to be a million dollar structure and will be the latest thing in that type of building. He explains that with the modern equipment in the new shops we have been able to speed up production and provide work for more men. We are two hundred thousand dollars ahead of last year. A fine showing, indeed. The new garage, where the prison's thirty trucks, three steam shovels, tractor and passenger cars are to be housed is ready for occupancy. It has been built entirely by prison labor and is a well-constructed building of concrete and steel.

Our visitor is interested. "What would you say is the value of the entire prison plant as it stands today?" he asks.

The Superintendent of Industries pondered the matter. "It seems to me," he replied, "if you include all appropriations for buildings and construction, the

188

value of the site consisting of forty-seven and a half acres within the walls of the old and new prison, and the land outside the walls, it is an establishment well worth $25,000,000."

"Quite an institution," the visitor remarked thoughtfully. "I can see how important its supervision and management must be and what practical problems must arise in its successful operation. The Executive of a $25,000,000 institution is indeed a responsible officer."

He turned to me and continued. "But your job, Warden, is much more than that, as I see it. You're not only running an industry with all the essentials and burdens of a huge producing concern, you must look as well to the care of your wards and their intimate problems. You've not only the task of regulating the relationship between officers and the prisoners but also between the prisoners themselves, their contact with the outside world and their relatives and families."

I pointed to a stack of vouchers on my desk. The bi-weekly pay checks for our officers and civilian employees. The Warden is the bonded fiscal officer of the institution; $3,000,000 flow through his hands annually. That authority cannot be delegated to any subordinate.

"Yes," I admitted, "and while you are here you will witness some of the Warden's daily functions. My next appointment is to hear charges against one of our uniformed guards. A sort of court martial."

I excused the Superintendent of Industries and called for the Principal Keeper. "I'll hear that case now," I told him. He ushered in two officers in uniform. One was the Captain of the Night Watch and the other a member of the night force. The charge against the officer was clear. Two nights ago the latter succumbed to Morpheus. It was his ill fortune that the Captain has a disposition for prowling at unexpected moments. The guard had hardly enjoyed his forty stolen winks when the Captain was upon him.

Now, prisons are peculiar places. The unexpected always happens. And it is as likely to happen in the early hours of the morning as at any other time. Alertness is the essential feature of prison administration. A steel file may be working overtime and surreptitiously. A prisoner may be taken suddenly ill and need medical attention. Despondency may have so overwhelmed another as to prompt him to suicide. Any of these things may happen during the night on any particular gallery. Wakefulness is the watchword of the night force. The soldier on sentry duty is court martialed if he is caught napping. The prison guard must also face the consequences of his neglect.

The Captain reads his report. The man was in his chair fast asleep and awoke only when the Captain shook him vigorously.

"Have you any explanation to offer?" I asked the accused.

"Nothing, Warden. I must have been tired. I can't understand how it happened."

"Weren't drinking during the day before you came on duty?" I suggested.

The man hesitated. "I might have had a drink in the afternoon," he finally admitted.

I had no alternative. The good of the service called for the man's dismissal. As a courtesy, he was permitted to resign. The hearing was over.

In the matter of prison discipline there can be no middle course. An officer is either conscientious and honest or he is dishonest and untrustworthy. We realize, of course, that we are dealing with human beings, not machinery; that now and then a man will be tempted and fall from grace. We have to allow for that, but do our best to prevent it and minimize the consequences. Yet it is an ever present source of worry.

One afternoon two lawyers arrived in my office summoned by the father of a prisoner. The prisoner is a man who was lucky enough to have escaped the death house. His conviction of murder in the first degree was reversed. He was given a plea of murder in the second degree and sentenced to a term of twenty years to life. This man had been in prison since 1921 and is due to remain there until 1941. He should not have been in a hurry about anything.

Yet his father received a telegram that morning with the time stamped on it showing that it took eleven minutes from the time it was dispatched in a town adjoining Ossining to the time it was delivered to the prisoner's father. The telegram stated that something new had turned up of vital importance to the prisoner and that he desired to see his attorneys at once to have something done about it. The father came. I let him see his son. The lawyers came. I did not let them see the prisoner. They demanded the right to see him to find out what new development had taken place in his case.

"Nothing new, gentlemen," I said, "since he killed that other man and was sent here for it. He made all the news then; none has been made since except the good news that he did not have to die in the chair."

The lawyers left. They had to. They had no legal

grounds to stay, although I have observed that that slight omission does not always stop lawyers from standing up and stating a forceful case. I reminded them that their imprisoned client could be punished for violating the prison rules.

"Yes," somebody wise-cracked, "he was in too great a hurry. With all the leisure he has on his hands he could have chiseled that wire on a glacier and it would have reached us in time."

I did not laugh at that one then or later. The man who joked about it wondered why.

"That isn't at all funny to me," I explained, "although I have no doubt that outside people may laugh at the idea of a life termer sending a telegram. With me, as the Warden of this prison, where twenty-five hundred men are confined, I have to worry that when a telegram can be smuggled out, something worse might be smuggled in. Some guard is a grafter, and to a thousand and one responsibilities, I have to add the thousand and second and find out who it is."

Such lapses on the part of the guards are not every day occurrences, or else the prison system would become one vast racket and a guard or for that matter the Warden himself, would hardly know whether he was locking cells one night or to be locked in one himself the next.

Out of the two hundred and eight guards in Sing Sing and ninety-five civilian employees that constitute the average Sing Sing administrative personnel, few have gone wrong, although those few have been exceedingly dangerous to the morale and peace of the prison. I like to think that most of these men, in a pinch, are like the one we will call O'Brien. This officer was on yard duty one day making the count with other officers. He knew there had been trouble on one cell tier, a row over a stolen cigar. That, in prison, can become a serious matter if the man who missed the cigar is ugly or the man who stole it despised. In this instance, both the thief and the victim filled the requirements for a maximum of trouble.

In the yard, the men of that tier were lined up for the count. It was the first time the thief and his victim had been within striking distance since the theft was discovered.

All O'Brien saw was a man dropping out of the ranks. O'Brien did not hesitate. He waded into that line of convicts, yanked out that big brute by the neck and started rushing him through the yard. There were murmurs, and the convicts moved in a self-impelled wave. The other guards walked coolly and slowly toward the bulge of the wave. It set back. In the meantime the man who had been knocked down scrambled to his feet, rubbing an injured jaw. And O'Brien did a smart thing. He checked the bruiser somewhere, returned, grabbed the stricken cigar thief and took him from the yard to face the prison bar of justice with his assailant.

That was intelligent and fearless action—and I see plenty of it in the course of the year at Sing Sing, where the guards, not extravagantly paid, averaging less than $175 a month, are faced by temptation to cowardice and to bribery, not as frequently perhaps as the temptation that assails the metropolitan policeman, but of a sharper degree when it does arise to sway his judgment and swerve him from the straight line of hard duty.

Common sense is an important asset to every prison official, whether in the ranks or higher up. An admonition, without infliction of punishment, will often go a long way toward correcting wavering impulses of prisoners. One of our officers took this means of straightening out a fellow who had been brought before him charged with fighting. The prisoner had a good record and had always been quiet and peaceful. It was his first offence since coming to prison. The prisoner explained that the man he had struck had aggravated him until he had lost his temper. "I won't punish you this time," the official said, "but I would advise you to keep away from that fellow in the future and have as little to do with him as you can. If you sleep with a dog, you must expect to find fleas on you when you wake up."

Our visitor was impressed with the prompt decision at the court martial of that unfortunate officer. "That was prompt and speedy justice," he remarked. "If the courts outside adopted that plan you would have less to do here. I'd be interested to know how you deal with malefactors among the prisoners."

"You'll soon see," I tell him. "The disciplinary officer is next. He is coming to review with me the cases that appeared in the last session of the Warden's Court. You've got to remember one thing, however. The members of our official staff are subject to suspension or dismissal. We cannot suspend or dismiss our prisoners—that is, not unless their terms are expired. They are with us to stay until then. Prisoner discipline is a wholly different problem."

The Warden's Court hears all charges against prisoners. The Assistant Principal Keeper, who is also the Disciplinary Officer, presides over this court. With him sit the Psychiatrist and the Doctor in advisory capacities. The record of the last session of this court includes the various and usual assortment of minor infractions; absent from school without good cause; neglecting to make beds in the morning before leaving cells; bars of cell door covered with dust; windows of cell unwashed; walking through the yard or on the recreation field without a top shirt; singing in a loud and discordant tone of voice in cells to annoyance of neighbors, and other violations of rules of routine. For the first offence, charges of this class are invariably disposed of with a suspended sentence and a warning. A second offence is more severely dealt with. There is the reduction in Grade, with consequent withdrawal of privileges. In aggravated cases there is the further and severer punishment of adding days, or months, even years to the minimum term. This is the penalty most dreaded by prisoners. A first offender with a term of five years to ten will, under the present law, be able to earn for himself ten months by the recently adopted "good time" law, which restored in small measure the procedure that existed prior to the enactment of the so-called Baumes Law in 1926, whereby prisoners could earn for themselves a substantial reduction of their minimum sentences by good conduct. Two months a year is the good time allowed under the present law; the old law called for three months a year. Two months a year makes hardly any perceptible difference to a man doing a fifty year sentence, certainly none at all to the life termer. Yet almost every prisoner is anxious to keep his record clean of loss of time. For the comparatively short termer, the man doing anywhere up to five years, or even ten, the loss of any portion of this good time allowance is a serious matter, especially as he nears the end of his term. But, of course, prisoners are human even in their infractions of rules and regulations. They will be guilty of acts of omission or commission even as the average citizen on the outside. Sometimes it is sheer carelessness. Often it is the result of nerves. There are the nitwit daredevils who are never happy unless in some fracas or another. There are those who, embittered by life, take the "devil-may-care" attitude toward the future. We have our troubles and worries with "big shots" who desire to impress their fellows and use dangerous and vicious methods in their purposeful campaigns.

It is the duty of the Warden's Court to unscramble this accumulation of behavior problems within the walls. Some of the men need straightening out. Others require more drastic attention from the psychiatrist or psychologist. Such cases are placed in the observation company for closer and more intimate analysis. Others may be physically incapacitated and are transferred to the invalid company. None of these three groups is permitted to work. They are quartered in the new cell blocks on the hill, with sufficient light and air, but no access. Each company has its particular location in the mess hall; is permitted exactly the same food as the rest of the population. They have their exercise periods. Visiting and correspondence are restricted. They are not permitted to attend picture shows or entertainments in the chapel and may not participate in athletic events on the recreation field. All this is a part of the responsibilities of the Warden's Court in cooperation with the Assignment Board.

There are, also, more serious problems. The Court frequently stands as the buttress between officers and prisoners. It must sustain the dignity of the administration and, at the same time, protect the prisoner from persecution. Officers as well as prisoners vary in mentality and personal responsibility. Every member of our staff, uniformed and civilian, is on duty eight hours daily and is subject to extraordinary duty at any hour of the day. On occasion men have been on duty for twenty-four hours of continuous service. No extra pay is allowed for such special duty. The prerequisite of a competent prison official is understanding human nature. That is perhaps as important, if not more so, than understanding fixed rules. Our entire force, except guards on guard posts, are unarmed. They do not carry blackjacks or sticks. We have had only one assault by a prisoner upon an officer, despite the fact that our count includes many long termers and lifers. Some of our officers, through long association with their men, take a personal interest in their prisoners. Not a few extend financial aid to men about to be discharged, and who are without immediate prospects.

But among three hundred men there are a few who have lesser appreciation of their responsibilities. Perhaps a sluggish liver will befog a man's judgment. Or he may be influenced by personal spite or antagonism. Charges and complaints by officers against prisoners must be carefully sifted. That is within the province of the Warden's Court. Often this sifting process results in change of personnel. Officers may not fit in with certain groups and fare better with others. This will become apparent from a review of the cases presented by that officer for attention by the Disciplinary officer.

Thus many of our departments dovetail. One affects the policy of the other.

There are also the more serious accusations which must be dealt with sternly and effectively. Among these are:

> Assault upon fellow prisoners;
> Carrying concealed weapons, razors, knives, etc.;
> Insolence to officers;
> Refusing to work at assigned tasks;
> Sending out letters through improper channels;
> Attempted escapes, and (strange as it may seem) Drunkenness.

I do not encourage the practice, prevailing in other prisons and in many municipalities, of looking passively on while dangerous situations develop into hazardous facts. I believe in the theory of "nipping the bud" policy. We act on suspicions and fairly reliable information. We do not always succeed in separating hostile groups. With our congested numbers it is not always possible. But when we learn of precarious relationships among prisoners, we do our best to break up the associations.

Word came to me recently that a life prisoner in the observation company was preparing himself for an attempt to escape. I ordered a thorough search made of his cell and all his belongings. Sure enough, we found among his effects a rope ladder. He had torn his bed sheets into strips and twined them up closely into strong rope. It took a lot of patience to do it, but there it was. Strong enough to hold his weight and, if opportunity arose, a handy contraption. We might have waited until the prisoner took advantage of an opportunity to scale the walls and shoot him down. It was more satisfactory to check the plot before it progressed to that fatal result. The Warden's Court handled the matter effectively by continuing the prisoner's isolation and forfeiting all his privileges.

Similarly, when one of these unfathomable rumors had it that a certain group of prisoners were hatching "something" against the peace and order of the prison, I made it my business to meet the "big shot" of that crowd "accidentally." I passed the time of the day with him and talked about generalities. Before he left me he knew that I was cognizant of the situation and familiar with plots and plans. Nothing further was heard about that particular incident. The institution was saved from any impairment of morale and the Warden's Court from possible action.

Now and then a prisoner is seen staggering uncertainly through the courtyard. He is apprehended and a doctor is called. The case is diagnosed as "booze." Liquor, of course, is strictly prohibited. An officer who is detected bringing in booze is instantly dismissed. And yet we do have our drunks, though they are, as a rule, few and far between. Prisoners have a way of making their home brew. It is a serious offence and severely punished. But desperate men will chance it. And so, periodic searches will yield cans of ill smelling, poisonous stuff that can kick one all the way to Paradise Lost. "Potato Water" is the usual concoction. A swill of that and your troubles are over for a day and a night. The imbiber usually comes to in an isolation cell, where he is left for a while to think it over and clear his brain. We have no bread and water diet. We feed the fellow, if he is capable of swallowing and retaining his food, but we leave him there to reflect on the error of his ways. Generally it helps. The ninety days that the Warden's Court adds to his minimum term, thus deferring his day of discharge, is probably more impressive. "Potato Water" is indigenous to prisons, and while not very common will make its odoriferous appearance from time to time regardless of most stringent regulations and supervision.

My visitor looked on as I examined each card with the Disciplinarian and marked my approval on his findings and punishments or commented on particular cases. One card I held up. I had received a letter from the accused prisoner protesting his innocence and contending that it was a case of mistaken identity. Some one on the gallery had yelled an insulting remark to an officer and this prisoner was charged with the offence. "Bring the officer and the prisoner to me tomorrow and I'll look into this," I ordered.

My visitor smiled. "I see that you are the court of last resort. A Court of Appeals, as it were."

It is getting well on in the afternoon but the sessions are not yet ended. Two more gentlemen are waiting for interviews. There is the Secretary of the Mutual Welfare League who will have his second conference of the day. He boasts the only leather portfolio among the prisoners. It is his badge of office, handed down from his predecessors. It is rather worn, but has done yeoman service in its days. It has carried requests from prisoners of a most intimate nature; demands from League officials promptly turned down by the Warden, despite veiled threats from the senders; it has brought pleas for aid for prisoners' destitute dependents; grateful acknowledgments for privileges granted the population as well as resentments because others were withdrawn or curtailed under especial circumstances.

The Secretary has the usual accumulation of requests from Grade "B" and Grade "C" men for special writing privileges. The records of all men are examined. Have they behaved themselves since their last appearance before the Warden's Court that resulted in their reduction in rank? Does their diligence merit consideration and encouragement? If so, these requests are invariably granted. This is a matter that cannot properly be delegated to a subordinate official. The Warden likes to know how his men are getting on. How they are reacting to disciplinary measures. The prisoner who is sincere about his readjustment is given an opportunity to show the stuff he is made of. I am willing to meet him half way and give him a deserving break.

Jimmy is the Secretary's prison name. He is a barber by trade. And like all barbers has a smooth manner and a glib tongue. He dresses immaculately and is the courteous and respectful messenger.

"The boys want a double header next Sunday, Warden," he remarks. "I suppose it's all right." It is not all right and I tell him so. Not that there is any real objection to it, as long as the team is willing to work, but as a matter of policy the boys do not always get what they want.

The Secretary smiles. "Denied, Warden?"

"Denied is right," I reply. Jimmy passes on to the next.

He tells me how well pleased the general population is with the action of the last Parole Board. "They gave everybody a break. The boys will live up to it, Warden," he assures me.

He fumbles among his papers. "There are several requests here for railroad fares to wives and mothers for visiting. Will you please O. K. them for me?" The records of these applicants will be checked to verify the facts. If the papers show that their dependents are unable to pay their own fares these applications will be approved and the League Treasurer authorized to draw a check to cover the item. As the Trustee of the League, I sign all checks on its bank account. Several additional requests and Jimmy withdraws.

"Clever boy, that," my visitor remarks. "But do you really have to bother with those details? Can't you delegate such matters to a subordinate?"

It could be done, I explain to him, except for two reasons. The boys in the yard like to feel that the Warden has passed upon their requests. If he denies any, they feel less aggrieved than if the denial came from a subordinate official. It is human to expect and hope for consideration by the highest authority. On the other hand, the Warden likes to feel the pulse of his prisoners. Wants to know what is troubling their minds. What are their reactions to variations in routine and regulation? How do they respond to the rulings of the Warden's Court, to diet, to supervised recreation and to various forms of entertainment? It is the Warden's duty to know his prisoners. That can be accomplished only by understanding their intimate troubles, the things that are close to their hearts and minds. Such responsibility cannot be delegated. The knowledge must be first hand. That is why twice daily the Secretary of the League is given an opportunity to present the prisoners' problems to the Warden.

"So," my visitor remarked, "in addition to being the head of an industrial plant, with all the practical problems of manufacturing and production, you are the Judge, Court of Appeals, and sort of Big Brother to your inmates." Yes, I admit. All of those and perhaps more.

It is past three o'clock. We shall have time for a tour of the Hospital Building before the shops close down for the day. Perhaps we can find the time to exchange greetings with the Chief Physician. We must give our visitor a complete survey of the prison.

We climb a steep, temporary wooden stairway to the top of the cliff. We are on the highest point of the Sing Sing property. Below us the old prison looks small and cramped, as it snuggles close to the river edge. Only the smokestack rises in a commanding gesture toward the heavens. It is said to be one of the highest prison smokestacks in the country. To me it is the symbol of what we hope to make of Sing Sing—an industrial plant where men will labor willingly and hopefully; where they will learn to perfect themselves in the ways of honest toil. One can follow for miles the wide sweep of the Hudson, as it eddies its endless flow and disappears around a distant bend, majestically unconcerned with the problems of the variable human who clings to its shore in intermittent cycles of its countless years.

The Hospital Building rises four stories above its bed rock. An imposing structure of red brick and steel. Were it not for the iron bars that betray its purpose, this hospital could be the proud possession of any normal community. The uniformed officer at the front entrance opens the steel barred gate. We stop for a moment to read the inscription on a bronze tablet in the lower foyer. "Nihil Humani Probis Alienum" (Nothing that is human is foreign to us). It typifies the spirit of the New Sing Sing. The Hospital was the first building erected on this high level.

We guide our visitor rapidly through the first floor. We show him the Eye, Ear, Nose and Throat Clinic; the well equipped Dental Clinic; the well stocked Pharmacy; the busy Pathological Laboratory; the examination rooms; the X-ray rooms; the general offices with its complete Kardex System where we can find exact and detailed information about the physical condition of every prisoner in Sing Sing and also a full record of all hospital charts.

We take the elevator to the third floor. Here we find the medical and convalescent wards, and the isolation wards for contagious cases.

On the fourth floor we look through the two operating rooms with latest equipment; the sterilizing, the cystoscopic and the emergency rooms; the surgical wards and several private wards used for serious cases that need especial care and attention. We are shown the diet kitchens on each of the third and fourth floors.

In the surgical ward we meet the Chief Physician. He is a gentleman who stands high in his profession as physician and surgeon, to whom the work among the prisoners is more the labor of love than merely a job. He, of course, is in full charge of the Hospital. His staff consists of an Assistant Physician, a Resident Physician, a Dentist, Pharmacist, Laboratory Technician, and two Civilian Nurses. All on full time duty.

They are assisted by fifteen inmate nurses and several attendants.

The Chief Physician is a patient gentleman. He tells us something about the workings of his department.

The daily first aid clinic is in the old prison within easy access to the shops. The prisoner in need of medical attention reports the fact to the uniformed guard in his shop or company. He is given a pass to the first aid clinic where he is examined by the Assistant Physician for particular diagnosis. If his ailment is slight he is given medication immediately. It may be some form of common cold that will respond to simple treatment. Or he may be suffering from a gastronomic disturbance for which the first aid clinic is especially well prepared. The more serious cases are sent up in a group to the Hospital Building where daily clinics are held in the Eye, Ear, Nose and Throat Department, the Genito-Urinary Department, and the Dental "Parlor." The X-Ray room is held in constant readiness for immediate use.

Anti-Syphilitic and Orthopedic Clinics are held weekly.

The average daily attendance at the first aid clinic is about seventy-five men.

Drug addict cases are immediately isolated and ultimately find their way to Clinton Prison for special treatment. Tubercular cases are given pathological tests and X-Ray examinations. If the diagnosis is confirmed they also are transferred to Clinton Prison, whose high altitude is peculiarly adapted for their care and possible cure.

Our informant tells us of the staff meetings of the prison doctors held monthly. Of the general meetings with surgical clinics of the Westchester County Medical Society; of the periodic meetings of the State Prison Physicians and of the Salvarsan classes. The average daily invalid population in the hospital is about sixty.

Our visitor is curious about the surgical work among the prisoners.

"I suppose you have many cases of prisoners who are suffering from deformities or ailments antedating their admission. How do you handle them?" he asks.

The Chief Physician explains that most of the newly admitted prisoners suffer from digestive disorders. They have either led hectic and nervous lives on the outside prior to their arrest and conviction, or they have been confined in the City Jails over long periods without exercise or recreation. Some of these prisoners find it difficult to adjust their systems without special treatment. Most of them, however, do correct themselves after the first few weeks out of Reception.

There are prisoners with physical deformities. A record is made of these and in the course of time detailed examinations are made. In hopeful cases the prisoner is advised to submit to the operating table. Generally he is more than willing and anxious to respond. A few of these deserve mention.

A prisoner was admitted not long since with a scar on the side of his face caused by a burn. The scar tissue, in healing, contracted the muscle and as the result his chin was pulled sideways toward his shoulder at an angle of almost 45 degrees. This was corrected by doing a skin graft with good result. Thus was a man, whose facial deformity would have convinced every Lombrosoan enthusiast of his criminal nature, restored

206

to normal appearance. Whether his mind was equally corrected is still to be determined. We shall have sufficient time to observe him. He is doing a sentence of ten to twenty years.

Equally interesting was the operation performed on the prisoner who came to Sing Sing minus his proboscis. What should have been his nose was an unsightly scar flat against his face. Plastic bone surgery restored his missing organ. His nose was completely rebuilt. You would hardly suspect the handsome member of the cast in the Prison Annual Show as the erstwhile noseless prisoner. As a precautionary measure our Bertillon Department was directed to take a set of new photographs for our records. The old ones were, of course, utterly useless.

A prisoner was asked by the Receiving Clerk to sign his name to the blotter sheet on his admission. He was unable to make more than an X mark and explained that his right arm was stiff. It had been broken in his early youth and improperly set, which resulted in total loss of function. He was later taken in hand by our Surgical Department which restored the use of his arm with about seventy percent function.

Another prisoner, a negro, came in on crutches. His was a peculiar case; born with a dwarfed foot hanging from a short leg. The operation consisted of removing the miniature member, using the remainder of his leg as a stump for an artificial limb. For the first time in his life this man was able to walk without crutches.

Hunchbacks in prison are rare. As a rule this deformity is incurable. When they do come in they are assigned to work in keeping with their condition. But in one case our physician was curious and made a thorough examination. He discovered that the hump on the man's back, directly between the shoulders, was really an enlarged cyst. It was corrected. Today this prisoner is one of the star baseball players on the prison team.

A prisoner asked to see the Surgeon one day. He had suffered for years with severe headaches. He explained that a policeman's bullet had lodged in his head and had never been extracted. An X-Ray examination disclosed its location. The bullet had entered slightly above the right temple, traveled around the front of the head between the brain and the skull and imbedded itself in the brain tissue over the left eye which was thereby rendered almost sightless. The skull was opened and the bullet removed. His headaches disappeared, and his vision was restored.

In addition to these major treatments and operations, our surgical records show a large assortment of hernias, partial blindness, mastoids, stomach ulcers, kidney stones, gallstones and, of course, the usual number of appendicitis cases; all of them successfully cared for in the Hospital.

The Chief Physician informs us that the death rate in Sing Sing compares favorably if, indeed, it is not superior to any other community of equal or greater size in population. And he points with justifiable pride, in which I join him, to the fact that the Sing Sing Hospital is the only prison hospital in the world that has been approved by the American College of Surgeons and is practically on a par with the finest hospitals in the land.

Our visitor is impressed, as he should be. "Isn't it a

fact," he asks, "that men with no real problems in life such as occupy the minds of the citizen on the outside, often exaggerate minor ailments and are difficult to handle?"

The Surgeon admits this. But, he explains, our policy of keeping the men occupied with their tasks during the day, followed by recreation and athletics after working hours, takes their minds away from the irksomeness that leads to depression and imaginary aches and pains. It has been well said that "an idle brain is the devil's workshop." It is also the mainstay of doctors and surgeons as many physicians with fashionable patients will attest.

The Chief Physician confirms this from actual experience. He points out that the three months following the Christmas holidays are devoid of physical recreation. We have no facilities for indoor athletics. With the baseball and football seasons ended, and the passing of the Thanksgiving and Christmas holidays, the first aid clinic has many more patients than during all other months. The early lock-up during winter months, generally at 4:20 in the afternoon, accentuates and adds to the sick list. Colds are more common and frequent; cases of indigestion increase immeasurably; the night nurse answers innumerable calls of prisoners who suffer aches and pains and are unable to sleep. With the coming of spring and the resumption of baseball and other outdoor athletics, and the lengthening of daylight hours which shortens the time spent in cells, the doctors and nurses breathe a sigh of relief. For the balance of the year their work will be less strenuous.

"Certainly, in the matter of physical care," our visitor remarks, "nothing seems to be permitted in

Sing Sing to interfere with the prisoner's normal development. But what are you doing for his mind? A great many of your men are doing long terms, ten, twenty, fifty years and even life. They are of all ages and classes. There are vicious men and those who have made their one and only mistake. How do you pick the chaff from the wheat? Do you make any distinctions in the care and treatment of each group?"

We shall try to find the answer on the second floor of the Hospital Building. It is devoted exclusively to our Psychiatric and Psychological Departments.

Both of these institutions are comparatively new to prisons as they are to the world outside. I doubt if either has really found itself in the broad field it hopes to conquer. They are doing fine work with the material on hand and the scope they have been allowed. It is a human science which depends in a large measure on the reactions of the subject and the approach of the practitioner.

We shall interview the head of this department, who will explain its functions and operations. The staff consists of the following members:

> Director, who is also the Psychiatrist
> Two Assistant Psychiatrists
> One Psychologist and an Assistant Psychologist
> Two Investigators
> Two Clerks
> One Secretary and an Assistant Secretary

As has already been told, one member of the clinic staff attends the weekly sessions of the Warden's Court. At the weekly sessions of the Assignment Board the clinic is represented by two members, a psychiatrist and a psychologist. One member of the staff visits daily the Reception Company to examine briefly the newly admitted prisoners assigned to that company. The Psychiatric Observation Company is visited daily by one member of the staff and the members of the Disciplinary Observation Company are visited at least once a week.

Every newly admitted prisoner is examined at length within several weeks after his arrival, both by the psychiatrist and the psychologist. Prisoners do not generally regard these examinations with favor or respect. Few persons will respond freely to a formal oral questioning. Prisoners are especially on their guard with anyone who asks things. This attitude was expressed pointedly in recent months by a prisoner who was telling of his experiences before the psychiatrist. "He asked me why I went wrong. I answered him, 'Don't ask me. Tell me.' "

Following the psychiatric examinations, prisoners are classified as follows:

Normal, feeble-minded, neuropathic-psychopathic personality, neuropathic-post encephalitis, neuropathic-epileptic, neuropathic-alcoholic, neuropathic-drug addiction, neuropathic-others, psychotic and potentially psychotic.

Of 1,550 examined by our psychiatrists, 585 were found to be of normal mentality; 246 were called feeble-minded; all others were divided among the remaining subdivisions. It is interesting to note that only sixteen were drug addicts.

To the layman the findings of the psychologists and psychiatrists are hardly consistent. Thus while the psychiatrist finds about one-quarter of all the men examined to be of normal mentality, the psychologist finds less than one-fourth of the men he looked over to be defective mentally. Seventy-five percent of the men he interviewed, or 1,459 out of a total of 1,937 were found to be either of superior intelligence or of average intelligence with mental ages of 11 and over.

My visitor pointed out this apparent inconsistency. "Which do you follow in handling your men? The findings of the psychiatrist or the psychologist? They seem to be widely divergent."

I confess myself at a loss at times to follow either report. I am in thorough sympathy with both of those branches of human sciences. In placing men at tasks, in passing upon infractions of rules and general conduct in prison, we want to have the benefit of their advice and observations. But as a prison administrator, facing practical problems of routine and individual responsibility, when I want a man for a special assignment besides looking for his mental age or psychiatric report, I send for the man and talk with him. If I am satisfied with him he gets the job. If he does not impress me he is passed up.

Perhaps, as one of our psychologists said to me recently, the results of present day investigations in both psychiatry and psychology in institutions is but a prelude to what is to come, and will be felt twenty years from now. It may well be that through its probing into sources of human behavior we shall find the right method of treating with it. For the present, I like to think of both sciences as helpful in guiding floundering minds and personalities to surer footing.

The programs psychiatrists and psychologists have set for themselves are purely negative. They ask questions. That is all the law and budgetary appropriations have enabled them to do. I would like to have them become positive factors in their relationship with their charges. Their personnel will have to be increased, their facilities broadened. Brain doctors rather than mind probers. Menders of characters, not merely analysts. That prisoner with his sense of droll humor may be right. It is not enough to ask questions of men as to the causes of their delinquencies. They should be told and guided and instructed sympathetically on the proper course toward amendment. Towards that end and with that purpose I am willing and anxious to go along with the schools of psychiatry and psychology and help them to attain their objectives.

My visitor laughed. "Well, Warden, I don't suppose colleges and books alone can teach you how to run a prison or take care of a lot of men."

In a sense he is right, I admit to him. While I am a firm adherent to the principle of a trained personnel for prisons and all other institutions that have to do with the care and training of men and women, I do maintain that all theoretical study must be supplemented with practical experience. I believe the man in the ranks should be taught the fundamentals of human behavior and all the problems incidental thereto. I believe that the average mentality of the prison personnel should be higher than the average mental age of its prisoners, in order that there may be the proper respect for authority; not a respect born of the bludgeon but of sympathetic understanding of intimate problems. I believe, further, that prison service should offer a career to the serious minded officer, just as the army or navy assures careers to the youngest cadet in the service. It is only by offering the uniformed guard an opportunity for life work with possibilities for promotion that we shall be able to attract the right kind of men for institutional work.

The prison official must learn to feel his way. There can be no set rules in dealing with emotions. During my prison experience I have faced many situations that required quick thinking and determined action. Often they were unprecedented, and I had to employ my own methods and make my own plans. There were no references or opinions I could look up, no decisions of higher authorities that I could appeal to.

One such incident shall ever remain vivid in my mind. It happened in the summer of 1929, during the period of riots in prisons all over the country and especially in New York State. Whatever the causes for those disturbances, and they were as many in theory as penologists in practice, the fact was that each prison had its own peculiar problems. No two riots or demonstrations arose from exactly the same cause. Sing Sing had been peculiarly fortunate in avoiding all disorders, although the tenseness of the general situation did seep through our walls and put us on edge for a while. It approached its climax in July on the day of the monthly meeting of the Parole Board.

Word had gone out that no man with a gun record —that is, who had been sent up on a case charging possession of a gun—would be paroled. Of the one hundred and eight cases to be reviewed by the Board twenty-three were gun cases. These men, I had been informed, would refuse to face the Board if the first man called was denied parole on account of this unofficial ruling—and it was rumored the whole prison was ready to start trouble in order to back them up.

The day of the meeting I had delayed the cases of the twenty-three men until after supper when all other prisoners were locked in their cells. Then, lacking the moral support of their comrades, they had sullenly accepted the Board's verdict against them.

Early the next morning, shortly after six o'clock, the officer in general charge of the prisoners thought he detected a mutinous or restless spirit among the men. He promptly, but without authorization, told them, "The Warden will talk to you boys today."

I reprimanded the squad leader for this assumption of authority, but nevertheless issued a notice that I would speak to all the prisoners at four P. M. that day in the old prison chapel. Directions were given that no guards were to be present.

It was an unbearably hot, muggy day—we had had no rain for several weeks. In the afternoon, for no reason at all, I donned a pair of white flannels. At about three-fifty-five, I went inside the prison as the last of the lines were going into the chapel.

About two thousand men were packed into a hall with a normal capacity of nine hundred. As I edged my way in and faced the crowd I saw a sea of faces that filled every nook and corner of the auditorium. Not all the prisoners could gain entrance and several hundred men had to listen in from a radio connection in the old mess hall underneath the chapel.

Meanwhile it grew darker outside with heavy clouds overhead, so that we had to turn on the electric lights. The surcharged air of the meeting seemed to find an echo in the approaching storm without. The thunder never sounded worse to me. Lightning flashed, and just as I was about to reach the microphone in the front of the chapel—something happened. A bolt of electricity struck the wires between the condemned cells and the chapel—out went the lights!

Well! There I was, all in white, facing nearly two thousand men in practical darkness. My reception was unusual; I could feel the tension—no applause but no "raspberries" either. There was not even the usual "buzzing" among the men—only silence.

In my many years of prison service I had faced unusual situations. This topped them all. The seriousness of the moment called for a human touch to break the tension. I told a story about the necessity for mutual understanding. It was a dud, went flat—no laughs, no comments—still silence. For the moment I half regretted that I had not used the prison "mike" for all the prisoners.

By this time I was worried—scared would be a franker word. Something out of the ordinary had to be done and I suddenly thought of a "darky" story, just a little off-color.

The story was not really new. It was merely human, and it worked. The prisoners laughed—the lights came on and I sighed inwardly with relief. We then proceeded to discuss intramural affairs frankly and, I may add, with more emphasis. Now, I haven't heard to this day whether the forces of nature were then arrayed for or against me. I am giving you the facts. Draw your own conclusions.

That night the Principal Keeper, the Chaplain, the Chief Engineer and other department heads were permitted to go on their delayed vacations and the next day my family of over two thousand had a moving day. We moved from the old prison to the new one and we

216

all have been so busy ever since that the incident is probably forgotten by all except me.

"Yes, I quite agree with you," my visitor commented, as I finished the story, "you couldn't find a precedent for that experience in any books."

It was getting late. After four o'clock, and the civilian employees were already leaving their offices when we emerged from the hospital and made our way down through the arcade that connects the new prison on the hill with the old prison down below. The prisoners had returned from their supper and were scattering over the prison yard and in the athletic field for their three hours of outdoor recreation allowed them during the summer months before the evening lock-up.

My visitor was still eager to see things. We walk leisurely through the yard. No officer is with us. Prisoners greet us respectfully. Men sit in the shade or in the sun as suits their individual preferences. Here is a group playing a game of dominoes, one of Sing Sing's favorite pursuits; there is another group intent on a chess game. Now and then we see a pair of elderly prisoners, especially Italians, throwing bocci balls; on another patch of barren ground several men have improvised a miniature golf course where they play at golf with crude sticks and hard rubber balls; one cross walk, lined with iron benches, has been specially adopted by a number of Jewish prisoners, most of them aged and not a few of them reading Hebrew newspapers.

We stroll on to the athletic field. It presents a riot of action and color. Two shop teams are playing a game of baseball. Apparently it is a good game for the grandstands are full and the crowd is yelling encouragement to its favorite players.

The four handball courts are busy. We stop for a moment to watch the men. They are agile and accurate.

Here are prisoners with tremendously long sentences. But in this period of play and healthful recreation there is no time or inclination to think of self. The body is too active, the mind intent on immediate contests and the aim to win.

"What surprises me," my visitor remarks, "is that all this can be done without a single uniformed officer looking on."

I point to the men on guard post who stand there watchful and alert. They are the sole guardians and the only symbol of authority. The men do not look up at them. They are entirely unconscious of their presence. I am gratified that they can find forgetfulness of prison and routine and uniforms during these hours of wholesome play.

My guest will stay for dinner. I want him to complete his day with us. It is an uneventful affair. Our butler is a fastidious gentleman, well mannered. Doing a short "bit" of two and a half to five years. He claims to have handled large affairs and talks of millions as naturally as I smoke my after dinner cigar. Yet he can mix a salad as expertly as the famous Oscar himself.

My youngest daughter, Cherie, comes over to whisper in my ear. "Is it all right, Daddy?" she asks. Her freckled little face is all aglow with eagerness, anxious for my consent. One of the boys downstairs in the kitchen is going home in a few days. The other prisoners who work in my house are giving him a little send-off party and have asked Cherie to be the guest of honor.

May she go? I am not superstitious or sentimental. But I do remember the famous words, "Out of the mouths of babes . . ." The parting good wish that the little girl may give the man who is going out to face his great test in life may serve its purpose. The memory of this child's faith may make him think hard of the old saw—

> "The saddest words of mouth or pen
> Are these—we're in again."

A steam whistle blows loud and long. It is 6:50 and the call for the evening lock-up. We leave the table and stand on the old wooden porch that fronts my residence. The sun is riding fast toward its setting. The shadows are lengthening as the men begin their climb uphill toward the cell blocks. An endless line of men it seems to be. The older men and those of failing health or convalescents have gone before them; cripples have been carried up in the prison bus. The rest are marching. It is not a precise formation. Men walk at ease and talk at will. We stand there twenty minutes until that line passes and the last man disappears in the entrance of the chapel through which the prisoners will wind their way through the various corridors to their respective galleries. A sudden quiet has descended on the prison. Up there on the hill in those large buildings we hear the rattling of locks and the clang of steel on steel as brake bars are put in place.

My friend is lost in thought. Suddenly he turns toward me. "I've heard it said that prisons have a soul. Where is it to be found? Down here in the shops or athletic field during recreation or up there in those cells behind the bars? Have you ever thought about it, Warden?"

Surely, Mr. Visitor. I have. It's up there. The prisoner's home for five or ten or fifty years or for life. It is there he feels the pinch of punishment. In his cell he finds the message from home. On his narrow cot he writes his letters to those who still remember. He may be the most trusted of prisoners, the most efficient workman; he may stand out among his fellows in character, in mentality, in thought and ambition—the turn of the lock and the settling down of those long, iron brakes reduce him to the level with the lowliest of his fellows. He may have won his spurs in the public eye as a notorious gangster or a power in the nether world. His cell is no better, the key turns just as quickly on his lock, the brake works just as smoothly.

I tell my guest of a letter that passed through our correspondence department some time ago. A prisoner, a former public official, was writing home to his wife.

"I listened in on the radio last night," the prisoner wrote, "and was surprised to find myself in the midst of old friends. A dinner was being broadcast and the speakers were (he mentioned several names well known in the public eye) and let me tell you my heart beat fast. It sounded so familiar and so close to home and life." That prisoner's soul was laid bare in that letter.

"Yes," I told him, "if a prison has a soul, it is up there in those cells, suffering all the torments of an age-old and unsolved problem of life."

My guest bade me good night. Apparently he had been well entertained and, shall I add, instructed. I settled down in my library to enjoy a quiet evening looking over an old volume of Houdini's. The telephone rang. It was the officer at the front gate.

"Warden," he asked, "did you have an appointment with a rat catcher tonight?"

A rat catcher! Heaven forbid. True, we have our share of rodents and we are constantly battling with them. But that is hardly up to the Warden. The yard master attends to that. I was about to explain that to the officer who continued:

"The man insists on talking with you. He has a lady with him and a child."

I was interested, curious.

"Put him on the wire," I directed.

"Hello, Warden," an eager voice called, "don't you know me? This is Mike, you remember—Mike the Rat Catcher."

Of course, Mike was welcome. His wife was with him, also their little daughter.

It was five years since I had seen Mike. He was then driving what was probably the only team of horses in Brooklyn.

I recalled our last meeting. He was about to be married and lacked sufficient capital to set up house. I was glad to help.

"It's only a loan, Warden. I'll pay it back."

I waved him away with my blessing and, frankly, forgot about it.

Now, five years later, here was Mike, his wife and three-year-old child. We spent the evening talking about old times. His horses had given way to the automobile. He was now an expert mechanic and doing well. It was near midnight when Mike rose to go. Before leaving, he called me aside.

"Warden, I have something for you. Remember the

fifty? Here it is." He handed me a roll of bills. I hesitated to take it.

"Sure you can afford to do this?" I asked him.

"It's O. K., Warden," he proudly assured me. "All my debts are paid. I held yours for the last. I was sure you wouldn't mind."

Mind? I seldom felt happier.

Mike hesitated, grinned and whispered in my ear.

"Fine, Mike," I said, as I grasped his hand, "if you need it again soon—you know the address."

Apparently he was well prepared. He needed no further help. Some time later I received his card. A bouncing baby boy! Mike the Rat Catcher was getting on.

After three years of hard labor the house for birds was finished.

(*Page 233*)

RECEIVING BLOTTER
SING SING PRISON

Number 69698

Sentenced ~~Jany 14,1919~~ Name *Charles E. Chapin*

Received *Jany 19 1919* Max

Grade *C* Min

Received from *N.Y.*

County *N.Y.* Court *Supreme Part I* Judge *Weeks*

Plea *Con.* Term *20-0 to Life*

Crime *Con. Murder 2d*

Term out by ~~Commutation,~~ ~~Expiration~~ or Parole. *January 16, 1934*

Where born *Westfield N.J.*

Age *60* Occupation *Editor*

~~Single~~ ~~Married~~ Widower ~~Divorced~~

Height Weight Education *R & W.* Religion *Prot.*

Habits { ~~Moderate~~ Temperate ~~Intemperate~~ } Uses { ~~Drugs~~ Tobacco } { ~~Idler~~ or Employed } { Father Living Dead / Mother Living Dead / No. of Children }

Residence when arrested *Cumberland Hotel Bway & 57 St. N.Y.C.*

Name of relative or friend *Marion A. Chapin Sister*
Don C. Seitz. Jr N.Y. World N.Y.

Office Card ✓ Supt. Card P. K's. Card ✓ Number Book ✓

PREVIOUS COMMITMENTS

No

I hereby certify that the above is my criminal record. I further certify that the above statements were made by me voluntarily and without any promise or threats being made as an inducement to make the same.

Record taken by _____ *Charles E. Chapin*

Sing Sing Prison _____ 191____ Witness

CHAPTER 6: THE ROSE MAN

Two pages in the official records of Sing Sing Prison mark the beginning and the end of an extraordinary prison experience. "Even as man comes into the world unwillingly, so does he leave it reluctantly." Thus preaches an ancient philosophy. It is only partly true of the average man who enters prison to serve his sentence. He comes in unwillingly, of course, but he looks forward impatiently to the day of his discharge. Of Charles Chapin it can be truthfully said that he came willingly, even eagerly, to Sing Sing. In the last months of his life, he was complacent about his going. He felt that he had lived his life.

Chapin was among the outstanding personalities of Sing Sing's prison population. Men have done heroic work within these walls but few of them have left a lasting impress on the spirit of the prison. Chapin accomplished just that. He helped to dispel drabness, he dissipated gloom and despondency. He removed Sing Sing's raiment of sack-cloth and ashes—traditional in all prisons—and draped it with a mantle of green verdure and fertility. Its freshness and beauty are symbolic of the purposes we hope to achieve among the men entrusted to our care; to infuse new life in the debris of human backwash that eddies with endless flow through the gates of the prison.

Charles Chapin was my prisoner, a confessed murderer. I first met him in December, 1919, in the prison hospital during my visit to Sing Sing immediately preceding my acceptance of the wardenship. He was then about sixty years old and had been in Sing Sing for almost a year. He was already frail and feeble. A forlorn, gray haired figure lay listlessly on the prison cot. But I noticed that his eyes were wide open and brilliant. They followed me on my tour of the ward. I did not know him but I stopped beside him and inquired after his health. We talked for a few moments. His eyes seemed to thank me for my interest, and it was not long before he told me his name. I disclosed mine. "Oh, yes. You are going to be the new Warden?" he murmured. I had not yet decided upon it and told him so. "I'm praying you'll take it," he said. "You know," he smiled, "you are the first man who gave me a kindly nod since I came here."

It was hard to believe that this man had been the City Editor of one of New York City's great dailies. From his editorial sanctum he had ruled over the destinies of men, formulated the policies of his newspaper, helped to build up careers. Rumor had it that his whim toppled men from dizzy heights to the very lowest depths of degradation and despair. An autocrat in his own little world, he made many enemies, as autocrats must and do. I had heard about the reputation Chapin had built up in the newspaper world. And I was not surprised to find in my mail one day the following letter:

"I knew Mr. Chapin long and from a certain angle intimately in the years he was at the *New York World*. That is, I knew intimately the anguished stories of the hundreds and thousands of young writers whose lives he made a living hell. He was the worst curse our reportorial craft ever enjoyed. I used to think him a sort of devil sitting on enthroned power in the *World* office and making Park Row gutters flow red with the blood of ambitious young men. If you enjoy him I hope you keep him long and carefully."

Since this is not intended as a biography of Charles Chapin the incidents of his crime are not important. Suffice it to say that he killed his wife. I have always been willing to accept his explanation that it was not a premeditated murder, but committed in a moment of despondency and despair.

When I assumed the wardenship of Sing Sing, Chapin was still in the hospital. He was not expected to live. He had lost his powers of resistance and was failing rapidly. It seemed a pity that that vigorous mentality should be allowed to disintegrate. Twenty years to life had been his sentence. Possibly he might not live to complete that sentence. But surely the few remaining years of his life could be put to some good service. The man was entitled to a spiritual comeback before he answered the call of his Maker to render an accounting for his earthly deeds.

I went to see him in the hospital. He was almost too weak to answer my greeting. But his eyes still burned with life. Through them one could detect the active brain. I made a bid to reach it.

"Charlie, how would you like to get out of bed?" His head shook, "No."

"I think I'll put you to work, Charlie," I continued. His brows contracted in a frown. Again his head signalled "No."

"Something that I think you will like," I suggested. "You will be the editor of the *Bulletin*."

The *Bulletin* was then the prison paper. A rather

haphazard publication. It needed a guiding spirit and Chapin was the logical man. He seemed interested. His eyes bored into mine. "But you will have to get well in quick order, otherwise the offer is withdrawn. We can't wait too long." He was out of bed in a week. And he took hold of the *Bulletin* with an expert hand. I gave him as much latitude as was possible under the circumstances and he soon built up a prison paper second to none in the country. Frequently he chafed under institutional restrictions. Having his editorials censored was something new to a man of Chapin's temperament. As Warden that was my duty, and I fulfilled it literally. Chapin thrived in his work. He found renewed interest in life. He was a man made over.

Circumstances worked against him. They decreed the discontinuance of the publication of the *Bulletin*. Chapin was again without a job. I was worried about him. It is a Warden's responsibility to consider his wards. To place them properly, so that interest in life may not fade with the years. To make the most of brain and brawn, for the good of the institution and to help men retain normal faculties. Here was a man groping for an interest in life. It seemed to me his heart longed to justify himself in the eyes of his fellows. Chapin was a man of positive talents. He had to do something and that something had to be identified with Chapin, peculiarly his own. Again he began to droop. He walked through the yard with lagging step. A man just turned sixty, a failing body, a brain still active and willing, faced with years and years of endless nothingness. I was convinced that we would have to find a task well suited for his driving powers or he would again take to his bed. Society was hardly concerned with this man.

It gave him to me as my own particular problem. "We're through," was the substance of its mandate. "You're to keep him for twenty years. See that he keeps well, that he retains all his senses, that he continues normal. It's up to you. We'll hold you accountable." But it made no provision for all this. With the discontinuance of the prison paper there was no job within the walls of Sing Sing that could hold the interest of Chapin's sixty years of active, virile life.

One day I found Chapin waiting for me in front of my office. "Warden, I'd like to be assigned to a special job. To take care of the lawn. I think I could do it." It was hardly the kind of work for a man of his talents. But I humored him. "It's all right with me," I laughed, "but you will have to look after it carefully." He agreed. He came in the next day with the request for tools. He would need a lawn mower, a sickle, a hose and a pair of clippers. Eventually they were purchased, and the purchase used up a quarter of the budget for the care of the grounds of Sing Sing that year. Then Chapin had to wait till another quarter rolled around before money was available for grass seed. The old Sing Sing is built on a foundation of crushed rock, trodden cinders and old scrap iron. It is scarcely the sort of thing to support plant life. But, as the summer passed, the lawn kept thriving and Chapin began to feel better. Ambition stirred within him. His one desire was now to force that still sterile soil to produce life. On a morning early the next fall, Chapin stopped me in the yard. "Like my gardening, Warden?" "Yes, Charlie. You are doing fine," I replied.

"Well, I have an idea, Warden. I'd like to build a small garden, a flower garden. How about it?"

I glanced over the yard. Not a blade of grass, not a tree. Nothing but dirt and stone and sand, and piles of debris, trodden under countless feet for a hundred years. It was a desolate looking place, an entire square bounded on one side by the age-old, bastile-like cell block, and on two other sides by old, cold looking buildings badly in need of paint and repair. It was as barren to the eye as it was hopeless to the heart. Across the river, on the far shore of the Hudson, the hills were covered with a magnificent coat of green, nature's own garment. Here all was naked. Suddenly I was ashamed. I turned to the slim man at my side. "Tell you what, Charlie. Do the whole job. Put some life into this yard. Cover it up. Let's have a real garden, trees and flowers. The boys will get a thrill out of it." And quick as a flash Charlie took me up. "That's fine, Warden. I'll make roses grow in that desert. Wait and see." And so Charlie Chapin became the Rose Man of Sing Sing.

Chapin entered upon his new duties with an energy that surprised me. I did not think him capable of such amazing vitality. He of course knew little if anything about gardening. He wrote to a friend who was kind enough to send him a set of eight volumes of Luther Burbank, the California floral wizard. He literally devoured them during the winter months. He envisioned the yard between the cell block and the work shops, as well as the odd spaces around, as one great garden. He found a few fellow prisoners who, like himself, knew nothing of gardening but were willing to get to work under his guidance.

First, piles of iron, wood and stones had to be removed. That kept him busy all winter. There was plenty of help available for this work, and soon Chapin had a gang of about thirty men working at full speed. And how he drove them! There was no loafing on the job when Chapin was around. It was his big task and he meant to complete it. The ground had to be ready for spring planting.

I sent out a gang of men to get a supply of dirt. I gave Chapin a pair of overalls and a yard sized farm hat; gave him some help from among the prisoners and an Italian boy who loved flowers and who worked with him from five in the morning until noon, and from noon until supper time. He needed fertilizer and grass sod. I gave him the necessary orders and up came a wagon load of loam and squares of grass. He worked harder and got increasingly excited over it. It gave him new life.

Toward spring, having made a bed or two, Charlie ordered some plants. There were no appropriations in the budget for this work. Nor was there any special fund to draw upon for this purpose. The supply was, therefore, rather meagre. Chapin sent his first order to a gardener in a nearby town. The plants were shipped as ordered, but the gentleman followed them up with a visit to Sing Sing to see what was being done with them. This gentleman met Charlie, interviewed him, and was shown over the site of the prospective gardens. Shortly thereafter Mr. F. R. Pierson of Tarrytown sent a truck load of plants.

Mr. Adolph Lewisohn, the philanthropist, was also an interested visitor. To him Chapin wrote about his troubles. "I hope to have some very beautiful flowers next Spring if only I can procure what I need in the way of bulbs, shrubs and plants. Seeds I am able to buy out of my own slender funds. Do you know that I actually get a heartache every time I look through the catalogue and read of the many fine plants in greenhouses and nurseries that I covet? I bought some geranium and gladiola bulbs from Mr. Pierson, and when a friend wrote him what I am doing he sent me a load of plants and also came over himself to give me some practical suggestions. Encouraging isn't it, to have such a busy man give thought to a convict? It's the greatest happiness I have found in the three and a half years I have been in prison. I am up at five every morning and am at it almost constantly until it grows too dark to see."

From Mr. Lewisohn's garden came another load of plants. Chapin was overwhelmed with his good fortune. Other floriculturists became interested and people in all parts of the country favored Charlie with seeds and plants.

Rose bushes were planted and also dahlias, a dozen varieties of cannas, a considerable variety of perennials, including peonies.

The yard, a little over an acre in area, was broken up into a series of beds and borders. Surrounding the cell block wall a long border was filled with peonies and other flowers. Seats were placed all around to permit the prisoners to rest during recreation periods. In the center, and separated from the border by a wide walk and again divided by cross walks, was a sweep of turf in which a series of rose buds were planted. Between two stretches of turf in the center, a cement fountain and basin were built, measuring fully ten feet across. On the plot toward the river, between the old mess hall and the central office building, another sweep of turf

The yard was broken up into a series of beds and borders. (*Page 230*)

was laid down, cut up with beds filled with snapdragons, tagetes, perennial and annual phloxes and asters.

One day while Chapin was fussing among his plants, a young Italian boy, a prisoner, came up and gazed at one of the flower beds.

"What's dat leetle flower?" he asked Chapin.

"That? That's some sort of little aster. Pretty, isn't it, Tony?"

"Yes. Maka me tink of my bambino. I gotta bebee, looka joost same dat."

For three years Chapin worked unceasingly on his flower beds and his garden. He toiled patiently and he did not spare himself. And he demanded similar service from the prisoners assigned to work with him. "I would suggest," he wrote me in 1923, "that all men assigned to work in the garden be given to understand that they are not to shirk. Most of them disappear if I am not around an hour before the whistle blows. I expect them to work from 8 A. M. until 11:30, and from 1 P. M. until 3:30, except in stormy weather, and they should be given to understand that shirking will not be tolerated."

There was the old Chapin—demanding results from his men, but asking no more than he himself gave. Men do not like to be driven. Perhaps that is how he got his reputation as an iron-fisted boss. Prisoners are no different. And Chapin was not altogether popular with his men. But he was after an objective. And it was a proud Chapin who walked into my office one morning in the late spring with a handful of roses in his arms. "First choice, Warden. A thanksgiving offering to you for your cooperation." It was a new Chapin who stood before me. That afternoon I walked with him to survey his world, the gardens and the flower beds, and the greenhouses which he had had built near the river front. It was all a riot of color.

Every day thereafter Chapin would personally bring his floral contribution for my desk and my home. The day that he did not appear brought word of his illness.

I do not claim that flowers reform men, nor that the gardens or the roses reformed Chapin. But they gave him a new perspective. And after all, is not that the aim of prison administration? To me the blossoming of Chapin's roses meant more than having flowers for my desk. It was a gesture to our prisoners—a message of hope. The most arid of spots, filled in with the debris of a century, could be made to produce life and beauty. Is there not hope for the most depraved? Is any heart hopeless? Men gathered around the shrubbery and the garden spots and stood for hours. What did they see there? Life talking to life. God's message to man.

And Chapin walked among the flowers. . . .

Often there came requests from magazines and editors for stories or articles by him. "I have been asked a number of times," he told me once, "to write for magazines, and for reasons that are personal I have always declined. If they want to know something about the gardens, I shall be glad to supply the material, providing the writer understands that it is the gardens he is to write about and not an inmate." He did not seek publicity.

But Charles Chapin was a sick man. Our hospital physician reported in 1926 that his vitality was low and his heart action weak, his general condition feeble.

Yet Chapin carried on. Again the autocrat. A kingdom of flowers. In the fall he would trust no one to attend to the care of the flower beds and their protection against the weather. Toward spring he was at it again, seeding, sowing, plotting the grass beds, trimming the trees.

His friends continued to send him buds and flowers for his gardens. One shipment came marked "roses." "They turned out to be English Ivies," he laughed, "but I'll give them the best possible care." Flowers were flowers to him.

Several years ago another friend sent him a three years' subscription to a magazine. "He is more optimistic about how long I shall continue to carry on than I am," he said, "for all of my subscription renewals are never for a period longer than six months. Three years! I must try and avoid pneumonia. My only ambition now is that I may live to see our garden blossom through the next season."

Then, one day, he stood gazing at his gardens. It was a bright summer day. The birds had discovered his tree tops and rose bushes. He was lost in thought. Finally he turned to a friend. "Why not a bird house? It will complete the picture." He came to me later with his idea. A bird house amid Sing Sing's gardens. I doubted if it could be done. But I let him try. He would have to do it on his own. The State made no provision for it. He got busy with friends on the outside. Contributions flowed in. And the boys in the prison, even some of those who disliked working with him, went to work and slowly after three years of hard labor the house for birds was finished. So now Chapin had another possession. But his pride and his joy were in the garden. And the task he preferred was to pick the roses for the hospital and his daily contribution to the Warden.

In the summer of 1930, a new drainage system for the prison was being installed. New pipes had to be laid. The contractor appeared with his large steam shovel to dig the necessary trenches. He was ruthless, and cut wide swaths in Chapin's gardens. Everything went down before that iron fury. Rose hedges were uprooted and destroyed—annihilated. Chapin looked sorrowfully on this carnage, but he was helpless. His province was being laid waste. I think it affected him deeply. He was never the same.

He was suddenly the helpless invalid, unable to carry on. His burden of life too heavy. I was with him in his final moments. "Is there anything you want, Charlie?" I asked him. "Nothing," he whispered, as he held my hand, "nothing. I am tired and want to die."

"I desire to be buried by the side of my wife," his sealed message to me read. His will was done.

Did Charles Chapin die friendless? Was he remembered only as the "hard driver" of men? Not so. Kind thoughts hallowed his memory.

"As an old *Evening World* man who owes whatever success he has attained to the fact that he received his early training under the greatest newspaper general in the world, I send you this word in memory of Charles Chapin."

And another: "I cannot pass this opportunity to send this message of sympathy in the passing of Boss Chapin, in remembrance of many kindnesses shown me when I was a young reporter on his staff."

And from St. Louis, where he made a niche for himself as an editor, came the message, "Just a word in memory of Charles Chapin."

And in Sing Sing—Chapin's province has been reconstructed. Rose hedges again stand guard at its borders. They are living, conscious realities. Breathing of the spirit and soul of their godfather, Charles Chapin—Sing Sing's Rose Man.

M 1490

HOSPITAL DEATH NOTICE

Sing Sing Prison, ...12-13-30....................

Name................Charles E. Chapin................

Consecutive No.......69690...........................

Sentenced...............1-14-19.......................

Crime...............Murder 2d.........................

Term..................20-0 to Life.....................

Died.................12-13-30.........................

Hour..................11:45 p.m........................

Age....................72.............................

Cause of Death.......Bronchial pneumonia.............

_____ Physician.

235

CHAPTER 7: TWENTY THOUSAND YEARS IN SING SING

"The judge gives a guy a sentence. When he arrives it becomes a 'bit.' Eventually it becomes a 'stretch.' Finally, on its last legs, it becomes a 'whisper.' That's when the guy begins to shout."

Thus wrote a prisoner to his brother. There is a tinge of humor in that thought. But there is more to it than humor.

What happens to that "guy" while the "bit" is being transformed from the "stretch" into the "whisper?"

Recently a wife visited her prisoner-husband in Sing Sing. They talked for a while about intimate things. Suddenly she asked him, "Jim, how old are you now?" "Twenty-nine," was the answer. "Why," she exclaimed, "you were twenty-nine three years ago when you came here." "That's right," he replied doggedly, "and I'm still twenty-nine. My time here don't count."

I think it was Tolstoi's wife who said, "I always wrote in my diary when we quarrelled. When I didn't write in my diary for a long time I always felt that I had not said anything about how happy I was in the interval."

And it was a famous historian who explained that history is nothing but the story of disease and crime and wars among men.

Most of us think about prisons in terms of riots, escapes, brutality. The prisoner is a brute and his

236

keeper a trainer wielding a whip-lash. When the trainer discards his whip, we expect the prisoner-brute to maul his keeper. Failing that, the picture is disappointing. Something has gone wrong.

The things that go to make up prison life rarely get into newspapers. They are not lurid, sensational or sordid. In our community of approximately twenty-five hundred men, life is intensive. "Abnormal," said one of our respected teachers, "is but the normal exaggerated." That is true, in a sense, of life within prison walls.

We stroll by a vacant field. Two local teams are swatting it out on the neighborhood baseball diamond. We may be interested and look on with enthusiasm. It is an ordinary occurrence. A similar scene in a prison arouses dormant emotions. Strange that prisoners should indulge in baseball. Figuratively, we pat ourselves on the back. We're doing pretty well by those fellows.

Yet a judge (recently in the public eye in some unsavory publicity) permitted himself to explain, back in 1922, "The idea of having baseball games at Sing Sing and bringing in a high school team to play with the crooks at Sing Sing! That's the way to encourage crime." To which I might have replied in the words of another publicist: "Practice makes perfect. Fourteen bases were stolen during the first game played by Sing Sing convicts."

We cannot visualize the normal in the abnormal setting. It was ever so. In the dim beginnings of the prison system of New York State a prison warden refused to permit his prisoners to attend school or to

237

learn to read and write. "That will make them know too much," he said, "besides, it's not hard labor."

Prison news from time immemorial is the story of the unusual from a physical aspect—a desperate attempt to escape, a riot, a fire with terrible loss of life, a murder within the walls, an execution. These are read with avidity, something akin to enthusiasm. We know then that prisons exist, that men are doing time —dangerous, sullen, defiant, brooding men. The incident passes. It has been crushed with an iron hand. Two thousand, three thousand, even four thousand men are locked securely in their cells. "We're going to be a tough prison from now on," the Warden announces. "Good boy, Warden," is the public acclaim, "go to it. What are prisons for, anyway?"

Whether prison life "counts" for the prisoner depends altogether upon the prisoner's reactions.

"I'm doing a life time," one prisoner wailed, "just think of it—three years."

His neighbor laughed. "Well, I've got thirty-five to go, but I'll be darned if I'm doing life."

Two prisoners were assigned to the same task, to sweep and clean one of the corridors in the new cell block. I passed them by one day. One approached me. He looked forlorn, sour and depressed. "Warden, it's getting me. Can't you do something for me?" "How long have you to go?" I asked. "One to two, they gave me, Warden. I've been here three months." I glanced at the other fellow, pushing his broom to the tune of a popular air. He seemed intent on his job. I called him. "What did you get, son?" "Ten to twenty, Warden," he answered grimly, "eight to go. I'll be doing a lot of mopping in that time."

Twenty-five hundred men saddled with an aggregate of twenty thousand years! Within such cycles worlds are born, die and are reborn. That span has witnessed the evolution of the intelligence of mortal man. And we know that twenty thousand years have seen nations run their courses, perish and give way to their successors. Twenty thousand years in my keeping. What will they evolve? Will they bring life and purpose to any of our twenty-five hundred men who are sharing in that tremendous burden? It is hard to say. Only by observing each man as he meets his intimate problems is it possible to understand whether those years are for him worth while or carrying him further into void and uncertainty. These are what we call the human sidelights of prison life. In themselves they may seem trivial and unimportant. Seen in perspective, they give us a sober impression of what this vast aggregation of years is accomplishing for the men who are threading their way through its enormous span.

There is George. He is going home soon. It's so close he is counting the days. So many days and a "get up." George is going to be an engineer. He is about to realize his ambition. Seven years he has studied. He enrolled in a correspondence school while still a boy. He had a job then and paid his tuition regularly. The time came, however, when he lost his job and there was none other to be had. Still there was his ambition to continue on with his studies. In a weak moment he took to petty stealing. He would thieve by day and worry over his lessons at night. He was caught, arrested and committed to a reformatory. There he couldn't continue his studies. On his discharge he was unable to get work. But he was anxious to resume his

239

correspondence course. The little technical knowledge he had acquired led him to opening safes when the police were not looking. Now he worked at night and studied by day. He paid his tuition regularly. It couldn't last, of course. He landed in Sing Sing. Here he has been able to continue his course in engineering. He has already completed it. A round-about way indeed. I wouldn't recommend it. Yet George will now begin life in earnest. A job is waiting for him.

"All set, George?" I asked him the other day.

"Sure thing, Warden," and he proudly displayed his certificate.

George, at the "whisper" stage of his prison term, is justified in shouting. He is on the threshold of life. He is probably a good risk.

I am not so sure of Mike. His term is also nearing its end. He is well beyond fifty and has spent the greater part of his adult life in jails and prisons. He started early, at the age of ten, at petty pilfering. Now he is an accomplished thief. Mike, strange as it may seem, has a splendid family. His son is a hardworking, respectable citizen, occupying a responsible position. Mike is also a proud grandfather. As a prisoner his record is hardly encouraging. He is charged with attempted escapes, and other things of an unenviable nature. Yet for the past several years he has made himself particularly useful in the prison service.

Mike is eager to leave us. He plans to live with his son and spend the evening of his life watching his grandchildren grow to maturity. Yet Mike isn't sure of himself. I am not altogether sure of him, but his son hopes for the best.

"Tell you what, Dad," he told his father the other day, "I'll fix you up a fine room. Everything the way you like. We'll make you comfortable, just what you've been accustomed to all these years. We'll fit your room out to look like a real prison cell, so you won't have to steal to get back into one."

Mike laughed when he told me about it. It may be worth the try.

I was more certain of Tom who was doing twenty years to life for murder in the second degree. He, too, looked eagerly forward to the day of his discharge. Almost sixteen years in prison, with never a report or complaint against him. A plodding, willing sort of fellow, and reliable. He was my official runner. But I don't remember ever seeing him "run" an errand. He was the champion walker, with a sure, steady tread. He left us and immediately went to work. His earnings were meagre, but he was frugal and the second week he opened a bank account. By the time he came to see me to tell me of his progress, he had already saved thirty dollars. It was a different Tom, I beheld. There was a steady look in his eye. His shoulders had straightened up. The creases in his face were ironed out. We talked about himself, his prospects, his happiness. I happened to mention world politics, international debts.

"Now look here, Warden," Tom interrupted me, "as a business man I want to tell you——" And he went on to elucidate on America's justification in insisting on Germany paying her obligations.

Tom, you see, had become a thinker of world problems. He was now a responsible member of society. His bank account gave him poise and confidence.

The prison population is made up of distinct personalities. Each reacts differently to his surroundings. Each is a distinct personality problem, and must be accorded individual treatment if there are to be effective results. Surprising as it may seem, the old procrustean theory must often be employed literally by way of mental suggestion. The exaggerated ego must be reduced; the man with narrow vision and low mentality lifted to levels never before attained.

There was the conceited prisoner, learned in the arts, and a linguist. He was called before the assignment board.

"What can you do?" asked the Principal Keeper.

"I can clerk in an office. I am also an interpreter. I speak fourteen different languages," he explained.

"No good," smiled the Principal Keeper, "we speak only one language here, and damn little of that."

Some prisoners quickly acclimate themselves to their surroundings, perform their tasks willingly, and even if they slip occasionally, manage to maintain a human attitude toward their superiors that helps all around. Edward, the porter, was that sort of a fellow.

He was a good natured, burly, coal black negro. He had met the Parole Board and was due for discharge in a few days. Edward had served six years. A second offender. Everyone thought well of him. Officers and prisoners were glad he was going, yet sorry to lose him. He had been an obliging, willing worker, was seldom grouchy and keenly relished a good joke— even on himself.

He was shining the Sergeant's shoes.

"Edward," the officer said, "you'll be back."

"No, sir," the colored porter answered with emphasis. "No, sir, I'm going straight. I got a home and I got work, good, steady work. No, sir, no more jail for me."

"Where's your home, Edward?"

"Hundred and Sixteenth street near Lenox Avenue. Suppose you come to see me, Sergeant?"

"Sure I will, Edward. What's the address?"

Edward hesitated.

"Well, now, Sergeant. Remember the day you reported me?"

"Yes, you bet I do, and you deserved it."

"Remember, Sergeant, the day you locked me up for being late for the count?"

"Sure, I do, Ed. You couldn't give an honest excuse."

"Sergeant," continued the porter, "remember the day you kicked me in the pants and told me to get the hell out of your office?"

"Sure, I remember that too. You were too fresh. But why do you rake up those things now?"

"Well, Sergeant," answered the porter with a sly wink at another officer, "you just remember those things, all of 'em, before you come to visit me."

Writing is the prisoner's traditional avocation. Almost every prisoner feels that he has a story to tell, an autobiography that is worth the telling. No sooner is he settled in his cell after his admission into the prison than he sharpens his pencil, somehow obtains a pad, and is at it. The enthusiasm generally wanes with the years. But during his first few months, even years, he works at it painstakingly. There is hardly a locker within the prison that does not harbor a ream of paper well filled with script, often illegible, about happy childhood and gradual fall from grace. Some of them are finally completed. They are submitted to me with the request for permission to send them out to newspapers or magazines. I make it a point to read them all. Very few, however, leave the institution. Most of them emphasize the sex urge that led them on to their fate. Somewhere there is the siren, the blond or dark-haired vixen whose charms were not to be resisted. He stole to provide her with luxuries. In justice to the ladies, I hesitate to make the story public. But some prisoners really have imagination. Once in a great while something comes along that has merit and is a real literary contribution. When the Sing Sing *Bulletin* was being published, many of these stories saw the light of day. They received favorable comment in the press and in the world of literature. The following little item was one of those. It is a Christmas story, and bears reading:

Here was Bill on Christmas Eve, still "doing time" and three and a half years yet to go.

His pipe went out and he laid there and thought about that picture of the convict getting a pardon for a Christmas present. If only the governor would play Santa Claus and put a pardon in his stocking. "In his stocking!"

Burglar Bill chuckled, and he kept on chuckling over the silly thought that had come into his head until he got up, knocked the ashes from his pipe, and deliberately opened the small locker that was fastened to the side of his cell. He rummaged about it and drew out an old woolen sock through which he ran a bit of string and fastened it to the steel bars. A "screw" came along and locked the door. He noticed that "Bill the Burglar" had hung up his woolen sock, but said nothing and passed along.

Burglar Bill fell asleep. He was awakened by voices at his cell door. An electric flashlight shone in his face for an instant, but Burglar Bill, still as a mouse, peeped through the slits of his nearly closed eyelids and said never a word. He recognized the voice as one of the night guards in charge of his gallery and he was pretty sure the other was the warden. The voice he took to be the warden's said to the other man, "I'll put it in his sock and I guess he'll be the most surprised 'con' in Sing Sing when he wakes up in the morning."

Burglar Bill was all a-quiver. He wanted to get up and inspect the sock, but the lights had been turned off and he had used his last match to light his pipe. Nothing to do but be patient until they turned the lights on again at five-thirty. He pulled the blankets over his head and snored so loudly that cries of "lay down, you bum, lay down" were shouted by disturbed sleepers in the cells nearby.

Five-thirty o'clock Christmas morning. The lights shone in every cell.

Burglar Bill sprang from his bunk and grabbed his old woolen sock.

Empty! He had only dreamed that the warden came in the night with a pardon from the governor. Only a dream!

"Ain't that hell," said Burglar Bill.

He told "Spike" about it while they were eating breakfast and "Spike" said, "Oh, well, easy come, easy go."

Sometimes prisoners' imaginations lead them into strange by-ways.

Night after night, as young Bob passed a certain cell, he was attracted by the beauty of the girl whose photograph adorned a prisoner's desk. Nightly he would stand, in the few available moments before lock-up, to gaze in rapture at the lady, to him the embodiment of female perfection. Then one night the picture was gone! Its owner filed a complaint. A reward was offered for its return. There were charges and counter-charges. It was not recovered.

Some time later Bob met the Board and was released. They cleaned his cell. In his bed, underneath the mattress, was the lady's portrait. I thought of the old adage about "strange bed-fellows." This problem of sex in prison is most troublesome, perhaps the most troublesome, for it is the root of many of our institutional worries and the cause of much grief.

In public discussions of prison problems the matter of sex emotionalism is politely ignored. The fact is, however, that it is one of the chief concerns of all prison administrators. They know that perversion exists, but it is difficult to detect and control. Investigations of conditions in jails and prisons, as also in reformatories, invariably avoid this question, and I have yet to see an adequate discussion of it with definite and constructive recommendations. A ray of hope in its ultimate solution may be seen in the recent innovations in some European countries whereby deserving prisoners are permitted periodic visits to their families. Certain it is that the overcrowding of our prisons retards any possible progress along these lines. It is still more difficult to understand how our legislators and responsible municipal and state officials countenance the doubling up of prisoners in one cell, as exists today in almost every city prison and county jail, without realizing how much they are thus contributing to the physical deterioration and moral perversion of the men. Seventy-five per cent of all our cases of sex perversion in prison can be traced directly to this custom of putting two or more men in one cell

246

where they are locked in together twenty-three hours out of every twenty-four.

Keeping the prisoner busy at his task is, of course, one of the methods by which his mind is swayed toward normal thoughts and outlets. But there are the after hours, when he is returned to his cell where he must remain until the following morning or be allowed some other form of activity that will engage his attention. I have tried to find the answer to that in wholesome recreation, in sportsmanship on the athletic field, in talking pictures, in radio, in letter writing, in a well-ordered library, in an occasional lecture by laymen with a worth-while message, in visits from close relatives, and, of course, in religious affiliation. I have found it, also, in permitting, to deserving men, a certain freedom of expression in their chosen avocations. Thus the prisoner with an inventive trend of mind, is given a measurable amount of leeway to work out his theories. One man in particular, during practically his entire term of imprisonment, experimented with a new model of a motor boat. I am informed that on his discharge he perfected his invention and is now actually manufacturing the product.

One young fellow, in his leisure hours, experimented with a perpetual motion contraption.

A well-known writer was admitted to the prison some months ago. His term was two to four years. Not long before that his latest book had been published and it was one of the "best sellers." I asked him one day, "What are you going to do about future publications? Are you through?"

"Oh, no, Warden," was the reply. "You see, I'm writing my new book now. In a way this will do me good. I was getting too lazy, too comfortable and had been neglecting my work. This is my chance to get back." I believe he will.

There is the prisoner of early middle age with a sentence of ten years. A very competent architect, with a flare for pencil drawings. He is of invaluable assistance in our general construction work. His work keeps him busy. Yet he finds time to do something that is probably unique among prisoners. Every month he sketches a drawing that illustrates a feature of the penal and parole problem. He, of course, expects favorable action on his application for earlier discharge, but if he should have to serve his full sentence the Governor's office will be greatly enriched by this collection of drawings and illustrations. His contributions tell the story more vividly than any word picture could describe.

Thirteen years ago, a young fellow, then a little past sixteen, was convicted of murder in the first degree and sentenced to die in the electric chair. There was considerable discussion about that case. The public generally protested against sending a boy of that age to his death. Eventually the Governor commuted his sentence to life imprisonment. That boy is now a young man of twenty-nine. All these years he has spent within the confines of Sing Sing Prison. During the first few years, following his commutation of sentence, he floundered; couldn't find himself. Then he began in earnest to improve his mental and physical status. To-day he is a man of good physique, an accomplished musician, a writer of a sort, a lover of literature and a competent critic.

Our present system of flood-lights which illuminate

248

every part of the prison walls and also every corner of the yard as well as the outside of buildings, was devised and installed by a prisoner recently discharged. His term was ten years. Not one day of the years he spent with us was idled away. He became an expert electrician, and today is earning his living in that trade.

Prison life has done something for these men. It has set them right. I cannot say that it has reformed them. Perhaps they did not need reform as much as introspection. It might have come to them outside the walls. But I do believe that prison has quickened its pace and given it more lasting effect.

Not all prisoners are so fortunate. Prison leaves its scars. Sometimes they are healed, often they are permanent marks, deep, reaching into the very soul, and are ineradicable.

My office commands a view of the road leading from the railroad station to the prison. Not infrequently I watch automobiles approach the prison gate. A woman alights, enters the prison for a visit with her husband. She may bring something, edibles or clothes, permitted under the rules. Her escort awaits her outside in the car. He is a patient gentleman, and he is duly rewarded. An hour or so later the lady takes tearful leave of her prisoner-husband and returns to town with the gentleman friend. We see these things daily. It is life, and "dear" hubby isn't due for discharge for perhaps five years or more.

Wives are not always patient with their erring husbands. Under the law the warden is required to permit the service of legal documents on prisoners, or serve them personally. So that when a titian haired wife of one of our wards called at the prison with a lawyer for the avowed purpose of summoning the defendant-prisoner to answer in twenty days why a decree of divorce should not be entered against him because of the facts alleged in the complaint, I had no alternative but to produce the prisoner. I had him called out. He shaved, donned fresh clothing, and appeared in the visiting room for the expectant affectionate greeting from his wife. He went in smiling and happy. The interview did not last long. "What a package I got!" he said ruefully when he emerged, as he exhibited the summons and complaint.

There came in my morning mail one day a letter from one of the Jewish Theological Seminaries of the City of New York, requesting permission to perform the usual orthodox divorce ritual for a prisoner. It was granted, of course. A room was set aside for their accommodation. On the appointed day came the rabbi, gray haired, with snow white beard, accompanied by his scribe. They brought with them a sheet of parchment, a quill pen and a bottle of especially prepared ink. Several other gentlemen came with them—witnesses as prescribed by the ritual. Then, naturally, there was the prisoner's wife and her parents, as also the prisoner's parents. Into this company a uniformed guard escorted the prisoner in gray. And in the presence of a representative of the State of New York in the person of the prison official, the rabbi spoke the necessary formula; the scribe etched the Hebrew characters on the parchment—an hour's task—the witnesses attested it. In accordance with Jewish orthodox custom, the prisoner-husband "without mental reservation" handed the wife the decree that gave her the right to remarry. The law of the land made no such fuss about the prisoner's marital status. Civilly he was dead and had no rights. He was doing natural life as a fourth offender. In the eyes of his faith he was still a man; his wife could not be free unless he willed it and—apparently—he did.

Sing Sing's visiting room has been called the hub of the prison, and properly so. The call for "visit" takes precedence over every other activity. Most important tasks are laid aside when that summons comes. Parents, wives, children, brothers, sisters, occasional friends, all come to add their mite of comfort and encouragement to their kin within the walls. Here contacts are maintained. Broken troths renewed, new ones created. Occasionally the prisoner finds there a new problem most difficult to face and overcome.

There was the fellow serving a term of ten years. He had just completed his second year. A quiet, well-behaved prisoner. He was married. His child, a son, was a little over a year old when he was "sent up." In the two years his mail had been regular, but his wife never came to see him. She could not leave the child, she explained in her letters. He understood and never complained.

Finally came the letter with the news that she was coming and bringing the child, now three years old.

He was a changed man; joked and laughed with the other prisoners; prepared clean linen and pressed his trousers. On the morning of the visit the barber took particular pains with him. Officers and prisoners in the shop were interested in his visit. Everyone knew that it was his first since his arrival at the prison.

The prisoner waited eagerly for the call. At last

it came. "Don't hurry back," the keeper said, "take all the time you want. Have a pleasant visit." He could have more than the allotted hour. He went forth, smiling.

Ten minutes later he was back. Face pale and drawn. Without a word he sat down at his table, bowed his face in his hands. The officer approached him. "What's the trouble, Joe?"

No answer.

A full hour he sat thus. No one could make it out. He did not answer the call for lunch. Left alone with the officer the latter questioned him.

"Yes, the wife came," he said, "and the boy, too. I hardly knew the child. He was so grown up and smart. But he was fidgety. I called him. 'Come to your papa,' I said. He looked at me, then at his mother. She pushed him to me. The boy held back, shy. Then suddenly he looked up at his mother and said, 'But, mamma, my papa is home!' "

Nor was Tony Barrata's visit more pleasant. Tony was a young prisoner doing ten years; well behaved; married. His wife and little son visited him regularly. They seemed a happy group. One day the officer in charge of the visiting room was startled by a sudden commotion in Tony's small circle. The wife stood up suddenly and began to denounce him in strong, emphatic language. "You——. You were never any good." Words tumbled from her mouth in a constantly rising crescendo. The poor fellow sat dumbfounded. Finally the officer succeeded in quieting the woman and escorted her from the room. As she turned away she gave him a parting shot. "And what's more," she screamed, "this boy is not yours. Now you know."

We never knew the reason for this outburst. Tony wouldn't talk. The woman left the building but returned later and approached the officer diffidently.

"I forgot to leave some money for my husband. Can I do it now?" She handed him ten dollars.

In this hub of the prison, life is raw and life is earnest. You see it throb. There are aches and pains, joys and sorrows. One sees hope and despair. There is here, also, viciousness and depravity, all jumbled together. To the casual observer they are but groups of men and women conversing with more or less intimacy. Yet, each of those groups has its peculiar problem. There in the corner sat a man and woman—husband and wife. They presented an extraordinary situation for the warden to solve. He was a newly admitted prisoner convicted of bigamy. He had married, not wisely, but often. Four trusting damsels he had led to the altar on as many occasions. How he had managed to keep the secret will ever remain a mystery. Finally, however, our Don Juan met his doom. One of the ladies discovered his quadrumus life, and after a few vexatious months he found relief, and a haven, within the walls of Sing Sing.

Now, this man might have had some peculiar love charm. A Don Juan par excellence. But he was far from an Adonis. It hardly ever fails. The bigamist is seldom the strong, handsome fellow; more often he is the frail, weazened shrimp of a creature who wears a size 13½ collar. The kind women like to lord it over. Well, after his discharge from the Reception Company, two women were clamoring to visit their "dear" husband—each claiming her nuptial prison rights (such as they were). Both averred they intended to stick by their errant spouse. But only one could possibly gain admittance. Neither would yield to the other.

As Warden—actually governor, chief of police, advisor and mentor—I was faced with a ticklish problem. The prisoner was entitled to a visit from his wife. But which one? Believe it or not, it was finally adjusted and everybody was happy. The older woman got the break. The younger, I felt, had the better chance for another matrimonial venture.

A stately looking woman, middle aged, and exquisitely gowned, walked into the prison one day and peremptorily demanded that she be allowed to visit her husband, a notorious prisoner doing time on a conviction for bigamy. Now, this man was already having visits from the lady whom he had designated as his legal wife. We were worried for the moment. Had the elderly bigamist put one over on us? We were about to check up his record when one of the men in the office pointed to a gray haired gentleman, a civilian official seated at a desk, and remarked jokingly, "There's your husband, madam. Don't you know him?"

The woman turned to "the husband," hurried to him and in a moment, much to that gentleman's amazement and discomfort, had smothered him with kisses.

"I've searched high and low for you," she cried as she held the struggling man to her broad bosom. She meant it, of course. Poor woman, her clouded mind led her to strange by-ways of life.

Our records show that only a small percentage of homes are disrupted by prison sentences. Most wives

254

are loyal. The kind that do not stick do not exceed ten per cent.

Joe was among the more fortunate ones. He was a full-blooded Irishman from Kerry County. His wife was a Jewess. He had been in his youth an exuberant, precocious boy. His was the usual case of "bad booze and bad girls." And though a married man, with two fine boys, he succumbed to the ancient lure of "wine, women and song." After a hilarious night, he found himself short of available cash and with two companions sauntered tipsily into a delicatessen shop, shooed the owner from the cash register and helped himself to its contents. Thirty-five dollars was the amount they found there. Hardly enough for more than several rounds of drinks, but it got Joe fifteen years behind the bars at Sing Sing on a conviction of robbery in the first degree.

Did his wife run to a lawyer and file her divorce papers? She had ample statutory grounds. The records in our correspondence department showed that this couple exchanged letters at least once weekly during all the years of his confinement. The record of our visiting room shows that the lady never missed her fortnightly visit. His card shows that immediately upon his admission to the prison he interested himself in mechanics. He became in time an indispensable adjunct of our machine repair department. No job was too hard for him and he saved the State thousands of dollars through his acquired expertness in handling machinery. His wage, during all those years (the present scale of wages had not yet been inaugurated) was one and one-half cents a day. I watched him during my periodic tours of the prison as he hurried from one prison shop to another in answer to constant calls for help on machines. Always he appeared the busy mechanic, grease and oil smeared the length of his prison uniform, his hands roughened and face blackened.

Meanwhile his wife was supporting herself and their two children on her meagre earnings. Hers was a scanty budget. She had the one thing that has saved many a prisoner's household from shipwreck. Faith in her Joe. He went home last Christmas. The State, through the person of its Governor, shortened his prison term. That little family is now reunited. The trade he learned in Sing Sing is earning him his living now on the outside. He might have been a safe risk long ago. He may not have had a high intelligence quotient, or the highest mental rating. But he had evolved into a social asset.

I escort a well known publicist through the prison. He wants to see things. He peers into the old, narrow cells, built over a hundred years ago. Dark, damp, cold. A gigantic filing cabinet of stone. We visit the shops where men bend over their tasks; we stop for a moment in offices where prisoners sit at desks thumping away at typewriters; we view the construction company out there in the open. Here they are laying a concrete road, there blasting rock on the side of a steep hill; at another point we see the chugging steam shovel levelling a pile of broken rock or hills that impede the progress of the new prison; we see trucks race over the roads that wind around the various buildings; there is the Reception Company digging into the coal pile. Out of 2376 men, twenty-three are not assigned to some definite employment. Our visitor is satisfied. He has witnessed a prison at work. No nonsense here. But has he really seen the prison? There are men in prison who work for mere pride of accomplishment. No reward awaits them, except in the satisfaction of doing a job well. The average prisoner works because he has to. He is generally happy to find forgetfulness in labor. To know a prison one must seek elsewhere than in the shops or at the rock pile. One must find the things that move men's hearts and minds, the perspective with which they view life; their interpretations of bars, cells, and lock-step existence.

Not infrequently men find peace of mind behind the walls. Gene did. He told me the story one morning. "I seldom dream, Warden," he said. "But I had the most awful dream last night. I had been mixed up in some kind of a scrape and the gang insisted that I do something. You know what I mean. Get the guy. I refused, told them I was off them for good. Intended to go straight. That night they came after me. I ran. They followed me. There were four of them and they had their gats with them. Gee, how I ran. There was no hiding place, and it was only a question of losing them. But they gained on me. I felt them coming nearer and nearer. They were almost on top of me when I awoke. I was sort of dazed, I guess. Didn't know just where I was. I looked around in the darkness. Then I gradually came to myself. Saw the cell door, the bars on the windows and I lay back on my pillow and sighed with relief. I was safe behind those bars."

Subconsciously, Gene felt safer with us than outside amid the dangers and hates of his former associates. Yet Gene will be anxious to leave us when his time is up.

If my visitor had the time and the patience I would

like to point out two prisoners. They are inseparable. They invariably walk alone. No one thinks of breaking up their intimacy. Father and son doing their "bits" together. The elder, in the late forties, had been careless with clients' accounts as a Wall Street broker. Tall, erect, with iron gray hair, sharp features, he walks with the stride of a man of affairs. At his side, trying hard to keep up, is the boy, sandy haired, pale of face, round shouldered, no more than eighteen. Only a messenger boy for a dishonest employer. But it had sent him to Sing Sing, where his father had preceded him.

The father talks rapidly and earnestly—he seems to have everything to say. The boy seldom answers.

The son is never out of his father's sight. It's lucky, some of the men remarked, that the boy will go out first. He is too weak to do time alone. Prison life would surely get him.

The other day they were called to the visiting room. Their "visit" was a woman. Mother and wife visiting son and husband. A doubly burdened wife and mother bringing her crumb of comfort to her menfolk.

She carries her burden well. She is not sad or harrowed. Kindly faced, patient, she listens quietly, indulgently to the father's rapid fire talk, smiles occasionally. Now and then she holds the boy's hand.

They seem oblivious, these three who are really four, to their surroundings.

Then when the hour is up she takes her leave. The husband grasps her arm, kisses her fondly. She kisses the boy and with head erect walks slowly to the door.

This woman bears her weight upon her heart. Her

head also unbowed, shoulders straight. Is not this one of the multi-mirrored views of a prison's soul?

I would take the visitor to the recreation field where a ball game is in progress. In the bleachers sit half the prison population. An alert team is on the diamond. "Natural Life" is pitching. He swings a practiced arm and sends the ball with unerring accuracy over the plate. "Fifty-nine Years" fans it. It drops into the glove of "Twenty Years," with ten to go. Ten and a "wop" (he's going home soon) calls "strike." The ball makes the round of the field. "Fifteen Years" stops it at first base; hurls it to "Life" on second; it goes to "Sixty Years" on third base, and then back to "Natural Life" on the mound. Another batter at the plate. A young, sandy haired, stocky fellow—"Twenty to Life"—with eighteen to go. He stoops, picks up a handful of sand, rubs it over the bat to insure his grip, feels for a firm foothold. "Over the wall, Tom," the crowd yells. Tom looks those eighteen years full in the face. He is a determined fellow. "Eighteen Years" hits the speeding ball a resounding whack; it climbs into the air, higher and higher, up and away from those yelling "Years" in the bleachers. The guard on post looks on with a broad grin. He wouldn't stop that ball if he could. Over the wall. And "Eighteen Years" has made the grade. He's home again. Here is a good, clean, wholesome sport. Depression falls away before the spirit of the game. The crowd is jovial.

Gene, a friend of the prisoners, struts up and down before the grandstand, engaging in breezy repartee with the boys. A genial personality his, sympathetic and witty.

Gene cannot boast of an extensive wardrobe. A voice

in the crowd yells: "Gene, why don't you lose that brown suit somewhere?"

Gene smiles broadly, his eyes twinkle.

"Listen, Buddy. I've been coming here for ten years; you've been here all along and I've never seen you sportin' anything but that gray outfit. You're not such a fashion plate either." The boys give Gene a big hand.

Contrary to popular notions, prisons do not always seethe with emotions. Prisoners do not stride warily along corridors or wait in dark corners seeking each other's scalps. Except for a small minority, prisoners are a well-behaved lot. Even the old type of prison slang is giving way to understandable and, generally, decent language except, of course, in fiction and feature articles. The lapses when they do occur are more in jest and imitation of earlier decades. The ordinary prisoner wants to keep out of trouble. "We have a head on us," wrote a prisoner-philosopher, "for the same reason that a pin has. To keep us from going too far."

Prisoners on their arrival at Sing Sing are analyzed by our psychiatrists. Their personal history is gone into in great detail. The whys and wherefores of their crime are sought. It is possible, however, that the father who was visiting his son for the first time had the right idea after all. The father was an elderly gentleman, a man of the old school. They sat in the visiting room talking things over. There were no recriminations. After a while there was a lull in their conversation. The father looked quizzically at his son, a man well in the thirties. "You know, son, I'm thinking," the old gentleman said musingly. "It seems to me that if

I had used the leather strap on you less sparingly when you were a boy you would not have been here today." And the son, himself a father, smiled grimly at his father and shrugged his shoulders. Who knows? Perhaps the younger man was thinking of his own children. I am not sure that the lash would have helped in that particular instance. The fact is that parental neglect does result in misadventure of children. There is no gainsaying that thought.

And yet, how often are children the comforters of their fathers in the visiting room! Fine, upstanding young men and women, engaged in lawful occupations, ambitious, hard working, visiting their prisoner-fathers. Hereditary criminals? Heaven forbid! One sees the affectionate greetings between parent and children, their concern for his well being. These children are old enough to understand that they are to suffer socially because of their father's plight. Convict's children. They contribute from their earnings to his welfare and do it without a murmur. Their task is to wipe the slate clean, to build anew and help their parent to steady himself on his discharge.

Prisoners resent being questioned about crime motives. That is why psychiatry and psychological treatment in prisons have accomplished little with prisoners. The trouble is that we expect too much of the man in prison. We want him to be better than we are, or hope to be. On a par with Caesar's wife—beyond suspicion. Let us be frank about it. We are mortally afraid of him. Some years ago the popular play "Outward Bound" was presented at Sing Sing. Later one member of the cast was somewhat embarrassed by his visit. J. E. Kerrigan, who played "Stubby," struck up an acquaintance with a prisoner of literary tastes and there was a long discussion about books. When Kerrigan left he promised to send the inmate a novel in which he had expressed great interest.

"You know, he sent the book back to me," Kerrigan told a friend several days later, "he wants my autograph."

"What's the harm in that?" his friend asked.

"Well, you see," said Kerrigan, "he's serving his third term in Sing Sing for forgery."

In the early days of my wardenship at Sing Sing a well-known judge of the General Sessions Court visited us. He had the reputation as a stern judge who handed out severe sentences. I wasn't sure of his reactions and asked him whether he wanted to go through while the men were in the yard. It was Labor Day and most of the prisoners were assembled in the recreation field for the annual athletic events. Nothing daunted, the Judge insisted upon witnessing the contests. He was recognized immediately and given an ovation. There were calls for "speech." He spoke to them from the grandstand. A sensible, straight-from-the-shoulder talk which drew a fine response from his audience.

There was one judge who did find himself in a tough spot. He came late, remained for dinner and stayed over night. In the morning I arranged for my barber to shave him. The barber was an old-timer, had served about fifteen years, with several more to go. He had always maintained his innocence and had no particularly friendly feeling for the judge who presided at his trial and sentenced him. The barber took pains with my guest who was also an old-timer on the bench. But the barber did not know that his subject was a judge. In keeping with the traditions of his calling this barber was loquacious. He was an Italian and his command of the English language was rather limited. But he found a sympathetic listener in the gentleman in his chair. He waxed eloquent about his case and the injustice that, he claimed, was done him. By this time the barber was scraping the judge's chin and was proceeding downward. The judge became interested.

"Who was the judge?" he asked the voluble prisoner.

The latter mentioned the name. The judge became tense. The razor was grazing his Adam's apple. The blood left his face. He held up his hand. "Wait a moment, my man," he said quickly, "I forgot to telephone to New York. I'll finish the shave later." And he made a rapid exit from the barber shop.

It was a ticklish moment for that judge and perhaps a fortunate one. For the prisoner did not recognize in my gray haired visitor the judge who had presided over the trial that ended with a twenty year sentence for him. When told about it later he simply shrugged his shoulders and smiled.

"Which are your bad men?" one of our visitors asked me as I escorted him through the prison. I told him the story of the two tramps who were promised a big feed if they would pick an apple orchard. They were each told to work in different sections. An hour later the farmer checked up on them. One had filled several barrels. "Fine apples," he told the farmer. "I'm pickin' the good ones an' throwin' away the bad ones." The second tramp had accomplished very little. "What's the trouble?" he was asked. "Don't know,

263

boss. I'm doin' the best I can. I'm throwin' away the bad ones, and there don't seem to be many left."

How are we to judge the good from the bad? Does the length of a prisoner's sentence determine that? And yet short termers are in trouble just as frequently as those facing long years ahead. As a matter of fact our "lifers" are our best prisoners and most dependable. Many of them have trusted assignments.

During the influenza epidemic Sing Sing suffered as did the rest of the country. Our regular hospital force was swamped. The hospital was crowded to capacity and more. Volunteers offered their services from all over the prison. They were burglars, robbers, forgers, murderers. Our head nurse was a "dope" doctor, his assistant was a druggist from New York's tenderest tenderloin. The physician's helper was one of the most famous safe blowers in the country. The cook who worked ten hours a day, while with two degrees of fever, had been described by a leading newspaper as the head of a dangerous gang of murderous criminals. He prepared food at break-neck speed for several hundred patients in a kitchen meant for forty. He was a kidnapper.

We have had several big fires in Sing Sing. The one that occurred on March 20, 1928, was the worst one in my experience. It started in the incinerator, and the sparks were blown into the mattress shop. It happened about 11:45 in the morning. The men were in line waiting to march to the mess hall. The officers had a hard time trying to get the men to go in and have their lunch. Most of them wanted to stay in the yard and help fight the fire. The fire department of the Village of Ossining was called in. But the prisoners did most of the fire fighting, and took most of the chances. The fire lasted until about two or three o'clock in the morning. More than fifty prisoners worked continuously. Smoke lay over the whole prison like a heavy fog. There was no excitement in the yard and no extra guards were required.

Being brave in the face of danger does not make good men out of bad. We have a waiting list of scores of prisoners who are ready to offer their blood for transfusion purposes in cases of necessity. We had occasion recently to call upon one of them. In order to prepare him for the operation the prison doctor ordered special food for him. That night he was tendered a chicken dinner. He waved it aside. "Give it to the patient," he suggested, "he needs it more than I do." Judged by ordinary standards that blood donor was a bad man doing a long "stretch" for a heinous crime.

"There's so much good in the worst of us" is a universally accepted preachment handed down through the years. Yet the theory of prison administration generally applauded is the one that frowns upon any attempt to bring out the particle of good. Baseball, recreation, talking pictures, music, wholesome entertainment are decried. They savor too much of ease and comfort. "Men will commit crimes to get into prison." Not long ago I walked through Union Square Park and saw hundreds of men lounging on the park benches. Most of them were ragged, unkempt, gaunt-looking individuals. All around them were hotels and restaurants. Well-dressed people passed them in endless numbers. Every one of them would have been better off, physically, in Sing Sing. Policemen patrolled the streets adjoining. It would take but a moment. An assault on a pedestrian. An arrest, and they would soon be on their way. Yet their liberty was worth more to these "bench warmers" than all confinement could offer them.

Prisoners have a way of consoling each other. One tried it on his neighbor, a newcomer, who had not yet acclimated himself to the prison routine.

"I've been here four years and I am a better man than when I came in. I have gained in weight as well as in sense, and I am in better physical condition than I have been in twenty years. Don't prate about the hardship of prison life to me. I know if I had not been here I would now be dead. The regular life we lead, tends to lengthen our lives. I believe that five years in prison will add at least fifteen years to the life of almost every man who tries it."

The man he was talking to replied, "Oh, hell!"

Courtesy Pathe News.

At each game more than two thousand men lined up . . . intent and enthusiastic

Annual Labor Day dinner given to the prisoner-winners of athletic events. (*Page 274*)

CHAPTER 8: MEN, MINDS AND MOTIVES

"On April 4, 1930, a prisoner by name of Torrello headed for the iron fence and jumped over it into the river. He failed to halt at a command and was shot by one of the guards while diving into the water and disappeared into the river. All the prisoners were in the yard at the time. The Principal Keeper and the Assistant Principal Keeper ran down to the water front. I saw them and said, 'Let's try to find him.' So I offered to go into the water if I could get hold of a fish-hook pole. I and three other guys went into the water looking for the body. I laid on my stomach in the water while the Principal Keeper was holding my feet. I got to the bottom and fished for the body. Suddenly my hook grabbed the man in the water by the crotch of his pants and I dragged him out. Then they took the body to the autopsy room and found there was a bullet in the shoulder blade."

This was Hugo talking. A prisoner who has been with us for eleven years. Hugo is a model prisoner. He has never had a charge against him in all the years of his prison service. Hugo is not much on books, but he is a good plumber. One of our night emergency plumbers. Yet Hugo is more than a plumber. As a prisoner he is a type. Young prisoners regard him with awe and a measure of respect. He is an old-timer. A prison aristocrat. Keepers are kind to Hugo. Officials go out of their way to do him a service. Hugo is thirty-eight years old. Nineteen of those years he has spent behind the bars. He remembers the changes that have come with the years.

Hugo has no use for "big shots" who are the bane of all prison officials and prison administrations. Big shots are always seeking favors. They seldom if ever get any, but that does not stop them from persistent and repeated requests.

A uniformed guard will mutter under his breath, "Who the hell does he think he is?" He is probably referring to a prisoner who has "hardly put his shoes under the bed" but who is already asking for privileges and courtesies and leniency accorded only to those who have earned them by long and faithful service. The big shot in prison is the man who tries to attract the spotlight, who boasts of influence and "connections," and who is the all-around sorehead when put in his place. The aristocrat in prison is the prisoner who has learned how to do his time; who is self-effacing, re-tiring, and jealous of the privileges that time and serv-ice have earned for him and his fellows. Hugo is inter-esting, therefore, not because he is Hugo, but because he represents an important type within the walls.

Hugo was doing an errand in the prison yard sev-eral months ago. An elderly gentleman approached him. A thick set, robust looking man of medium stature, who was my guest for the day. "Aren't you Hugo?" the white haired gentleman asked the old-timer. Hugo looked closely at the man. His face broke into an eager smile. "Why if it ain't Sittin' Bull!" They had not seen each other for eighteen years since Hugo was in the Tombs awaiting trial on an indictment for larceny and my guest a keeper on his tier. The latter had

268

climbed high in his profession and is now retired. He has health and leisure and comfort commensurate with his station in life. Hugo is getting ready to leave Sing Sing after almost a score of years in prisons and jails and reformatories, aiming to start life all over again.

These two talked for a while. Then my gray haired visitor bade the old-timer good-bye. "Think you've had enough, Hugo?" he asked.

"You're right, I have," Hugo answered. "I've seen the light. I'm going straight."

My old friend and I talked it over late that night. What has brought about that change of heart in Hugo? Was it hardship endured during his prison service? Hardly. He has been a model prisoner and never incurred the ill will of his keepers or officials.

Was it fear? Apparently not. For Hugo was never placed in the position where threats or intimidation were necessary to good conduct.

Was it the sense of duty to dear ones? Yet this same sense of obligation had not influenced him in his earlier years.

Was it religion? Hugo is not strong on prayers or rituals.

None of these factors has influenced Hugo in his determination to leave the life of chance in which he has been the consistent loser. It is merely that his course is run. That a period of his life has been rounded out. I would call it the danger age, the age of gambling with fate, the daredevil age. This corrected vision of life is not new with Hugo. It has been with him for years. His last prison sentence was too long. He could have been discharged with perfect safety to society five years ago. But our penal code is straightjacketed and inflexible. Hugo has to do his full time. But Hugo's new sense of responsibility seeks an outlet. He is eager to impress it on his fellows. He is a sort of an evangelist. Circumstance provided that opportunity for him during these last years of his prison life. Hugo is not strong on syntax or rules of grammar. But his words carry a distinct punch. They have a ring of sincerity. Let him tell his story in his own way.

"I took on my own responsibility the job of instructing all new men that come from the Reception Company after a period of putting in fourteen days there. The Principal Keeper sees them first and then he turns the men over to me. I bring them into the annex and sit them down and tell them that they can smoke and be at ease. I tell them that 'I have something very important to explain to you in regards to the institution, the League and the officials.'

"I start off in telling them about the League. What it means to every man, be he a long-termer or a short-time man. I tell them about the privileges we have lost through a few individuals who did not care about the welfare of the men. Several of them went out in the yard and committed two murders in six days. The Warden said if these prisoners die, he will close the place up. His attitude was justified. We couldn't expect anything else.

"All of us old-timers, numbering about twenty-five, went up to the chapel and talked the matter over among us. We couldn't come to an agreement as to what would benefit the entire population. We called for the Warden. He came up and told us that it was up to us old-timers to try and see what we can do with the new men in the general conduct of the prison. So I took the job.

"I explain to every new man my past experience in prison life. That I am here a long time and never lost a day for violation of the rules. And that I want them to know that the Warden here in Sing Sing has three orders to fulfill. Work us, feed us and lock us up. What other things we get, we get from him.

"I tell them not to carry knives, either on their persons or in their lockers. Not to let anyone 'steam them up' to cut another prisoner or use a weapon. The last murder that happened here was committed by a prisoner who was 'steamed up' by someone else. In fact, I don't believe the man who done the stabbing even knew the victim before he stabbed him. That fellow is now in the death house, probably waiting to be tried for murder in the first degree. The reason I am telling you all this is that you mustn't let anyone else do your bit. Do your own time. Be careful of the wolves in the institution. They will try to give you cigarettes and tell you they want to be your friend. I say that only to the younger boys of the institution. The older boys know better.

"Don't leave your shop without a pass. It means a report. If at any time you want to leave your shop all you have to do is to ask your officer for a pass, and if it's on the up and up he'll give you one. Don't walk around the yard in your undershirt. It means a report.

"You will stay in the old cell block about five months. Then you will be transferred to decent cells on the hill. Every man goes up there in rotation. While in the old cell block you will see no pictures, but when you are moved up there you will see moving pictures twice a week. When you're up in the chapel, conduct your-selves like men and not kids.

"We have a visiting room here that is the best in the State, if not in the country. When you are there, conduct yourselves like men, not hoodlums. All you men are in Grade A. You are allowed five visits a month. If you're in Grade B, you are allowed two visits a month and one letter a week. If you are in Grade C you are not allowed to have any visits or write letters unless by written order of the Warden. Don't click up too easily with fellows you don't know. If you pulled any jobs on the outside, don't be telling your stories to anyone.

"Any of you men here that are thinking of making an escape, keep it to yourself. If you can beat the Warden's machine guns you're going some. During the last few years three men were shot trying to make the wall or fence. It's your own funeral if you try it. But this I want you to remember. If any of you thinks he can hide out somewhere in the prison and get away you're mistaken. I have never seen a hide-out that was successful. My advice to you men is don't take a chance.

"Now I keep a record of all you new men I inter-view. I have a book here and I put all your numbers in that book. Each week we have a Warden's Court here and if I find your number on that Court list, I will see you that day or on the following day and tell you you are a bunch of bums for getting in trouble after my talk to you. I'll ask you all about your trouble. And I'll want you to be frank with me. Several of the men I have interviewed have gone to Court already for something they could have avoided, a very minor offence, just a little neglect on their part. I want to

272

see if my talk to you is doing any good. I'm looking for results. I do not wear a badge from the League or any other kind. I'm taking up my time in instructing you men as I believe in the proper way and putting you wise how to do a bit. You can take it or leave it. Use your own judgment.

"Just one thing more. Bear this in mind. The Warden didn't send us any letters requesting us to commit crimes so as to come to Sing Sing and help him hold his job. You hear a lot about Big Shots in the place. There is only one Big Shot and that's the Warden."

Hugo checks carefully the records of the Warden's Court. And he points with pride to the fact that out of a population of about twenty-five hundred men, all of them supposed to be intractable and many of them with reputations for viciousness, there are only about twenty-five men in line at the weekly sessions of the Court and most of them for only minor infractions of the rules.

Yet this man is an ordinary prisoner who is guarded and counted just as any of his fellows and who follows the prison routine day after day without deviation or special privileges. He is not a polished gentleman. He never was. I remember him from Elmira where he served a term while I was Chief Guard. On the day of his discharge from the Reformatory I was waiting for the train to New York to keep an appointment. Hugo was at the station smoking cigarettes incessantly to make up for lost time. At noon I started for the dining car. Hugo sat in his seat in the smoker, looking rather forlorn. I invited him to accompany me. I ordered lunch for him. It was a fine treat for the youngster. He was nervous and excited. Finally the finger bowls were passed to him. Without waiting for explanations he picked it up and drank deeply of its contents. Then he set it down with a sigh of contentment. His face flushed a deep red when he noticed me dip my finger tips into my bowl. He looked around toward the other passengers, some of whom were smiling their enjoyment of his confusion. I had quite forgotten the incident but was reminded of it at the last Labor Day dinner given to the prisoners who participated in the athletic events. Hugo was there. As I passed his table he looked up at me and whispered in my ear: "Say, Warden, don't we get no finger bowls today? Remember?"

It takes a long time to develop the Hugo type of prisoner. He has become institutionalized. Whether he will be able to stand on his own on his discharge is problematical. That he is eagerly hopeful and sincerely anxious to join the ranks of normal men and assume the responsibilities of normal life is beyond question. He will need a steadying hand in the first years of his new experiences. Are we ready to furnish it?

Helpful guidance was especially needed in the case of an old bank robber who was discharged from Sing Sing in 1920. He took with him his three cunning puppies. He was over seventy years old and had spent more than half of his adult life in prison. He knew the value of companionship. Because he was old and too feeble to do mischief, the Governor set him free. He had the reputation of having robbed banks of millions, but when he left the prison all he had to show for a lifetime of crime were his dogs and a ten dollar bill. The first night he was in New York he

274

fell in among thieves and when he awoke in the morning his three dogs were gone as was his ten dollar bill. Also his coat, hat and shoes. Institutionalism had done something to this man. Robbed him of all except the ache for companionship. Hundreds, if not thousands of prisoners are equally helpless when they leave the prison walls. Yet we seem to be unable to do anything for them.

But there are more difficult types in prison. They stand at the other extreme. They are our real problems. Cynical, resentful, selfish, they constitute the small minority. Yet they are the most dangerous of our men.

In most prisons throughout the country routine and administration are planned solely with an eye towards the subjection of this small group. In Sing Sing we do just the opposite. Our own policy is planned for the good of the ninety per cent who are reliable and trustworthy as well as appreciative of the benefits they derive from a sympathetic administration. Often we are able to reclaim some of these "bad" fellows. I was particularly happy one day about the reactions of one of them.

It was one of the happiest days of my wardenship at Sing Sing. A day when it was my pleasure to shake hands with more than a score of commuted prisoners and send them home for Christmas. Yet it brought me as severe a shock as I have ever suffered. The prison population never seemed more tranquil. Favorable action by the Parole Board on many requests for Christmas releases had produced good morale.

At that time only one man appeared to me to be a very dangerous character. He was a big brute of a fellow, as tough as any that New York has produced.

In for robbery and atrocious assault, he was the type whose premature release can become a great embarrassment to the political powers. With the ever familiar cry of "crime wave" it was hardly politic to give him his parole. Like many of the utterly hard-boiled he had a soft spot for a common law wife and her two children, who may or may not have been his. I never could find out. Wives must have their "marriage lines" before we permit them to visit prisoners in Sing Sing.

This man came to see me, and I had to give him bad news—that the Parole Board had refused his plea. I have seen few sights more terrible than the working of that man's face. He was mad clean through. I let him brood over it for a day, then sent for him. I gave him a cigar to smoke and reasoned with him, pointing out that at the next monthly meeting of the Board I should urge favorable consideration of his case.

"Here," I said finally, "is a Christmas box for you."

It was a box of candy and pastry sent by his woman and carefully examined for contraband—dope, drink or blades or tools of any kind.

He took the box, shook my hand and thanked me. Later that evening he asked to see me again. An unusual request, rarely granted, for it demoralizes the men to know that any prisoner has too easy access to the warden's office.

He had in his hand the box I had passed to him that morning.

"I'd like to give you a Christmas present, Warden," he said sheepishly, although there was a meaningful glitter in his eye. We parried; but it ended by my accepting the gift. This was shortly afterwards opened by my little daughter. Beneath a row of doughnuts and candy there lay a .38 calibre pistol. That was my Christmas gift from him. It shocked me; but I have never received a present more gratefully.

If this man had been put on the rack he would never have revealed how that gun came into his possession in Sing Sing. He had absolved himself by surrendering it. I went through with my promise to urge his parole —and he got it. Every Christmas brings a greeting from him. He is evidently meeting the conditions of his parole.

I have always had a deep admiration for the old philosopher who suggested the thought that if you would make a friend of a dangerous man have him do you a favor. I have tried it out often with most satisfactory results. One was especially gratifying. It happened in the summer of 1929, in the aftermath of the riots in Clinton and Auburn Prisons and in the Colorado State Prison at Canyon City. The Governor sent for me while he was reviewing the cadets at West Point. He took me aside on the parade grounds and showed me a letter. It was very disturbing.

We exercise censorship over mail to and from prisoners, just as we scrutinize carefully all visitors during their contact with inmates. But this letter had escaped us—some letters always do, no matter how vigilant we may be.

Its purport was clear and uncompromising. It was also unsigned. In effect it warned the Governor that the riots in other State prisons would be mere picnics compared to what would happen in Sing Sing if food was not improved and if the Parole Board did not practice less discrimination, releasing men as men and not judging criminals by their crimes. Needless to say, the Parole Board was following the fairest policy it could adopt in view of public opinion and limitations fixed by law, although disappointed prisoners will never agree with any Board or anybody but themselves.

Back at the prison I summoned the guards. They were prepared; but one of them was honest enough to confess that while working with a road gang he had lost his gun. When a policeman in any city loses his gun it's a trivial matter. When a guard in charge of convicts loses his gun—there is an immediate threat. That explained the warning letter from the prison—a gun was loose.

It was time to think and think hard; to think of some way to get that gun. A canvass of the prison—of that road gang—would be a joke. Only hard, determined men would have that gun or know who had it; and that kind never talk. Nobody could help me much. A public plea to the prisoners would be poor business—a confession of weakness.

There was only one thing to do. Pick out, not the man I thought had the gun, but the man best fitted to get it back. I summoned a former gangleader, a man with many bullet marks on him and in him, a veteran of innumerable roof battles and of numerous street fights. He was in for manslaughter and had become a power among the prisoners.

"There is a gun loose," I said. "You know what that means. Of course, if anybody wants a fight, it will come—if it's to be to the last guard, including me, and the last prisoner. I want that gun."

"You're on the square, Warden," said the gang-leader. "If you get that gun—no questions asked?"

"None," I assured him.

The gun was placed on my desk within an hour. I went to bed easier in mind.

Such "inside" power is exercised by some man or men in every prison, usually a character who had achieved renown as a gangleader outside. Know these men; make them few promises, but keep the promises you make, and they exert a strong influence for law and order within the prison.

There is an interesting sequel to this incident. Not long afterward this prisoner was discharged in the ordinary course of his prison term. Several months later he was taken suddenly ill and was compelled to submit to a serious operation. I called to see him at the hospital during his convalescence. We talked about himself, about the depression and about the sudden communist flurry which was then blazoned in the metropolitan press. Meetings were daily held in New York. He was lost in thought for a few moments. Then he turned to me with a smile on his lean, pale face. "Do you know what, Warden? If the cops would give us fellows a chance we would clean the town up of Bolsheviks in quick order. Let them appoint us deputies with power to act, and we'll have New York clean and safe in no time."

Despite his former antagonism to the forces of law and order he still had a sense of civic pride.

Wholly different was the reaction of the prisoner who had somehow learned about the missing gun. He wandered about the yard seeking information. He was not successful, but he sympathized with me in my worry. Suddenly he hit upon a plan to ease my mind. He confided in a few of his intimates. "I'd like to get a gun in and give it to the Warden," he told them. "It would make him feel satisfied and, gee, what a big shot I'd be!" The grapevine brought the story to me. Naturally, his plan failed.

No one realizes more profoundly than the prison Warden the truth in the old adage about the "best laid plans of mice and men." We feel that we have as good and perfect a system of checks and counter checks as there is to be found anywhere in the world. Yet we are always prepared for the unexpected, with an eye on the ten percent who are unresponsive. On the same day that we opened the Sing Sing recreation field to football, we received a large consignment of tear gas bombs and ammunition. On the first night of the annual show week at Sing Sing, when I permitted a selected number of inmates to mingle with the guests in the chapel, I dismissed an officer from the service for a violation of the rules against contraband. He was detected in bringing in several pint bottles of bootleg whiskey.

I am willing to trust a man on his honor, but I expect him to live up to the exact requirements of that trust. The committee of prisoners who arranged the cast and the costumes for the performance were allowed to meet the costumer, and agreed upon a price, subject to my approval. They reported to me that they had been able to secure a bargain. Five hundred dollars for all the costumes. It was much less than we had paid in previous years, but greatly to the chagrin and disappointment of two members of the committee I withheld my approval. I had discovered that they had received the usual "rake-off," customary in all similar ventures in the outside world.

I telephoned the costumer and asked him to come

up to Sing Sing for an interview. He was too busy. "Well," I told him, "you owe me an explanation. You committed a misdemeanor and if I press the charges you will be buying the costumes for our next show instead of selling them." He came up by the next train.

He brought with him check stubs and a large sheaf of records. They showed that in practically every case where he had furnished costumes for banquets and entertainments, whether they were for church functions or lodges or Masonic organizations, the committee in charge always received an honorarium from him. "It's an accepted fact," he explained, "and I had no other intention than to do the same thing in this case."

I sympathized with him, but advised him that prisoners must be more circumspect than their friends on the outside. If a man in prison is put on his honor, his conduct must be beyond criticism. I confronted him with the guilty prisoners, and the money he had paid them was turned over to me and applied to the proceeds of the show fund. The prisoners received their punishment (loss of seventy-five days) under the rules. The fact that they were important members of the show cast did not save them.

As a matter of fact, during the last twenty-five years most prison administrations throughout the country have advanced more rapidly in moral tone than other public, quasi-public institutions, or even mercantile establishments. There is a minimum of graft, and many lapses that would scarcely be noticed on the outside are severely condemned and punished within the walls. An executive of a large department store in New York City, during a recent conference on penal affairs, deplored the graft in public institutions. I replied that

his own organization was probably no better. He be
came very indignant. The following week I sent some
one to his employment manager and found that the
only successful applicants were those who were able
to give him a gratuity of five or ten dollars. The gentle
man in question maintained a splendid yacht for his
family and friends. Inquiry developed that for every
hundred dollars paid out for supplies thirty dollars
were refunded to the steward in the employ of the
owner. The scrutiny with which every capable prison
administration regards the daily life of its wards and
the official conduct of its staff precludes the possibility
of many irregularities that are accepted as matters of
course in other environments.

Some prisoners have a peculiar sense of honor that
leads them into strange situations and causes me no
end of worry and grief. Such was the case of the
trusted clerk with only a short time left to complete
his prison term. He was a capable worker, had received
a high mental and intelligence rating from our psychiatric department. He was young, not over twenty-
three. In the course of time he became acquainted with
several longtermers who boasted long and spectacular
records. They worked on his imagination. To him they
were the perfect "bad" men, daring, brave and true.
What he did not understand was that these men were
using him for their ulterior purposes in perfecting
their plans for an escape. The setting had all the details of a thrilling western movie stunt. They had guns,
four of them, one for each man. There would be shooting and possible killings. They had provided themselves with a large iron hook attached to a stout rope.
As soon as they reached the foot of the wall this hook

was to be thrown over the top and all four would climb up and over to safety and liberty.

My family and guests were dining in the Warden's quarters on what seemed to be a particularly quiet night. There had not even been the customary prisoners' complaints about food and jobs, and the rest of the routine matters that bother both inmates and their keepers. One of the guests was commenting upon the atmosphere in Sing Sing—how unlike it was to other prisons he had visited; that even the convicts seemed reconciled to surroundings that gave them a glimpse of green gardens and a breath of fresh air on a high site which overlooked the lordly Hudson at its lordliest.

"Yes," I was well satisfied enough to agree, instead of following the old Irish advice of not whistling so loud and being proud when the devil's around. "We have had good luck here," I went on while the distinguished guest followed me with flattering attention. "Our prison population, while not exactly docile, is amenable and appears surprisingly free from really vicious characters. At least we have no evidence that there are many wickedly desperate men here, now."

The words, as the fiction writers say, had barely left my lips when shots cracked through the prison. Trusties, house servants, stepped quickly and quietly to their posts to protect the women in the house. A guard dashed in to report.

"Four men with guns in 'A' Block," he blurted, "rushed the keepers and are shooting their way out."

I left my guest immediately. In a few moments our forces were organized. The four desperate prisoners were rounded up. Shots were exchanged. Several of the group of prisoners were wounded. One of them, realizing the hopelessness of their situation, committed suicide. One officer was slightly wounded. Tear gas bombs ended the battle. It was over in ten minutes. It was extremely fortunate that the gunmen had picked a dull time of the day for their attempt to escape. And what was more, they showed a surprisingly low conception of strategy and planning.

With this flare of mutiny over, my work began. True, it was simplified by the failure of the attempt. But where did those guns come from? I remembered with kindness that prisoner who handed me that Christmas box with the gun hidden underneath a layer of doughnuts. Also the gangleader who brought me another gun within an hour after my demand. Yet those four guns had been secreted within the walls, had somehow filtered in, and had wrought these tragic consequences.

For the first time in my life I hit upon a new idea in tracing lapses. I began to suspect myself.

My movements from the prison were fairly well advertised when the appearance was public, such as lectures or giving testimony before courts or legal and sociological bodies. If I returned by automobile through some nearby town, as is my usual practice, many trusties and prisoners could see me leave and return, unless I returned at night. My own car left and returned to the prison wall without being searched. Wouldn't that, I thought, be the most certain method for guns to be smuggled into the prison? I go to a nearby or distant town. Sometimes newspapers mention the fact. The news is picked up by argus-eyed persons deeply interested. My car is identified while waiting somewhere and a quick hand can tie guns underneath it

—somewhere—and tip off Sing Sing inmates by means best understood by crooks in the know, in and out of prison. No other vehicles are allowed to enter or leave the prison without being searched. But, knowing the enterprising among those made hopeless by long prison terms, I am inclined to believe that in that particular instance, my own car was selected to carry those guns.

Serious and important as this event was to me, more interesting was the fact that one of my trusted men had joined in the plot. Had that prisoner really wanted to get away, he could have picked surer and easier ways to accomplish his purpose alone and without the aid of conspirators. And without a gun.

He stood before me late that night. He was bleeding from several wounds and presented a sorry spectacle. I cross-examined him. His youthful face wore an air of bravado, although his most intimate friend lay dead in the prison morgue, the victim of the futile and foolish escapade.

"What surprises me is that you could have gone without all this fuss and trouble," I told him. "Why didn't you take advantage of it, instead of risking your life and those of the other men?"

He looked me straight in the eye. "I couldn't violate a trust, Warden. You put me on my honor out there and I would not betray you."

It was hard for me to reconcile this man's reasoning. Yet this is one of the most difficult tasks of a prison warden.

Chance plays an important part in every walk of life. The prison warden also gets his breaks. But snap judgment has little or no place in prison administration. Things may get out of hand occasionally; they require careful thought. The Warden knows no fixed hours. Twenty-four hours a day, seven days a week; in or out of the prison grounds, he is always on active duty. Sleepless nights are not uncommon. This is how they happen.

The recall whistle blows for the nightly lock-up. Twenty-five hundred men are supposed to march to their cells, to remain there until the following morning. The line passes in review, as I stand on my front porch. The uniformed keeper ends the procession and I breathe a sigh of relief as I join my family at the dinner table. Another day without untoward incident.

My efficient butler serves a cocktail—"tomato juice." "A nerve tonic," he explains. I appreciated it a moment later when the evening count shows that two men are missing. That was all the dinner I had that night. The entire uniformed force is called in and the man hunt is on. No, the siren isn't sounded. We know the prisoners cannot have scaled the walls. They are hiding out within the grounds. Therefore "Big Ben" is silent. It is an all-night job, with extra duty for all of us. Every foot of the prison area is combed fine. Torch lights peer into the dark corners, unused vaults, underground tunnels. Even wooden floors are lifted. No trace of either of them. We are about to give it up as a bad job and wait for daylight. Apparently those fellows have found a new wrinkle. We may have to starve them out. As it happens they are smoked out. For when the furnaces are stoked by the morning shift, two bedraggled, sooty, half choked boys clatter down the tall chimney and land in the power house. They are chimney sweeps by profession. It was nothing for them to climb up the inside of the

286

tall smokestack to the very top where they perched the night long. "What was the idea?" I asked the black-faced pair. "We wanted to inspect the chimney and didn't hear the whistle," one answered sheepishly, with the ghost of a grin on his face.

It was no laughing matter to us who hadn't slept a wink that night. But then—we were glad it wasn't more serious.

There was that other night when I sat in a chair reading. This time it was one of Edgar Wallace's latest. About a prisoner doing time on what seems to me a frame-up and the story becomes decidedly absorbing when the hero plans a daring escape from the prison. Inwardly I find myself sympathizing with the victim of a dastardly plot—hoping he will make his get-away and turn successfully on those responsible for his sufferings. It is near midnight and everything is quiet. The window of my bedroom faces the east wall of the prison. I hear a shuffling noise outside. I switch the light off and stand by the window. In a few minutes I see a black shape moving along the top of the wall and drop to the ground, twenty feet below. Then another shape looms in the darkness, and another drop. Two thumps. I get busy on the telephone. The guards on post are notified. The attempted flight is checked and the men apprehended while still in the yard. Nothing very serious happens except that those two prisoners' lives are saved. Had they been spied by the guards on the wall before I heard them, they would have been shot at and probably killed. The net result to me was the loss of another night's sleep.

These things disturb one's peace of mind. But they are more or less expected. If months go by and nothing happens, we begin to get restless. Something is due soon, we suspect. And we spend endless hours trying to figure it out. We do not always succeed.

We didn't that night when a prisoner actually got away. I organized my entire force immediately, and distributed them through Westchester County. Squads patrolled the highways and scouting parties examined every by-path and all side roads. After waiting an hour or more in my office for reports, I joined the hunt and drove my car out of the prison grounds for a tour of nearby roads. I passed a number of men who reported "No clues." On a chance I turned into a sort of private road. A man stepped out of the darkness. I slowed down. "How about a ride, Mister?" the man called. "Sure, jump in," I stopped the car and he sat down beside me. He didn't know me, but I recognized him. He had changed his shirt, but not his trousers. "Going all the way to the big town?" I asked. "Sure thing," the man replied eagerly. "Is that where you're going?" The fellow wasn't familiar with directions and after a few turns I reached the main highway and drove rapidly toward Ossining. In a few minutes I was at the prison gate, where a guard hailed me, "That you, Warden?" "I'll be damned," shouted the prisoner. "You will," I answered as we passed through the gate.

I do not want to create the impression that escapes are a Warden's major worries. They are, as a matter of fact, so infrequent as to constitute an infinitesimal part of his troubles. In the twelve years of my wardenship at Sing Sing, only three escaped prisoners are still at large. Three out of a total prisoner population of over 15,000 is a pretty fair average. A friend of mine facetiously remarked, "It is harder to keep men out of Sing Sing than in." There is more truth than jest in that sentiment. At the rate we are going, we shall soon have to turn them away.

The man in the prison service is in danger of becoming either sloppily emotional or iron fisted and hard boiled, with nothing but contempt for his wards. It is often difficult to find the well-balanced prison official, either in the ranks or higher up. I confess that I have often been tried, mentally and in spirit, with vexing situations that have arisen during the years of my prison work.

Ironing out twisted thoughts and ideals. One must live with the problem. One must sense it and grope his way along to possible solution. Back of it all is the soul torment which survives despite all physical comforts. That soul torment exists in every prison. I felt it keenly that night when three lives struggled to achieve their ultimate of hope or despair.

It was on a Thursday night—as usual, execution night. I had received final word from the Governor's office that there was no hope for a reprieve or respite for the condemned. All the witnesses were gathered in my office and I was checking the names to make sure we had the required number and also that no one had been admitted without proper credentials.

A guard suddenly appeared in the doorway and motioned frantically to me. I left the witnesses and turned to him.

"Warden," he gasped, "a fellow in the old cell block tried to commit suicide, and we cut him down in the nick of time."

I accompanied him to the first aid clinic to look at the would-be suicide. He was unconscious. Nurses were already on the spot with one of the prison doctors, all doing their best to revive him. I remained there until I saw his eyes flicker and was assured that the man would be saved. He was sent to the main hospital and I returned to the witnesses waiting to proceed to the death chamber.

We had just saved one man from self-inflicted death. Now we were about to execute the mandate of the law and put another to death. One wanted to die and couldn't. The other wanted to live and had to die.

But the night was not quite over. There was the autopsy required by law. The head surgeon made ready to perform it, when the telephone called him and the night nurse asked him to hurry up to the hospital immediately. "We have a case of acute appendicitis, Doctor. I think you will have to operate at once. We'll get him ready."

And from the autopsy room, where the surgeon made his incisions on the body of the man who lay in death, he hurried to the operating room where well nigh similar instruments and skill made incisions that were to save another's life. Three men, three lives and a Warden's responsibility.

CHAPTER 9: WHO'S AFRAID OF THE CHAIR?

RECENTLY two men were electrocuted in the death house in Sing Sing on the same night. One was a young fellow, not over twenty, convicted of a particularly vicious murder. The other was an older man, near thirty, the central figure of a triangle tragedy—a passion murder. A clergyman accompanied each of the condemned to the execution chamber.

The younger man went first. He paid little or no attention to the priest, strode rapidly to the Chair, with a swaggering gait, and seated himself, all the while puffing furiously at a large cigar between his lips. He gazed sneeringly at the witnesses while the attendants fumbled with the straps. Suddenly his eyes blazed. With a quick movement he threw the lighted cigar toward the nervous group. It struck one of them between the eyes. "You're a bunch of — —," he yelled, and died with a curse on his lips.

Before the startled witnesses regained their composure (things move rapidly in the death chamber), the door opened and the second man was escorted into the room. He walked slowly, the clergyman of his denomination beside him, both praying audibly. He did not falter at the Chair. I felt that his eyes were unseeing, fixed on things beyond our ken. The prayers continued while the straps were being adjusted. He died with a blessing on his lips.

One acted the hero stunt. He had committed murder to prove his gameness. Aimed to be a big shot with the gang. Had it been possible to stage that last act out in the open, with multitudes looking on, he would have died happy. That so little fuss was made at the moment of his passing was the breaking point of a drab waiting period in the death house. A braggadocio even in death.

The other died in expiation for his crime. Though convicted of murder in the first degree, his were not criminal instincts. He knew the nature and quality of his acts; therefore he was legally guilty. The law decreed his death and I had to carry out its mandate. I think he was glad to go. He wanted peace.

Another night two men died in the electric chair. Both, of course, guilty of murder.

One, a prisoner doing life, had stabbed another prisoner and killed him. It was a killing, committed almost in the shadow of the Chair, just outside the death house walls. My duty was to lay the facts before the district attorney. The murderer was tried, convicted and sentenced to death. Later, in the death house I visited him often. He was in turn morose, irritable and abusive. I soon discovered the reason. He had parents living, but they never came to see him. They had practically disowned him. I knew that he had a brother in another prison.

"Harry," I said to him one day, a week before the date set for his execution, "I have good news for you."

"A commute?" he asked eagerly.

"No. Not that. There isn't much hope, I'm afraid. But you will be glad to hear that your brother is coming down here."

"Here? What for?" he asked suspiciously.

292

"Why, to see you, of course," I assured him.

"Nothing doing, Warden. I won't see him. I don't want any visitors. I know it's the finish. So what's the use?"

The brother didn't come. Harry was difficult to handle. During his eight months in the death house he had quarreled with every keeper. He had taken a sudden dislike to his chaplain and ever after refused spiritual consolation. Not that the minister neglected him. It was rather because the reverend gentleman was too deeply concerned about Harry. An errand of mercy took him to the condemned man's parents, in the hope that they would relent and pay their departing son a visit. Harry had heard about it and resented it deeply. The chasm between parent and son had widened beyond all hope of repair. And so Harry spent his last days alone and, I am sure, in despair.

Now Harry, although guilty of a heinous crime, wasn't inherently vicious. At some time during his formative years something had snapped; something that had bound him, though the bond was slight, to the love and affection of his parents. He drifted on with bitterness in his heart. He never indulged in heroics, but was always disgruntled. He suspected everyone.

"They're all against me," he was heard to say once, when one of his unreasonable requests was refused. "They want to see me burn. Well, they'll soon have their way."

And so on the morning of the last day, when the men who are to die at night are permitted to make up their own menu, Harry wouldn't order anything. Didn't care about eating. I went to see him about it, but he was obstinate.

293

"Let me be, Warden," he insisted. "I'm all right. Don't want a thing." As a last resort I suggested that he could share his last meal with one of the condemned men with whom he had been friendly. He was interested. His eyes lit up. "Say, Warden, the kid'll have a good time. O.K. Send in all you've got. We'll finish it." And they did.

In all his twenty-nine years Harry probably never shed a tear. He might have been a happy-go-lucky youngster. Or an unconscious fatalist as an adult. Neither lends himself readily to emotion. Toward evening on that day a woman, whose identity cannot be disclosed, handed me a note. "Please give this to Harry a half hour before the end. It's confidential. Tell him to destroy it after he's read it. It's marked that way, too." I violated the strict rules of the Prison. I didn't censor that letter, and handed it to Harry as directed. I sat a short distance from him while he read it slowly. He must have read it over and over again, for it was some time before he looked up. As I approached him he tore the paper carefully into small bits. I don't know what was in that note, but there were real tears in Harry's eyes. All he said was, "Thank you, Warden," and turned away.

Harry's minutes were numbered. It was time to say good-bye. We sat eyeing each other. "Smoke, Harry?" I asked and handed him a cigar. I lighted his and smoked up mine. Finally, I rose to go. I held out my hand to him. But I had just one more question.

"Tell me, Harry," I asked. "What made you do it? Didn't you realize what it would mean?"

"Didn't give it a thought, Warden," he answered. "Just wanted to get my man."

"Was it an outside quarrel?" No. It wasn't that.

"Had he attacked you?" Harry had pleaded self-defense at his trial. But now he shrugged his shoulders.

Then his eyes clouded. He was again the sullen youth.

"No use, Warden," he mumbled, "you wouldn't understand."

"Bad man" Harry went to the Chair without heroics. Though Harry didn't know it, the minister whom he had spurned, followed him and prayed, not with him, but for him.

"What's the trouble, Searge? Nervous?" he smiled to the officer who adjusted the straps. Apparently the bitterness was gone from his heart.

I lay in my bed far into the early hours of the next morning struggling with Harry's last mortal thought: "You wouldn't understand."

Would Harry have been different if his parents hadn't disowned him? Who knows? It's hard to judge between parents and children. And yet, to me, as the warden of a prison with twenty-five hundred individual human equations, this is always a keen problem, pregnant with ever-pressing responsibilities.

I felt it poignantly some time later. A woman, a mother sat in my office. Three hours later her son, an only child, was to tread the "last mile" to his doom. She was a lady of middle age, intelligent and soft spoken. She did not betray her emotions. As usual, on the night of an execution, I kept the wires to Albany open. There may always be a chance. But that night I had little hope. "Do you think there's a possibility,

Warden?" the mother asked. She did not make me feel uncomfortable. There were no tears or hysterics.

"I know you have done everything possible," she added. I could only nod in acquiescence.

The condemned man had ordered his final meal. The last item was a peculiar one. "A dozen roses." The guard asked me about it. Here was a stunner. I couldn't imagine what the roses were for. Did he intend to walk to the Chair carrying a bouquet? Condemned men have been known to make peculiar requests. There was that fellow who insisted on wearing a white shirt; another wanted a tie. One tried to walk to the Chair on his hands with his feet in the air. But roses? That was a new one. Nevertheless, I ordered them and directed the guard to find out what the condemned man had in mind.

"They're for my mother," he said. "She loves roses."

I looked at this modest woman who sat facing me. Did she regard me as the executioner of her child?

"You're only doing your duty, Warden. I know and understand. You've done your best and have a mother's thanks."

I recalled the flowers. "Did you get the roses?" I asked her. "I left them with the guard," she explained. "I'm going back to say good-bye and I'll wear them, so he can see."

"You know, Warden," she continued, her eager voice anxious to give a motherly portrait of her son, "he's not really a criminal. I don't know what made him do it. He was always such a good son, and thoughtful. He worked steady, and on pay day, Saturday, he would stop at the grocers to buy things for Sunday. He would always come home with a big package. He knew I loved flowers. So every Saturday he brought me a bouquet of

296

roses. They were as important to him as the loaf of bread he bought." She paused for a moment. "I'll get them when I go in," she repeated, and rose to go. I escorted her to the door.

"This was the first time he was ever in trouble," she continued. "He was a good boy, Warden. But I suppose it's hopeless now. I know what it was, though." For the first time her eyes were hard, with deep lines showing around her mouth. "Bad booze and bad girls. They ruin more boys than we have any idea of." She left to get her roses.

A good mother. A thoughtful son. The death house and the electric chair. An incongruous setting. I tried to figure it out. I recalled Harry's sullen words, "You wouldn't understand."

Another condemned was a married man who would leave behind him a wife and two small children. This prisoner was from a city in upper New York. Two or three weeks before going he wanted to send for his wife and two children. He had been a laborer, just a coal shoveler, and had come from West Virginia. One Saturday night he went out to a speakeasy. He had some booze, and while in the speakeasy became acquainted with another fellow and his "girl." After a few drinks the other man suggested that they do a "job." They did. A man was killed and the other fellow who was a professional criminal turned State's evidence. The prime mover in these escapades quite often hides in the background or is the first to "tell" on the rookie in crime, who is made to take the "rap." Well, this fellow wanted to see his wife and children before the end, but he had no funds; his wife was destitute and they had no friends upon whom they could call in their distress. Tickets were arranged for by the Mutual Welfare League, by contributions from among a number of the prisoners who could ill afford to help out, but cheerfully did. The little family came to Ossining without funds, and I permitted them to stay over at my home. There were two children. I had one of my own of the same age. We had a big, old-fashioned bed and the three children were sleeping peacefully that night of the execution. The sheriff and the district attorney were there. The warden was ordered to kill and the man had to die. I had a talk with him a short time before the hour set for the execution.

"I am not afraid to die," he said. "We've all got to die. I've never had a headache, never had tuberculosis, or rheumatism, never been sick. I'm glad to die in the possession of all my faculties, but I am worried about those two children of mine. They will be marked for life." He paused for a moment, then he added thoughtfully. "And what is more and harder to bear, Warden, is that killing me won't help anything or anybody. This business of capital punishment is all wrong." He shrugged his shoulders.

"But what's the use, Warden. All I ask is that if it is at all possible try to do something for the kiddies." He went to the Chair gamely. Later, several of the witnesses to the execution sat around in my library discussing, naturally, the futility of it all. I motioned to them to follow me upstairs and led them into the spare bed room on the third floor, and switched on the light. "Two of them," I pointed to the sleeping children, "are our orphans. They will pay the penalty for their father's crime."

Hours later we separated. I had told them about

Harry's last grim words. "You wouldn't understand." It was the only thought we could agree upon.

Not long afterwards I was making my usual rounds of the prison. My course led me to the death house. As the keeper opened the heavy steel-barred door, I was met with a burst of song. At first I thought it was the radio and stopped to listen. A strong musical voice, followed by a male chorus. I soon discovered that it was not the radio, nor the phonograph, but the chorus of the condemned. The song these men, waiting for the final edict that was to bring them life or death, was none other than the popular refrain, "Happy Days Are Here Again."

Was it a gesture? Was it a soul song bringing its momentary relief to shattered hearts? Was it mere brazenness?

I remembered Harry's parting message: "You wouldn't understand."

It was Thursday. John's last day on earth. He was being escorted to the "dance hall," the prison term for the pre-execution chamber to which all condemned men are transferred on the morning of the final day. John stopped at each cell to shake hands with his fellow condemned who were to follow him later to the chair. One of his neighbors, Dan, grasped his hand firmly. He had more than a word to say to the man who was leaving.

"John," he asked. "Do you believe in Jesus Christ?"

"Sure, I do," the doomed man replied.

"Then kneel down and I'll give you my blessing."

John obeyed, and while three husky guards looked on, the man who had two weeks to live prayed over his fellow with less than twelve hours to go.

Did Harry's shade hover over the scene and point smilingly to the uniformed trio, "You wouldn't understand?"

It is hard to see a young man die. The electrocution of one young man stands out as the most poignant memory of all. His crime had been one of passion; he had killed the girl who had scorned him. He came of good, self-respecting family, a clerk with a record for industry and honesty in his employment. He was handsome, of athletic build and only twenty-three years old.

I came to like the lad because he had no friends, was reconciled to his fate, quietly professed his continuing love for the girl he had slain, deeply regretted the act, and recognized the justice of his sentence.

During his six months' confinement in the death house—the automatic interval between conviction and confirmation of sentence by the State Court of Appeals —he had displayed none of the moody bitterness of the average condemned man. If not actually cheerful, he had been pleasant. We of the prison who could reach beneath the surface of a man's conduct knew this boy had courage. Three men went before him to the Chair and he gave them words of comfort without reviling the State that sent them there. That is a sign of self-control.

The day before he was to die he asked the guard if I would see him. I went to his cell and found him unusually tense.

"Warden," he said in a low whisper so that his cell neighbors couldn't hear, "I don't think I'm going to do so well tomorrow night when the time comes."

"You've borne up bravely," I answered. "Don't give way now."

300

"I've had to struggle, Warden," he said. "Watching other boys go by this cell toward that outer cell where they wait for the Chair—that hasn't been easy. Somehow I feel I'm slipping."

"You'll have the Chaplain at your side. Let me bring you a book or two to read."

"No, thanks, Warden. But you can do something else for me."

"Anything within reason that the rules permit."

"Warden," he touched his forehead as if tipping an absent hat, "you can do me a favor if you'll give me a stiff drink of whiskey just ten minutes before they take me."

"That's against the rules, son," I replied.

"It's all I ask, Warden," he pleaded. "I want to bear up to the end. Just one stiff drink."

I hesitated. His eyes were unutterably anxious.

"All right, son," I said. "You'll have your drink."

After dusk the next evening, mindful of my promise, I went to the infirmary and secured from the doctor a two-ounce bottle which I filled with pure rye whiskey. I slipped this in my pocket, a trifle uncertain. By strict rule we never give stimulants of any kind to a condemned prisoner on his way to death. But I had made my promise and I liked the boy.

When I faced him thirty minutes before he was to die, he turned his head to see if the murmuring Chaplain was watching him. He whispered: "Did you bring that drink?"

I nodded. Then for the first time in my experience the sight of a man going to his death gave me qualms, nausea. He was young, virile, brave. It seemed a sacrilege that so very soon this stalwart, clear-eyed youth would become a corpse.

My mood must have been reflected in my face. The young man scanned me. Just before the walk to the Chair down a narrow concrete path to the door behind which twelve men sat to witness his death, I stepped close to him so that nobody saw me. I passed him the tiny bottle of whiskey.

He smiled. Took a step aside. As the guards turned to cover him he passed back the bottle.

"You need this worse than I, Warden," he said. "Please drink it."

I did, and he went to his death—smiling.

In the twelve years of my wardenship I have escorted 150 men and one woman to the death chamber and the electric chair. In ages they ranged from seventeen to sixty-three. They came from all kinds of homes and environments. In one respect they were all alike. All were poor, and most of them friendless. To what end or purpose were these victims sent to their premature deaths? Ordinarily the answer would be simple. They killed, therefore they had to die. A logical point of view, indeed, if it were applied equally to all who committed unjustifiable homicide.

The trouble is that sentiment plays too great a part in all judicial processes where life is at stake.

"You shall be put to death in the manner prescribed by law." The Court is pronouncing the sentence of death. The judgment is mandatory, for a jury of twelve men have convicted the prisoner of murder in the first degree. Several months later, at the hearing for clemency in the Governor's chambers, a bulky document is presented to His Excellency. It is a petition signed by

302

thousands of citizens endorsing the application for a commutation of sentence. A significant appendage is the special plea signed by the twelve men who constituted the jury that convicted the condemned.

Which judgment of the jury is more dependable? Its conviction of murder which carried with it the certainty of the death penalty or its subsequent plea for mercy? This is one of the incidents that emphasize the fallacy of the death penalty. In both instances the jury was swayed by sentiment. First by hysteria, later by undue sympathy. Where sentiment predominates, whether of hate or pity, the scales of justice are not evenly balanced.

Deliberate murder is the most heinous of all offences. It should be punished to the utmost limits of the law. Men do not differ about that. The doubt that assails the mind of the thoughtful citizen is what that limit shall be.

Since time began man has been struggling with the problem of behavior. In early days, when almost every human attribute had its counterpart in celestial spheres, with favorite gods who presided over particular human emotions, an offence by a mortal was interpreted as an affront to the Deity. Only the death of the offender could propitiate the anger of the offended god. It is not surprising, therefore, that a parallel has been drawn between the ancient custom of human sacrifice and capital punishment of today. Human sacrifices by way of propitiation to the old nebulous fancies of theology; capital punishment in deference to the modern, nebulous god known as public sentiment. One was, of course, as impotent as the other is fallacious.

The fact that the death penalty is the peculiar province of the public official, the prosecutor or even the judge, becomes more clearly apparent when these public officials on their return to private life do not hesitate to fight for the lives of clients accused of murder and, in the event of conviction, carry their cases to the Governor's chamber in their plea for avoidance of the extreme penalty. The self-same faculties that theretofore demanded "stern justice" are now employed in an appeal to the sympathies. Here, then, lies the weakness of capital punishment.

Governor Harry H. Woodring of Kansas stated the case admirably in his veto message of the bill to restore the death penalty in that State:

"The possibility of the infliction of the death penalty in any case dramatizes it before the public. What should be a solemn deliberation becomes a public spectacle, with the resultant brutalizing effect upon society. It is not desirable to have our communities divided, with one faction demanding the life of the criminal and another faction going to the other extreme of sympathy for the accused, thus greatly increasing the possibility of error, and there is no remedy in case of error."

The death penalty, in all its varied forms of accomplishment, has never effectively shaped the course of human conduct or destiny. Thus the human torches of the ancient Romans did not succeed in suppressing Christianity. It was not the sword of Mohamet, but the culture and philosophy of Islam that converted millions to Mohammedanism. Nor did the secret tortures and deaths of the Spanish Inquisition succeed in annihilating Judaism.

Peter I, Czar of all the Russians in 1720, put to death eight thousand of his subjects in his effort to

304

enforce his edict that moujiks shall shave their beards. Yet now, two hundred years later, we can hardly associate a Russian with an unadorned chin.

Neither the threat of death, nor its infliction, has ever halted the march of moral progress. Nor has the fear of death been able to impress a new order of living for which the people were not prepared by education and culture.

Our forbears did not understand that. Not all of us in this enlightened day appreciate it. And so the gallows, the electric chair, the guillotine, the lethal chamber and all other forms of execution still stand firmly imbedded in our scheme of government and civilization.

"After walking eleven hours," a traveler of the early centuries relates, "without having traced the print of human foot, to my great comfort and delight, I saw a man hanging upon a gibbet. My pleasure at the cheering prospect was inexpressible, for it convinced me that I was in a civilized country."

Perhaps the most effective of all indictments against capital punishment was heard in the great Parliamentary debates on the abolition, in England, of the death penalty for simple thefts. Strangely enough, the indictment was uttered by the proponents rather than opponents of the extreme penalty. Learned jurists, eloquent preachers, anxious prosecutors warned Parliament against the removal of the death penalty for the theft of forty shillings from storekeepers. "Our merchants will suffer such depredations that they will become bankrupt and the land will be ruined."

At first Parliament hearkened to these dire forebodings and refused to pass the abolition bill. Several years later, in 1837, the matter again came before the

House of Commons and this time, despite all protests from the opposition, the bill to abolish the death penalty for petty thievery was adopted. The immediate effect was exactly the opposite of the predictions made by opponents of abolition. Not only did merchants and storekeepers report a cessation of larcenies, but the improvement of the moral tone of the people and law enforcement agencies was felt throughout the country. England began to assume her envious position as the most law abiding people in all the world. It is a fact little understood that though the courts of the Eighteenth and early Nineteenth Century England often went out of their way to avoid convictions followed by the sentence of death in very much the same way as the modern district attorney or judge permits the accused to plead to a lesser charge (the amount involved was frequently reduced from 40 shillings to 39), it was really the large number of capital cases and the too general use of the gallows that finally turned the people of England against capital punishment except in the case of homicide.

Sir Edward Coke writes of "the lamentable thing it is to see so many Christian men and women strangled on that cursed tree of the gallows; insomuch that, if, in a large field, a man might see together all the Christians that in one year throughout England come to that untimely ignominious death, if there were any spark of grace and charity in him, it would make his heart to bleed for pity and compassion."

Dr. Frederick L. Hoffman, the statistician and consistent opponent of capital punishment, struck the same note in a letter to me in which he asks: "What would be the attitude of the American people if by good or ill circumstance the ten thousand men and women who in any one year commit our murders and manslaughters in these United States, would all be convicted of murder, sentenced to death and that punishment actually inflicted?" What, indeed, but an almost universal cry for abolition?

From every point of view, therefore, the death penalty is futile. Its wide and frequent application would arouse public fury against it; the practice prevailing in many jurisdictions to avoid it and the refusal of juries to convict in the face of undisputed evidence of crime, is reflected in the general disrespect of all law and procedure, and is an undoubted influence for crime.

My opposition to capital punishment is not based on sentiment or sympathy. I am not altogether impressed with the religious enthusiasts who talk about the sacredness of life and oppose the death penalty on the ground that man, whether by law or otherwise, has no right to take that which belongs only to God. It is useless to argue that point when men do not hesitate to make war and kill each other on the battlefield where none of the personal animosities or emotionalism of the private feud prompts the aggressor.

I am opposed to the death penalty because the evasions, the inequality of its application, the halo with which it surrounds every convicted murderer, the theatrics which are so important to every court proceeding where the stake is life or death, the momentary hysteria, passion and prejudice aroused by the crime which often make it impossible to weigh the facts carefully and impersonally and, finally, the infrequency of its application—all tend to weaken our entire structure of social control. They make for cynicism and disrespect of all law enforcing agencies, and encourage the desperate criminal toward the extreme crime. He knows that his gamble with the death penalty is safer than with a long term in prison for a lesser offence.

There is an inherent weakness in any system of law and procedure that does not recognize the reticence of citizens and prospective jurors to invoke the penalty provided by statute.

Jury panels have been exhausted time and again because of the court's inability to obtain twelve men willing to pass upon the guilt of a defendant accused of murder, because of their opposition to the death penalty.

That hysteria and periodic public clamor play a large part in capital punishment cases was brought home to me forcibly in the recent arrival at Sing Sing of a young man sentenced to a term of two to ten years for manslaughter. The crime for which he was permitted to take a plea was committed twelve years ago. A bank robbery in the perpetration of which two men were killed by this prisoner and his accomplice. It was a sensational case. Public indignation was aroused and justifiably so. The press demanded the immediate arrest and conviction of the murderers, who had succeeded in making their escape. The usual hue and cry followed. Several months later one of the murderers, Gordon Hamby, was captured. He was tried for murder, convicted and sentenced to death. Hamby was probably the most intelligent man who ever occupied a cell in the death house.

Newspapers had built him up as a dangerous criminal, a desperado of the worst type. His calm philosophy did not desert him in his final moments. It was he who staggered our death house guards with his unusual and theretofore unheard-of request to be permitted to wear a white shirt in the electric chair. There were murmured protests when I consented. It disturbed tradition. It was he who sent out the message from the death chamber, "Tell the folks out there the little green door is brown." Men breathed a sigh of relief when this bank robber was executed. Public opinion settled down until the next sensational crime would startle it out of its complacency.

Meanwhile, his accomplice remained away. He had disappeared without leaving a trace. He was seventeen at the time. Twelve years later a young man in San Francisco mentioned the fact of his English ancestry to a neighbor. For some unknown reason the immigration authorities were notified. An investigation disclosed the fact that this mild mannered, apparently harmless fellow was none other than the hunted bank robber of 1918.

He had managed to obtain honest employment. His motto, as he explained it to the officers who came for him from across the continent, was "live right and work hard." He had made new friends and apparently had lived up to his self-assumed code. When apprehended he made no effort to hide his identity. Readily confessed to the robbery and murder in 1918. He explained that his share of the booty was $5,000. His contention in extenuation was that his partner had compelled him to join in the robbery and had threatened him with death if he refused.

Had this man been captured twelve years ago nothing could have saved him from the electric chair. He

309

would have been a "dangerous" criminal, a bank robber, a killer, whom police, prosecutor, judge and jury would have sent to the Chair with the assurance of a duty well done. Twelve years changed all that. Hysteria had calmed down. To the press he was more or less a shadow of the past. He had apparently proved his ability to lead an honest and normal life. Why not give the young man a chance? And so, though he had participated in a felony which resulted in a murder, invariably punishable with death, every conceivable advantage was allowed the prisoner. Judge and prosecutor consented to allow him to plead to manslaughter upon which a sentence of two to ten years was imposed.

It is not the fact that this man escaped the death chair that concerns me. Rather that scores of others, no more guilty and no less, have paid with their lives for murders committed under similar circumstances. It is significant also as a commentary on the "viciousness" of men who commit murders, which is so widely emphasized in moments of hysteria fanned by sensational reports but which invariably wanes with the lapse of time.

A typical case was that of Ruth Snyder, the last woman electrocuted in the death chair at Sing Sing. During my wardenship, five women have been sentenced to the extreme penalty. Three of them were later either commuted or acquitted after a second trial following the reversal of the original judgment. The execution of Ruth Snyder and her paramour, Judd Gray, aroused more furor than perhaps all other executions in my experience. Neither prisoner saw the other after entering the condemned cells. Just before their death permission was granted them to exchange notes. Three thousand people milled around the gates of Sing Sing Prison on the night of the execution. This host was not actuated by the desire to witness the even course of justice. Nor did the one hundred thousand words flashed over especially installed telegraph wires on the hills overlooking the prison deal with law's impartiality. It was pointed out at the time that the crowd at the prison, as also the readers of those newspaper accounts, derived as much sensual pleasure out of the incident as in watching a spectacular fire, regardless of the tragic loss of life and property involved.

But in the death house all was quiet. Both prisoners bore up bravely and calmly in their last moments. Ruth Snyder entertained high hopes for a reprieve or commutation until almost the very end. The day before the execution she seemed to lose this slender hope and gave way to hysteria. She was in a coma most of that day. But towards evening she revived. The Bible, which had become her constant companion, and her religious devotion seemed to give her strength. Thenceforth she looked calmly for the final drawing of the curtain. On the last day she asked the matron to dress her hair and played cards when she was not reading, until just a few moments before she was to go to the Chair. She trod the "last mile" bravely, if not with dignity.

Actually, it was the woman guard, her matron, who succumbed. She had been instructed to take her stand immediately in front of the chair facing Mrs. Snyder, so as to shield her somewhat from the eyes of the witnesses, all men. The matron accompanied the condemned woman into the death chamber and assumed her position. A moment later, while the straps were being adjusted, she was overcome and had to be led from the chamber. Had this not occurred, the now notorious picture incident—a photograph showing Ruth Snyder in her last throes while the current was passing through her body—would not have happened.

In the hysteria occasioned by the execution of this woman, the original crime for which she was paying the extreme penalty was almost entirely forgotten. The judge who presided at her trial imposed the death sentence most reluctantly. He recognized its futility.

Its demoralizing influence reached into every community and affected numberless morbid minds of all ages. Certainly it was no deterrent to other passion or triangle murders. Its immediate effect was to emphasize stage play and showmanship in courts, and through imaginary and mythical descriptive details, in the death house.

During her stay in the death house many offers of marriage came for Mrs. Snyder. For a week prior to the date of the execution hundreds of newspaper reporters, feature article writers, and general nuisances, made the prison and its environs practically their domicile.

Reports of imaginary interviews with the condemned, invented and prepared in local speakeasies, were telegraphed from Ossining to various newspapers throughout the country. The measure of sordidness was, of course, dependent on the quality of the liquid imbibed.

On the day of the execution there was bedlam in the vicinity of Ossining, occasioned by the hundreds of visitors attracted to the prison gate by the impending execution.

It was impossible for me to answer the innumerable

312

telephone calls requesting information about the details of the procedure in the death house and the attitude of the condemned.

I was grateful to Ruth Hale, one of America's foremost women of letters, for her telegram: "Have tried all day to phone you but you very sensibly do not answer. I have wanted to say that my heart is heavy with yours and that since you do this hideous job for all of us, I would take my part if I could."

No less interesting and pointed is the case of a young boy, nineteen years of age, recently executed in the death house at Sing Sing. Francis (Two-Gun) Crowley arrived at Sing Sing in a burst of glory. He had been publicized far and wide as a daring murderer and a criminal of the most vicious type. His impressionable mind aimed to measure up to the reputation built up for him by a gullible public. A chance reportorial phrase gave him his cue. And so from a mere bad boy he became the notorious "Two-Gun" bandit. It is perhaps no answer to the practical problem of law enforcement to point out that this murderer was since his infancy the ugly duckling of society. That he was neglected at school; that his home influence was bad; that no attention was given to latent and special abilities. Nor that despite all this indifference toward the maturing boy the latter was actually engaged in honest and gainful employment until shortly before his entry upon his criminal career.

What is important to me is that this youthful bandit entered the death house imbued with the spirit that urged him on to do his vicious killings. He had about him the pompous air of bravado and a dare-devil mentality, which were displayed in minor and unimportant obstinacies.

Owing to his spectacular, though stupid crimes, Crowley was well press-agented before his arrival at Sing Sing. I was amazed to see him—small in stature and of low grade mentality. In a different setting, his clear complexion and general appearance would have marked him as a choir boy. His eyes were small and indicated stolidity.

Immediately upon his arrival in the custody of several deputy sheriffs, he was searched as are all men coming into the condemned cells. The long handle of a table spoon was found concealed inside one of his socks. The sheriff was later permitted to question Crowley about it. He claimed to have taken it from a person who was eating while watching him.

"Two-Gun" Crowley was hailed in the death house as a tough boy who could make his presence felt even in that prison within a prison. He cursed and jibed the guards who brought him food. Some of the other boys laughed and applauded. Thus egged on, Crowley set out to show us just how tough he could be. I learned later that his insensate fury was provoked by a letter from his girl friend who was with him when he killed a policeman and when he was arrested. In the letter she called him yellow. That was enough to arouse him.

Several days after his admission he removed portions of the bed spring, twisted the wire around a copy of a bulky weekly magazine, and he soon had a crude but formidable weapon. He was admonished and advised that he would be treated just as he deserved; that no one desired to make his short stay with us any more nerve-racking than was necessary. The warning served no purpose.

Death house inmates are denied matches; but Crowley managed to set fire to his bed at night with a cigarette ignited for him, as is the custom, by a guard. The officer should have been suspicious because Crowley had never used tobacco in any form. Strong-armed men put out the fire, while others restrained the prisoner. Left alone, he proceeded to smash everything in his cell; he tore off his clothes to stuff up the plumbing.

Crowley was then removed to another section of the death house where he was practically isolated from the other prisoners.

For a while he continued to disport himself in the same way. He again stuffed the toilet, and as the result his cell was flooded. His clothing was then taken from him; his bed was removed, and a mattress was furnished only at night. So there was our death house hero, tough "Two-Gun" Crowley, naked in his cell. He spent his time catching flies to kill them. He would take grains of sugar and wait patiently for the flies to assemble. Then he would pounce upon them.

We let him alone. There was no one to applaud him in his isolated corner of the death house. He had no opportunity to parade himself before his fellow inmates.

About three days after we put him in his new cell, a guard appealed to me to let Crowley have a new bed and clothes.

"Something's happened to him," the guard explained. "It sounds like hokum, but it's true. A starling hopped into his cell. He didn't kill it. He fed it. The bird keeps on coming back to his cell and he's interested in it."

"I'm glad of that," I said. "But we'll see how Mr. Crowley behaves tomorrow."

The following day I went to see the young murderer. Physically, he seemed none the worse for his cave man isolation. His appearance was animal-like, but tamed. He spoke normally, promised that he'd be on good behavior if clothing were given him and a mattress to sleep on. And if he could keep the bird. I consented.

The starling kept flying into the prisoner's cell day after day. Always it received its daily ration. The prisoner had tamed the bird. But more surprising was the fact that the tiny bird tamed the bandit. Our prisoner became a normal person. He began to spend his time in drawing and sketching, and making miniature buildings and other things out of newspapers. His language became moderate.

He showed an aptitude for drawing and his sketch of the death house was, on the whole, quite accurate and comprehensive. He drew a picture of the death chair, which he pasted on the wall of his cell. He also drew a picture of a coffin, showing the figure of a man lying within, and on the sides he printed the name—"Francis (Two-Gun) Crowley."

Several weeks before he was scheduled to die, Crowley was sent to New York City to appear as a witness in a case in defense of the defendant who, Crowley claimed, was innocent of the crime charged. Crowley assumed the responsibility for the robbery. He insisted that he was the guilty party. He again sensed the opportunity for stage play. Before leaving the death house he called to one of the porters: "Take all my

316

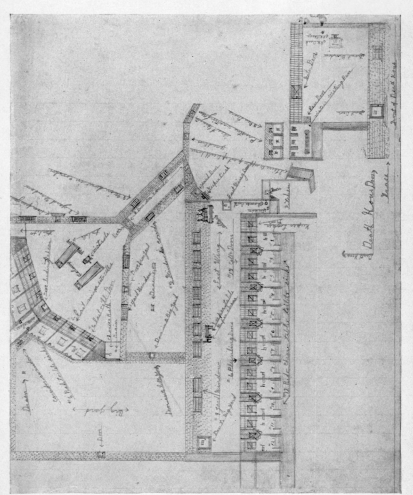

Crowley's sketch of the death house.   (Page 346)

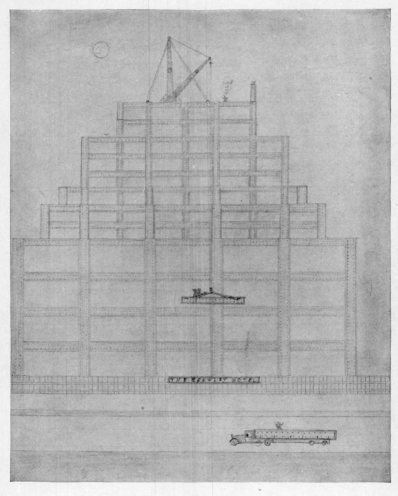

The Crowley Hotel. (*Page 318*)

things. I won't need them again. Once I leave here I won't come back. You can be sure of that." He apparently planned a spectacular break from the guards or in the court room.

All the way from Ossining to New York (a thirty mile ride), Crowley expanded on his exploits. He was apparently unconcerned with his mission. But he made no attempt to break away. I doubt that he expected to accomplish anything. But the thought occurred to me that he might possibly grasp at the chance of being shot down and die in his tracks rather than wait for the end in the Chair. The latter was too tame.

He soon realized that there was to be no opportunity for theatrics. He entered the court room without attempting any disturbance. He waited quietly until he was called to the witness stand.

During intermission he called for "something to eat." There was a slight delay before he was served. Finally his lunch arrived. When he had finished, he turned to one of his attendants. "You know, Sergeant," he laughed, "it's lucky they sent that stuff. I had almost made up my mind to fool 'em. No eats, no testimony."

It was a contented and satisfied Crowley who resumed the stand in the afternoon. He fenced with the district attorney and lawyers for the defense. He made what he later called "wise cracks." Sometimes the audience laughed at his sallies. Crowley was delighted with the response. He would glance at the reporters to make sure they took down his words. "Did you notice how busy those newspapermen got every time I made a hit?" he asked his guard.

Crowley was returned to his cell in the death house. That porter did not inherit his possessions.

On the way down through the busy streets of New York, the car in which Crowley was traveling was stopped by a traffic signal. Immediately in front of the prison car, an armored truck was waiting. A moment or two later two men emerged from a bank close by. One was carrying a bag, the other followed him holding a revolver in full view. Crowley noticed it. He turned and grinned to the officer at his side. "How easy that would be. Wouldn't take long to get into that."

He marveled at the sights that were passed on the way. His one glance at the new George Washington Bridge was sufficient to impress it on his mind. When he returned to the death house he asked for several newspapers. From the rotogravure section of a Sunday paper he constructed a skillful reproduction of the bridge. Another section of the paper he used for a miniature of the Empire State Building. A day or two later we permitted him to have some light white wood with which he built a structure which he called Crowley's Hotel. He managed to set up elevators and made small figures of workmen, which he placed inside and outside the building. He somehow got hold of a water bug or a species of beetle and for several days, with a thread tied to it, the beetle was compelled to do watchman's duty in Crowley's Hotel.

Crowley did not smoke or chew or drink; nor was he a drug addict. But he was very fond of hard candy. During his last six months in the death house, he was perfectly happy by himself. When he was in the section where the other men were confined, he would be the "fall guy" or "lobby gob" for them, always pulling their own chestnuts out of the fire in order to live up

318

to the reputation he had established and desired to continue. Left to himself, he was a well behaved, somewhat studious and an altogether likeable boy.

Crowley explained to me that he had been brought up to have a fierce hatred of policemen. He was an illegitimate child and a grandson of a police official. His father abandoned the infant and his mother, a German household worker. His mother placed him in a foundling home and later deserted him. The woman who took him from the home was the only mother Crowley ever knew. His schooling had ended with the third grade. He was practically illiterate. Yet the woman who had brought him up and whom he called "mother," managed to steer him to honest work during his adolescence.

This woman sat in my office the day before Crowley was to be executed. "He was a thoughtful boy," she said. "He would bring his pay envelope home and give it to me. No, I did not suspect anything wrong with him during all those years, and I'm sure there was nothing wrong."

During his short, eventful but stupid crime career, he often came to Ossining, within the vicinity of Sing Sing Prison and the death house. An incident that is of peculiar interest was that he rented garage space for his automobile adjoining that of one of the keepers of the prison. And it was this very keeper who watched over him in the death house in the months preceding his execution.

Strange as it may seem, Crowley did occasionally attend Church services. He was always fully armed, even on those occasions. Always with his two guns. He talked with one of his guards about a service he at-

319

tended in an Ossining Church and told of the revolvers that were secreted in his pockets. The officer was shocked.

"Why didn't you shoot the minister?" he exclaimed.

Crowley smiled. "I never shoot my friends. Only my enemies—policemen."

What relation, if any, was there between Crowley's "toughness" and his policeman grandfather whom he knew only by hearsay? Crowley was a boy of fourteen when he saw a woman enter his home and talk for a while with his "mother." He was too young to understand the subject and nature of their discourse. When the woman left, he asked his "mother," "who is that woman?" It was then that he learned for the first time about his parentage and his illegitimacy. The woman who brought him up from infancy explained it all to his boyish and immature mind. "And that woman is your real mother," she told him. The boy listened quietly. Then he shook his little head. "I don't care if she is my mother. I don't like her."

An ugly duckling of society. I sometimes wonder if this boy, born out of wedlock and without half a chance in life, could not have been saved from the electric chair if someone could have understood his liking for drawing and mechanics and had developed it.

But the public was hardly interested in that feature of this step-child of society. Spectacular, though foolish and stupid crimes had turned Crowley into front page material. Sensation writers, as well as sensation readers, had found a new outlet for their sordid curiosity. It was not surprising to me that I began to receive the usual number of crank letters several days prior to the date set for the execution. One syndicate that featured special articles was insistent upon interviewing Crowley for the purpose of preparing a series of articles having to do with his sensational crimes. Naturally, this was impossible under the law, as only those with court orders are permitted to visit condemned men. But these enterprising journalists would not take "No" for an answer and continued their requests for several days. Finally, on the night of the execution, a telegraph boy came to the prison with a telegram which, he said, "he would have to deliver to the Warden personally." He was permitted to enter the prison to accomplish his mission. The telegram was a lengthy one. It was from the same syndicate, and rather hysterically repeated the former request for an interview with Crowley. This time, however, the message explained that the articles had already been prepared. All that was now necessary, at this late hour, was to have Crowley sign his name to them. For this they were prepared to offer Crowley fifty per cent of the proceeds of the sale of the articles which they agreed would be not less than ten thousand dollars. For Crowley's signature he was to receive five thousand dollars—the money to be disposed of as he directed. I read that message with increasing nausea.

What was there about this man condemned to death that warranted this outburst of emotions? What was there about this stupid boy that had so aroused a large portion of the public to this moronic display? Incidents like these help to make the death penalty farcical either as a deterrent or as a practical solution to a serious problem. Farcical to every one but the man who is to go to the Chair. When Crowley was told about this offer he made what was probably the first philosophic comment in all of his youthful life. "If mother (meaning his foster mother) had that five grand when I was a kid, maybe things would have been different."

I was with him until almost the last minute. He talked about his former escapades, about his erstwhile companions for whom he had little, if any, respect or affection. During a momentary pause in our conversation he pointed to a large water bug that was scurrying to and fro on the floor of his cell. "See that?" he said. "I was about to kill it. Several times I wanted to crush it. It's a dirty looking thing. But then I decided to give it a chance and let it live." He didn't smile or brag about it. I doubted even if he understood the significance of his remark or his thought.

Crowley went to his death calmly, without braggadocio, without swagger. "Give my love to mother," he called, just as the hood was placed over his head.

Society, an interested public, represented by twenty-five newspapermen watched him die. "He was a game kid," was the unanimous sentiment. The boy who had terrorized the police force of a great metropolitan city, the youth who lived with bitterness in his heart against something he "knew not what" but could only sense, died with love in that heart and on his lips. An ugly duckling gone to rest.

Crowley was a bad boy. So was the ten-year-old Chicago youngster who, while playing "hold-up man" with his five-year-old brother in his father's delicatessen store, seized his father's pistol and shouting, "I'm going to shoot you," actually shot and killed the child. Underneath the veneer of hardness and swagger, Crowley was a playboy, certainly a very dangerous playboy. Society's failure to provide an outlet for his

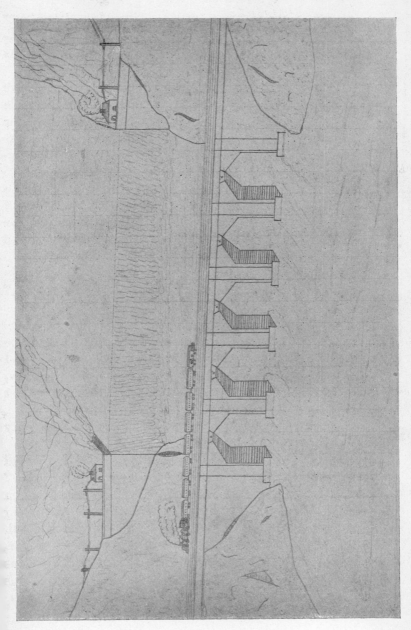

Crowley showed an aptitude for drawing. (*Page 316*)

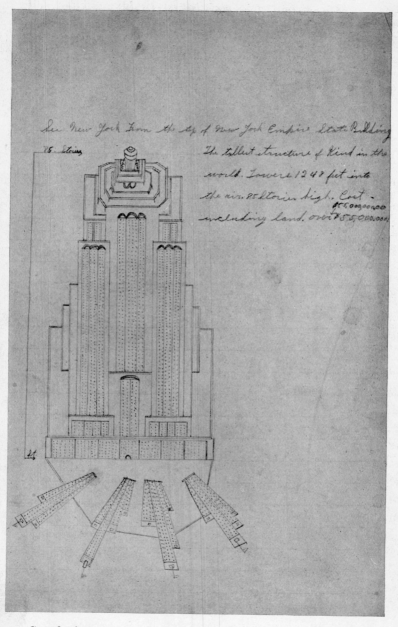

See New York from the top of New York Empire State Building

The tallest structure of kind in the world. Towers 1248 feet into the air. 85 stories high. Cost including land. over $5 5,000,000.

85 stories

44

Crowley's miniature sketch of the Empire State Building.

(*Page 318*)

normal desire for play, its neglect in failing to provide proper training and schooling—these constitute the answer to the problem of the Crowleys. Certainly, the answer is not to be found in the death chamber, or in the electric chair. An evidence of that appeared in a morning newspaper several days before the execution of Crowley. It told of another youngster who outdid Crowley. He became the "Three-Gun" bandit who left behind him a crimson trail of two murders in one night.

I have more than a faint suspicion that a large part of our public dotes upon murders and murder trials and executions just as an equally emotional class of people find relaxation and mind food in the gross exaggerations of intimate life that come out of Reno or Hollywood or other well known pivotal social centers. I see it daily.

Some years ago our executioner tendered his resignation without notice, and to take effect immediately. Seven men were then awaiting execution in the electric chair. Notice of the vacancy was made public. The next morning's mail brought hundreds of applications offering to take the place of the man who resigned. Almost all explained the reasons that prompted the writers to ask for the job. A number were apologetic. They were opposed to capital punishment, but they were without employment and had families to support. Others, especially ex-service men, told of their experiences at the front. "I was sent to France to kill and I killed," wrote one. "I am hardened in this killing business. This job won't feaze me."

"These fellows knew what they were doing when they set out to kill. Why then should I have any compunctions about doing the same to them? I'll take the job, and do it with vigor and efficiency."

"I'll take the job," one letter reads, "if there is no publicity attached to it."

"I am opposed to the death penalty," another is careful to explain, "but the law is law, and as long as someone has to do the work, why not I?"

We finally found our man. I have never asked him his opinion on capital punishment. It is a topic that we never discuss.

Not less interesting, and somewhat more complex, are the many letters requesting permission to witness an execution. They come from men in all walks of life. Physicians who are prompted for professional reasons. Lawyers, newspaper men, social workers, ordinary laymen and last, but not least, gentlemen of the cloth.

"Would it be asking too much of you to extend to me an invitation to the next execution that is held at Sing Sing Prison? I am very much interested in the abolition of capital punishment, and I belong to the League of which you are a member."

This is a typical letter. It puts me in mind of the men who are strongly for Prohibition, but who are anxious to obtain jobs as "samplers," to find out whether the stuff has a real "kick."

"I am very much interested in capital punishment. To see the execution itself will be of inestimable value to me," writes one anxious prospect.

Strange to say, I have never received a request from a district attorney to witness the execution of the man whom he prosecuted, or from a judge to attend the execution of the man whom he sentenced. Under the law, invitations must be sent out to a judge of the

Supreme Court of the district from which the condemned man was sentenced, also to the district attorney who prosecuted, as well as the sheriff of the County. It is not, however, obligatory for them to attend. As a rule they do not.

Several months ago a judge of the Supreme Court, the only one since my wardenship, attended an execution. The judge came as an interested citizen. At the risk of seeming immodesty, I quote from his letter, which came shortly thereafter:

"If men must kill according to statute, certainly it cannot be done with less offence to men of sensibility and understanding than you did last night. I believe the words of the last poor fellow who spoke in your praise were sincere and a just measure of the regard which you have earned by years of kind and fatherly treatment."

Numerous requests do come from policemen. Whatever it is that prompts them, whether curiosity or revenge, or plain morbidity, the fact is that the policeman does not shrink from witnessing the operation of the electric chair.

Since my term as warden, we have had but one woman witness in the death chamber. She was Nellie Bly, who represented a New York newspaper at the execution of Hamby. She was so overcome that we literally had to carry her out of the death house. The next day she wrote a highly emotional story of her experience.

Some years later I received the following letter from another woman reporter:

"Is there any rule of the State Prison Commission to prevent a duly accredited reporter from witnessing

325

an execution at Sing Sing, if that reporter happens to be a woman? Her reactions would make a far more interesting story than that of a man."

I agreed with the lady that her story would be interesting and good reading. But, with the concurrence of the Superintendent of Prisons, we thought it best to refuse her the desired permission. Women may be excellent jurors, even in capital cases, but as witnesses to grim tragedy, they have their failings. The merely morbid woman might stand it. Certainly we should not encourage that type of feminism.

Letters to the condemned from all manner of people are especially heavy in cases that have become notorious. They come from emotional women who send their messages of sympathy and advice to the prisoners. A great many are prompted by hysteria and religious frenzy. Some assume that the warden has the choice of executing or "saving" the condemned and insist that I refrain from carrying out the mandate of the court. Comments on the particular cases are numerous; also epithets, slanders, libels, curses, blessings, warnings.

A letter was addressed to a prisoner nearing the end of his patient vigil for death. His appeal had been denied. It came from a friend of the boy's family, and read as follows:

"I saw in the paper just what happened. I have been hoping it would turn out better for you, but it seems inevitable now. Now, Morris, inasmuch as it must happen, do you think your mother would agree to have you laid out in my place? Most of your friends are in this neighborhood. I don't know what arrangements have been made, but if it isn't too late, I would take pride in making everything as pleasant as possible."

This bid for business came from an undertaker of the boy's home town. The letter, of course, never reached the condemned. Its writer, a lady, unconsciously plagiarized an incident that occurred in 1727 in London. One Major Oneby, the records disclose, was condemned to the gallows. Several days prior to the execution, he received a letter from an undertaker in Drury Lane, who, having heard that the Major was to die shortly, promised to perform the funeral "as cheap and in as decent a manner as any man alive."

How history does repeat itself!

Commercialism plays a great part in whetting public appetite for the morbid in capital cases. In the latter part of 1927, two well advertised homicides whipped the country into a frenzy of sordid interest in murder and execution. The death chamber and the electric chair received their undue proportion of publicity. The question of the efficacy of electricity for executions was debated anew on hundreds of public forums and in the press.

One morning I received a notice signed by a theatrical manager who claimed that he could prove beyond doubt that the electric chair does not kill. He explained that the performer, who was a "scientist and electrical genius," would, "if allowed one hour with anyone sentenced to be electrocuted (possibly he had in mind Snyder and Gray) teach the condemned how to withstand the entire voltage of the 'hot squat.' "

The "scientist and electrical genius" intended to demonstrate on the stage of the Hippodrome in New York City on Tuesday, December 20, 1927, at 11 A. M., and I was asked to send a representative to witness the demonstration.

"Mr. Johnson," the notice continued, "as you know, is not a fake side show attraction. He is a highly paid consulting electrical engineer who invented the wireless phone at the age of 17 (he is now 35), and has contributed in a large way to the scientific advancement of radio and electricity."

I promptly sent a representative, Mr. George Ogle, Consulting Power Engineer of the General Engineering and Management Corporation, to witness the performance. On December 22, 1927, I received the following letter from Mr. Ogle:

"Complying with your request I investigated Fake, now appearing at the Hippodrome, who advertises himself as the man who defies the electric chair. Mr. Johnson was rather indignant at first and said he welcomed such scientific investigation, but broke down after a few minutes and admitted that he was nothing more than a pure and simple fake.

"Inspection of his electric chair and equipments developed the fact that this demonstration was carried on with a standard 18 volt arch, welded transformer. At no time during his act does he take as much as one volt of electricity. In fact, absolutely nothing, as the low voltage current fed to the head gear is short circuited and shunted back to the low voltage transformer by means of a trick connection on the back of the head gear, which engages with conductor concealed on the back of this fake electric chair.

"I did not publicly expose this faker on promise of both Mr. Johnson and the manager of the Hippodrome Theatre, that they would cut out all references to Sing Sing and its unfortunate inmates, as well as to eliminate from this act all statements that may tend to cause the general public to feel that a man was not scientifically and instantaneously killed when electrocuted at any prison."

All of which illustrates to what lengths men will go to capitalize on the sordid. Thousands of people were attracted to that performance by the misrepresentations contained in the notice which was sent out through the regular United States Mail.

In weighing the pros and cons in the matter of capital punishment it is wise not to let sentiment affect judgment. A famous sob sister once came to Sing Sing and asked me for a record of last words uttered by men about to die. The first words she received were a flat refusal. This morbid romanticizing of prisoners is a hindrance to sane solution of prison problems. The public is led either to weep over them or grit its teeth at them; led, indeed, to do everything but view the problem in its right perspective.

Prisoners, especially death house prisoners, are too often prone to romanticize their plight. One of the most callous gangsters Sing Sing has known, following to the Chair another member of his gang, actually made a grandstand play in the death chamber. When his turn came he asked for a rag, carefully wiped off the Chair and said:

"I've got to rub it off after that rat sat in it."

And something of the same flair for showmanship was in the hymn-singing negro who almost ran to the Chair, kissed it reverently and sang a sermon on how, to him, it was a chariot swinging low to life everlasting and a harp among the angel choirs.

I know of few instances where a convicted murderer did not have the loyalty of a mother, wife or sweetheart to sustain him—and also to make his going more bitter. In some cases I have had to stand silently and take the abuse of an outraged woman for what the State exacted of the man she loved; but as a rule the women are even more philosophical than the men: they seem to realize the practical impossibility of escape from the Chair once the lawyers have decided that nothing more can be done. But deep in the breast of every woman whose man-child or husband or lover has gone to the chair is resentment. Not resentment at his punishment so much as at the unevenness of justice that permits a rich slayer to remain alive, even free, while lowly men of perhaps no more guilt go to their doom.

The most trying part of the hapless task of ridding the world of the condemned is the contact with their womenfolk. When you have steeled yourself, as I have, to supervise the death of a young and healthy man; when you try, as I try, to let routine rule while doing everything within the law to make the end as merciful as possible, it's heartbreaking to run against the raw of human suffering. A mother called me—the mother of the young man—on the telephone after we had waited until the eleventh hour for her to come to the prison and make her last farewell:

"I can't bear to come, Warden," she said. "But will you do what I should like to do? When my boy is dead please put a white rose in his hand."

Of course, it was done.

It would serve no purpose to explore the heartaches and miseries inflicted on women when the Chair exacts its toll. Always back of every executed man, and, indeed, back of every imprisoned man, is a chain of suffering women and children who feel, not only th disgrace of the man's punishment, but the actual economic hardship this entails.

There are those who oppose the abolition of capital punishment because of sentiment for the family of the victim. "Think of the poor widow, suddenly bereaved, and her orphaned children." They are indeed deserving of every sympathy. Innocent, helpless victims of passion or hate or downright lawlessness. But are we competent to judge between two groups of equally innocent victims? Between dependents of the murdered and those of the murderer? How many of us really sympathize with the kin of the victim who begs for permission to "pull the switch," or "spring the trap?" We have outgrown and abandoned mere vengeance in the treatment of crime.

Two men went to the Chair on the same night. Both had been implicated in the same crime. When they came into the death house after their conviction they were apparently friendly. As the end approached their relations appeared strained. They were heard to abuse each other. Investigation disclosed the circumstance that one, a married man and father, had asked his accomplice, an unmarried man, to "take the rap" for the murder. The latter refused, saying, "If I go, you go." Both did go, carrying their hostility with them to the Chair.

It was during the governorship of Alfred E. Smith that four men were doomed to die in one night. Their cases had been affirmed by the Court of Appeals, and there seemed to be no hope. Toward evening of the night of the execution I received a call from the death house. The boys wanted to see me urgently. I hurried over. One of the condemned handed me without comment a letter. I read it carefully. It was a message to the Governor.

"For God's sake, Governor," it read, "save the other three boys. Clear my conscience. I am to blame. Save the three boys. Don't let four families suffer. One is enough. Please clear my conscience. I done the shooting. Please consider this."

The message was telephoned to the Governor's office. A respite was granted. Investigation followed, but the facts apparently were not convincing and all were subsequently executed.

On another occasion a prisoner sent for me a short time before the final hour. He seemed to be perturbed about something. I waited for him to speak. Finally he explained the reason for his agitation.

"Warden," he said, "if you found yourself in my position and there were extenuating circumstances; if another fellow did the actual shooting and he got away with it, would you tell?"

It was a difficult question to answer. I told him that it was a matter for his own conscience and told him to think it over before he took any further steps. He thought it over and several hours later went to the Chair apparently determined on his course of silence.

Thus the human drama that begins with the arrest of the man suspected of murder and continues through the trial, appeal and clemency hearings, is extended to the death house and into the electric chair.

Generally, however, the life of the prisoner awaiting execution is a drab affair. With the exception of a short exercise period, they are in their cells throughout the day and night. They are permitted to play cards, not permitted to the rest of the prisoner population, and checkers. Naturally only men in adjoining cells can play together on boards extending across both cells. Checkers are sometimes played by calling numbers which indicate certain moves. Ingenious prisoners have been known to use this method for compiling codes by means of which they were able to converse about intimate matters without the knowledge of their keepers.

Cells are searched (frisked) regularly and prisoners are moved frequently. Food is passed to each prisoner through an opening in the steel-barred doors which are not opened except for visiting, bathing, shaving and the daily exercise.

Men are permitted to smoke, but are not allowed matches. One of the most arduous duties of the keeper in the death house is to keep cigarettes, cigars and pipes lit and fuming.

Knives and forks are not allowed. A specially constructed soft spoon is used. Felt slippers are the only foot gear, except during the exercise period when they are permitted to wear shoes, specially made, without metal in the soles.

An old tradition of the death house called for monthly hair cuts for the condemned. But even a man who sees nothing ahead but the electric chair can be sartorially exact. So that I was hardly surprised several years ago to receive the following request signed by all the condemned men: "We would like to have two hair cuts a month instead of one. The reason we, the undersigned, beg this favor of you is that on account of the weather getting warmer, the hair grows faster than usual and if we don't get two hair cuts a month we not only look unkempt but we feel very uncomfortable."

Today the men in the condemned cells are shaved frequently by an inmate barber with a safety razor and are "hair cutted" twice monthly all the year round. The State does not want men awaiting execution to look scraggy or feel uncomfortable.

As a rule prisoners in the condemned cells are well behaved and give us little trouble. It may be surprising to know that one of our worst cases in the death house was a woman. She spent months with us awaiting the decision on her appeal. The judgment in her case was finally reversed and ultimately she won her freedom. But she was a holy terror all the while she was with us. She bulldozed the matrons who for some reason never reported her. She could swear like a trooper, smoked cigarettes incessantly, stampeded around in her cell like one bewitched and kept her wing in the death house in constant turmoil.

Only when I threatened to withdraw her visiting and writing privileges did she show any improvement. When she left the prison I breathed a sigh of relief, not only because she won out, but because we were genuinely happy to be rid of a petty tyrant.

It is a standing and unwritten rule of the death house that during the week preceding an execution all other condemned surrender their visiting privileges to the one due to die the following Thursday. On the day of an execution the radio is completely shut off from the death house.

The condemned men are watched carefully against suicide. Now and then, despite extraordinary vigil, prisoners do succeed in "cheating the Chair." The health of the men is looked after by our prison physicians who make daily rounds and the civiliar

334

nurses who respond instantly to first aid calls. Teeth are looked after. One particularly meticulous prisoner insisted that the dentist insert a gold cap on a defective tooth the day preceding his execution. He explained grimly that he wanted to get accustomed to pain so as not to flinch when the current was turned on the next night.

As a matter of fact, however, electricity is the most painless death producer yet devised by man. Death is instantaneous. The shock to the vital organs is infinitely faster than the speed with which conscious pain travels over nerve fibres.

From the standpoint of physical care the State of New York, as doubtless all other jurisdictions, leaves nothing undone to make the short lives of their condemned as comfortable as possible. Their spiritual wants are cared for by the regular prison chaplains who conduct special services for the men of various denominations.

For mental relaxation they are permitted books from the prison library, newspapers and magazines.

But while these men are passing their final days in drab existence, emotion, hysteria, sentiment, theatrics are playing their part in final attempts to avoid the extreme penalty. To me it is not the individual case that is of vital importance. It is the fact that all this is but a gesture. And a futile gesture at best.

Over ten thousand murders are committed in the United States every year. Not more than two percent of the murderers ever reach the death chamber. The ratio of convictions in prosecutions for murder throughout the country is less than 17 percent. In the eight States of the Union where capital punishment has been abolished there have been no excessive murders. In the balance of the States where the death penalty is still on the statute books, there has been no diminution of homicides. Periodic and short lived indignation aroused by particularly vicious crimes prompts prosecutors to bring the accused to an early trial. Yet when he picks his jury, at least fifty percent of the panel will ask to be excused from service on the ground that they are opposed to capital punishment. One thousand men have been examined before a jury of twelve could be finally chosen to sit on a capital case. What, after all, has the method of punishment for particular crimes to do with determining the guilt or innocence of the man at the bar of justice? And yet courts and lawyers struggle with this problem in every case where the death penalty is involved.

Capital punishment in the United States may be regarded as practically abolished through indifferent enforcement. But, by retaining the death penalty in its penal codes, it necessarily goes through the theatricals of the threat of enforcement. These very theatricals lend glamor to the accused fighting for life. The offence, no matter how heinous, is frequently disregarded in the new drama portrayed in the court room where prosecutors demand death for the prisoners and counsel pleads for mercy. These theatricals reach out beyond the atmosphere of the court room and weaken law enforcement all along the line.

The crime of which they were accused faded into insignificance at a recent murder trial where two defendants fought for their lives. The new sensation whetted the appetite of a morbid loving public which was appeased by fifty photographers on duty around the court house and one hundred and twenty newspaper reporters and special feature writers on constant vigil in the court room.

Remove capital punishment from the penal code and substitute life imprisonment, and judges, prosecutors, jurors, lawyers, the press and the public will be able to pass upon the merits of each case without passion or sentiment or emotion.

The force behind every murder does not stand out separate and apart from all other influences that have to do with human behavior. It may mark the beginning as well as the climax of a criminal career. It may be an incident to a life of crime indicating a latent mental or emotional disorder. Unless this is more widely appreciated, homicide will continue unabated.

The answer to our excessive murder rate is not to be found in "murder on the heels of murder." It is to be found rather in a revised penal code and a simplified criminal procedure that shall aim at speedy rather than hasty justice; that shall render judgment in an even, calm and deliberate proceeding; an aroused public conscience that shall demand more adequate measures of prevention. Every murder, whether instigated by passion, criminality or even gang warfare, reaches back to some form of social disaffection. Why not reexamine the fundamentals that have to do with shaping and strengthening the guide posts of good living and right thinking?

CHAPTER 10: IS THERE A WAY?

"They tell me," said a well-known educator, speaking to a University convocation, "you are a tough generation and you are. And so were your fathers and mothers. I knew them."

The 1929 Harvard Class slogan summed it up in a line. "Each age achieves its own damnation."

During the last decade, the American people have been literally smothered under an avalanche of voluminous data, tables of percentages and comparisons. Usually, each set of figures represents an enormous outlay of funds. It is difficult for the ordinary citizen to digest these often complicated and perplexing reports. Facts and figures are important only as we understand their application.

Fundamentals in the study of human behavior need no labyrinthian researches. They are understandable and clearly apparent to the layman. The course leads to the ranks of our youth.

In the last analysis, if there is to be any permanent diminution of crime, we shall have to look to our adolescents. Digesting, collating and comparing statistics and ratios we find that not every non-conforming child develops criminal traits; not every boy who steals an apple from a fruit stand or breaks a window becomes a burglar or a robber. Boys and men go through life under the constant handicap of an inferiority complex and remain law abiding. Men grumble and pro-

338

test against man's inhumanity to man during a lifetime of toil and hardship, but spurn the thought of a dishonest dollar. Even abnormal mentality is not symptomatic of social antipathy. The children of poor, ignorant parents have risen to leadership among men as champions of the humanities, or in the fields of practical research and social advancement. Nor has education, as we understand it, deterred criminal tendencies where there exists definite maladjustment to environment or intimate contacts. Such maladjustments may occur in the homes of the wealthy as in poor homes; it may exist among the children of the finest homes and most pleasant physical surroundings as in the slums of our great cities.

The ultimate source of behavior is in the individual. There is no royal road to the diagnosis of human emotions. Whether crime is the result of responsible or irresponsible motivations can best be left for determination by scholarly criminologists with a preference for didactics. We cannot hope for the total elimination of social non-conformity. We may, however, achieve a measure of abatement if we apply ourselves through every possible agency to mitigating the maladjustment by sympathetic measures during formative years.

"If we take the ordinary child," wrote a noted jurist, "that we see in our schools today, we must realize that those little hearts, those little minds, those little bundles of emotions have their difficulties, their suppressions, all those dark, mysterious turns of the workings of the heart and mind and human soul, which, when unaccounted for and unheeded, result disastrously."

Youthful delinquents as well as adult offenders have

been adjudged cowardly or precocious depending upon the approach of the investigator. It is always difficult to find a common denominator in human behavior.

"It strikes me dumb," Carlyle exclaims in *Past and Present*, "to look over the long series of faces, such as any full Church, Courthouse, London Tavern Meeting, or miscellany of men will show them. Some score or two years ago all these were little red-colored infants; each of them capable of being kneaded, baked into any social form you chose; yet I see now how they are fixed and hardened—into artisans, artists, clergy, learned sergeants, unlearned dandies, and can and shall now be nothing else henceforth!"

The criminal career of Adam Worth, one of the most notorious of criminals, is said to have begun in his school days when he was cheated by a schoolmate who gave him a new penny in exchange for two old ones. When he discovered his loss he determined never to be "done" again. He recovered those two pennies millions of times during his criminal experiences.

An executive of a social welfare organization in Connecticut was telling me of his boyhood days.

"There were six of us," he said. "We always studied together. Buddies, in fact. Three were daring fellows. Nothing feazed them. The other three, of whom I was one, were quiet and retiring. I believe we lacked the courage to do things and so we preferred to remain at home or spend our time in the library. All six grew to manhood. The three precocious youngsters reached the top—their names appeared frequently in the newspapers as notorious gangsters and racketeers. All are doing time in western penitentiaries. The other three are also well known. One is a famous surgeon, one a divine, the third—myself. So you see," he added smilingly, "it was probably lack of courage that kept us from going wrong."

I recalled a conversation I had with Francis (Two-Gun) Crowley. We were talking about the chances he took, about his gun fights. He told me about the first revolver he bought. "I knew when I bought that gun that it would land me in the Chair," he said. Yet that thought did not deter him from carrying and using it in the course of his escapades.

Another prisoner doing natural life put it differently.

"I was sixteen when I was arrested for murder. My associations at home and my environment generally were wholesome and led me far away from that sort of thing. I did not take kindly to the proposition that resulted in the killing. As a matter of fact, I refused to have anything to do with it. The two other fellows, there were three of us, walked me around for hours and asked me if I was turning yellow and all that. I had an idea that things wouldn't turn out right, but I wasn't going to be called a coward. I went with them and—here I am. Thirteen years in prison behind me and goodness knows how many more ahead."

A public official, much in the public eye, confided in me. "Pride did not let me be a cheap crook and I realized early in life that I hadn't the intelligence to be a successful one, so I remained honest."

The head of the forgery department of one of the major surety companies is quoted as saying that ninety per cent of the population of the United States are potential crooks and ninety-eight per cent are potential liars. A sweeping statement indeed, explanatory of

Bernard Shaw's thought on man's "marginal conscience." Yet it was Emerson who said that "I have never heard of a crime which I might not have committed."

Two elderly spinsters, after a lifetime spent in the service of their church, lost their fortune and took to forging checks in order to maintain their standard of living. They continued praying and asked for divine aid in their forgeries. Seventy-six million Bibles were distributed by a Bible Society in the last seventy-five years. Bibles can be had for the asking, yet a librarian in Brooklyn reports that the Bible is the most stolen book in her library.

Important Church and Religious Organizations do not always depend upon the tenets of their faith to persuade their agents and employees toward integrity and honesty of purpose. Treasurers, office employees, even ministers are bonded against larcenies and embezzlements. Surety companies, in seeking new clients, proudly maintain that they have paid out large sums against losses by churches and affiliated organizations.

The president of one of our large Eastern Railroad Systems is heard to say that if he were starving he would not hesitate to steal. Yet six million people who are out of work stand patiently and wearily in the long bread lines, preferring to wait their turn for alms rather than to forage on their own for money or sustenance. Hunger knows no law, but hunger is not responsible for extensive crime. As a matter of fact, the present drastic penal laws of the State of New York were enacted during a period of the greatest prosperity in the history of America.

Broken homes are responsible for much of our crime

problem. Yet the sons of millionaires, of educators, of clergymen, even bishops with presumably every advantage of education and fine living are involved in scandal and murder and drunken orgies that frequently startle the public.

Society matrons make luxurious and expensive trips to Europe. On their return they stand nervously by while customs officials ransack their trunks for undeclared importations and resent discoveries of jewelry and fine clothes that were omitted from the usual customs declarations in order to avoid comparatively small customs duties.

Gerald Chapman, notorious and unsuccessful bandit who was hanged in a Connecticut prison several years ago, explained that "stealing and going to prison seemed to be natural and ordinary events in my life."

It has been estimated that forty million people in the United States are persistent violators of the Eighteenth Amendment.

Students of penology frequently contend that our high crime rate is the result of the last wave of immigration from eastern and southern Europe which brought to these shores large numbers of immigrants from the so-called inferior races. Nordics from Western Europe are more desirable, they claim. Yet in the year 1860, while the Nordic immigration was at its height, 58,067 persons were actually convicted of crime in what is now a single county in New York City, 80 per cent of whom were foreign born. And in 1862, when nearly half of New York's population of 800,000 was foreign born, generally of Nordic origin, fully 80,000 or 10 per cent of its inhabitants were arrested for crime.

With a population of 6,930,446 in New York City in 1930, 29,646 reports of felonies were followed by 9,891 arrests. Foreign born in 1930 were 2,621,106 persons, mostly of non-Nordic races. Of these 2,006 were arrested for felonious crimes. Thus although the foreign born population of New York City is more than a third of the total population it produces only a little more than a fifth of the persons arrested for felonies. During the same year, foreign born prisoners in Sing Sing were 637 as compared with an average total prisoner population of 2,345.

President Hoover is an enthusiastic angler. Addressing the Izaak Walton League he said whimsically: "I assure you the increase of crime is due to a lack of those qualities of mind and character which impregnate the soul of every fisherman, except those who get no bites."

If Mr. Hoover meant by that sentiment that contentment is a safeguard against crime, he was right. Discontentment may not always lead to crime. In some cases it is the urge that prompts one to greater effort toward successful endeavor. In others it arouses a desperation that breaks down all moral barriers and sane thinking. Despite its great wealth, there is more evidence of this discontent in the United States than in any other country. The high standard of living which has become so intimately associated with American life is in a large measure responsible for the discontent that leads to crime. The luxuries of yesterday become the necessities of today. There is a sudden derangement in the economic structure. People are forced to change their living conditions. Erstwhile comforts have to be dispensed with. There is resentment. Bread alone will not satisfy. Some people find a sufficient outlet for their discontent in the ballot box; others are so overwhelmed as to lead them to suicide; still others take to crime. Thus we find that the ranks of criminals are greater in all countries with high standards of living. The higher the standard the higher the crime rate.

A peculiar sidelight on this problem of standard of living brings us into the realm of Prohibition which unwittingly changed the life and habits of the criminal classes.

There is no doubt that many thousands of heretofore honest men and women have been induced to join the ranks of law violators and criminals by the huge profits offered in the booze racket. The fact that the violation of the prohibition law has been declared from the bench to carry with it no moral stigma has, of course, encouraged new recruits to the ranks of illicit and ill-smelling and poisonous liquor trade. But it has had a more far-reaching effect. The lure of large and easy profits opened a new field to the professional criminal who, at the same time, was able to add to his retinue and followers by dangling before them hundreds and thousands instead of the mere tens or less of the lean days preceding the Volstead Act.

The old-time crook was lucky if he could afford a dingy furnished room in a disreputable part of the town. Automobiles were, of course, out of the question. Their consorts were habitués of equally disreputable environments. Photographs of beautiful women might have adorned the bare walls of their hall bedrooms, but the pretty woman of the stage and elsewhere would hardly notice the unkempt and sallow-faced fellow who stood at the stage door or stared at her on the street.

If it was ease or money that she sought, certainly she could not find it there.

Prohibition changed all that. The small change crook became the prosperous bootlegger. He began to move in different and higher circles. He supplied his barber with merchandise for his speakeasy and received, in return, in part payment the most careful sartorial treatment. He bought only the best in clothing and wearing apparel. To do his errands safely and quickly he must have high-powered automobiles. The rapid and constant inflow of money enabled him to spend lavishly. Impressionable women, some of them of respectable families, were attracted to the fashionably attired young man. Now he had a new standard in life to maintain and he sought a new home in luxurious apartments which he furnished with a lavish hand. The cheap crook had come into his own.

But like all good things, this does not last. The day comes when the profession finds itself crowded. Too many are after this easy money. Business is slow and after a while competitive and somewhat hazardous. Profits are lean. Our former cheap crook is hard pressed. His woman is peevish. His landlord insistent and his clothes are fraying. Something will have to be done. Rather than give up all his new possessions and his new standards, he will forage for big game. And so he takes to robbery. It is quicker than burglary and surer. The young fellow in the corner pool room hears all this. Between drinks in the back room he learns about the luxurious apartments and the lovely ladies. He begins his apprenticeship as a delivery boy for the prosperous bootlegger. He is an apt pupil. He learns quickly. He, too, goes foraging. He wants

346

his money, and wants it quickly. A hold-up takes but a minute or two. He is not as deliberate as his older prototype. His heart beats faster, the hand which holds the revolver is nervous. His victim responds too slowly. The young robber is terror-stricken. His fingers tighten convulsively on the trigger. For months he will linger in the death house wondering how it all happened. If he could reason it out, he could explain that it was the high standard of living among crooks.

Prohibition may be responsible for a large percentage of our crimes of violence. But violent crimes do not, after all, constitute the sum total of our problems of behavior. As a matter of fact, out of 41,023 complaints for felonies and misdemeanors in the City of New York for 1930, only 1,166 were for robbery. Compared with the total value of stolen property, the fruits of robbery as of all crimes of violence are almost negligible. One robbery resulting in a prison sentence of twenty years yielded twenty cents. Another, attended with murder and a conviction with the finale of the death house and the electric chair, yielded exactly one dollar. The more spectacular crimes of violence involving large sums are as a rule desperate battles ending in death for the aggressors as well as the defenders. And from an economic standpoint, crimes involving large sums of money and property are non-violent and have to do with commerce in its varied branches and aspects.

I read in the morning newspapers of an impending crash in Wall Street. Inflation is about to be deflated. Bulls will soon become lambs. Millionaires will be reduced to paupers. Affluent brokers will stare nervously at their diminishing bank balances. There will be a wave of suicides. There will also be a procession of brokers to Sing Sing. I admonish my Principal Keeper. "Better clean out some of those empty cells. We'll be needing them soon. And how are we fixed for clerical jobs? Stenographers, typists and the like? We shall be getting a lot of them when the dust settles down." Here are crimes that involve millions, if not billions of dollars annually.

A bank is closed. More millions lost. The press clamors for investigations. There are sure to be indictments and convictions and—additional prisoners for Sing Sing. And so more bankers are added to our already large population.

The Legislature orders an investigation of the judiciary and lawyers generally. Its activities will be reflected in the group of lawyers who will find their way to the prison gate.

And so each social, economic and political upheaval is mirrored in the composition of Sing Sing's prison population. The average citizen reads about it in the newspaper over his cup of coffee. If he is at all socially minded he will wonder about it. Crimes by rich and poor, by educated and illiterate, by those of high as well as low birth, by skilled and unskilled. What can be done about it? Isn't there a way, a definite, determined way of coping with the problem?

Whether he is a psychologist or a psychiatrist, or an ordinary physician, the investigator will find it difficult to determine the exact moment when the crime thought entered the brain of the offender.

Scientists, in seeking cures for disease, spend years in trying to identify and separate the germ in order

348

that they may experiment with preventive measures. Not so with human emotions. Passion will not lend itself to experiment and will not stay within set rules. Men will withstand temptation at one moment and fall the next. One of our prisoners at Sing Sing, a former public official, is said to have scorned a gratuity of $50,000 a year or two prior to his conviction of bribery for a much lesser sum.

All the woodwork in the old prison office at Sing Sing was carved by a prisoner about twenty-five years ago. It was an extraordinarily fine job and displayed excellent workmanship, and still excites the admiration of visitors. The prisoner toiled patiently. He apparently possessed every capacity to make good on his release. Yet when he was discharged at the expiration of his prison term he could not adjust himself and was soon returned for a new crime. Was the fault entirely his? The fact that he could, while in prison, be the splendid workman would seem to indicate that there was no opportunity to give expression to his art and workmanship outside.

A prisoner who spent the better part of his adult life in prison is about to be discharged. He stands before me waiting for a word of encouragement. "Don't come back, Jim," I caution him. "It's the book for you the next time. Remember." He will be a fourth offender and sent up for life if he is again convicted of crime. "Gee, I'd like to go straight, Warden. I'd like to be like other fellows. I hope I can get a job." He hesitates, then adds: "But you understand, Warden, I've got to earn enough for a living." How much is his living, I ask. He expects at least fifty dollars a week. If he can earn that he would be safe. And he would give value received for his wage. There is no use telling him that he will find it hard to obtain employment. He is not skilled in any trade. No use explaining to him that eighty-five per cent of the American people earn less than $1,500 a year. No use telling him about the standard of living so difficult to maintain on that average earning. He will answer that there is nothing wrong with the standard, but something radically wrong with the unequal distribution of wealth that makes it impossible to maintain that standard.

Yet it is a fact little appreciated by the average citizen that three out of every four prisoners from State prisons do not return for new crimes. That fact is not as widely publicized as is the failure of the fourth. First, because arresting and prosecuting authorities do not hesitate to acquaint the public with their successful campaigns against experienced offenders; secondly, because the public likes its sensational news served frequently and well adorned.

Utopia, as pictured by Sir Thomas More, was a world without crime. Certainly without lawyers for whom that philosopher had little or no respect. I am not so sanguine about the possibility of a human society without the temptations that lead to offences against the social order and authority. But I feel that, except for the person who is the occasional offender, such phenomena as crime waves may be altogether eliminated. Crime may not be a disease, as it is commonly understood, but there is no more reason or necessity for so-called crime waves than for epidemics or plagues.

The average citizen, complacent in his philosophy of life, shrugs his shoulders. "I know the reason for all this. There is no respect for law." Perhaps not. How are we going to create that respect? Preach that doctrine to the adult prisoner and he will argue that he can have little respect for a law which punishes only the sap and the bungler and does not seem to be able to reach the rich and the powerful. A law that gives the convicted man the right to appeal but withholds it from the fellow who is unable to hire counsel or who cannot afford the expense of a printed case on appeal. A law that depends for its interpretation upon the ability of the accused to retain proper counsel. A law that permits the affluent to continue his place in society while he is out on bail pending trial and appeal, while the poor and unfortunate languishes in prisons and jails without recourse in the event of his acquittal or reversal of conviction, if he is fortunate enough to carry his case to the higher courts. A law that regards the deed rather than the man; that disregards dependents who are left destitute while their provider is "paying the penalty." A law that compels a man to spend years in comparative idleness, refusing him the human right to help in the support of his dependents with the labor which he is anxious to perform during his incarceration.

"You cannot be heard to complain," is the answer of society, "you should have thought of all that before you committed the crime which landed you in prison."

A legislator in Albany put it tersely to me when I argued for the restoration of time compensation for good behavior in prison, which had been abrogated with the enactment of the so-called Baumes Laws in 1926. "We did not send for them," he commented. "We don't owe them anything."

It is blind justice talking. The kind of justice that the civil law has long abandoned. For side by side with the law of property and contracts there has grown up the equally, if not more important, institution of equity. It was discovered by inspired and far-sighted jurists in the early centuries that law, standing alone and relying upon its own precedents, must work injustice and hardships upon litigants. Equity stands higher than precedent because it interprets statutes in the light of current necessities and with due regard to human emotions. That is lacking in criminal jurisprudence. A logical, common sense view of the problems of behavior must lend itself to the equities of every situation: The complainant in a court of equity, if he is to be successfully heard, must, in legal parlance, come into court with clean hands. Society, represented by the State, is the complainant in our criminal courts. It does not require elaborate research to establish the fact that our complainant does not come into court with clean hands. Has it not, in a large measure, contributed to the condition of which it is complaining?

A man in the thirties stands before the bar. He has been convicted as a fourth offender and the court has no alternative but to impose a life sentence. The law demands that. It is its due and there can be no deviation. Who is this man? What are his antecedents? What has he done?

The Judge regards him with compassion; the prosecutor with a measure of pride in accomplishment; the jury with sympathy; the newspaper representative with impersonal curiosity. He is good copy. This man is not vicious. He seems to be a quiet, well-mannered person. There is a sudden hush in the courtroom as the judge reads the reports handed up to him by investigators. Not that they will affect the disposition of this man's case. But they will give the Judge an idea of the development of a life which he must now remove forever from wife and children and perhaps parents. Let us look over the Judge's shoulder and read with him.

Max (the name will do for the class we have in mind) is a native born American of foreign born parents. He attended the public schools of a congested section of the metropolis. He was a fairly good student. He was a part of the great army of children, thirty millions of them, who were undergoing the process of Americanization. He was being trained in the traditional method. Lessons had to do with reading and writing and kindred subjects. A thoughtful comment on the American School system is that of John Dewey: "Moral Education in school is practically hopeless when we set up the development of character as a supreme end, and at the same time treat the acquiring of knowledge and the development of understanding, which of necessity occupy the chief part of school time, as having nothing to do with character."

Mass education that disregards individual inclination and response has long been denounced by educators. Yet nothing has been done to correct it. The responsibility of the school ended with the close of the session. Thereafter the boy was permitted to roam at will. The home, where the spirit of America was still unfelt, did not satisfy the boy's mind. The privately controlled boy's clubs in the neighborhood were not within his reach or were already overcrowded.

Max sought companionship elsewhere. He found it

with other youngsters of his age and neighborhood on the street corner or in back alleys. It was the kind of association that led to truancy. Truancy led to court which in turn led to Protectories or Children's homes. A short term in an institution and Max was again returned to his home and his school. Meantime he had learned new lessons in life. Old gang friendships were renewed and new ones encountered. Another turn in an institution. Max was developing into an unsocial and ungovernable youth. He completed his school course and graduated from the eighth grade without a steady purpose in life, without a trade, skilled or unskilled. He took on odd jobs, but he was now old enough to join the gang in pool rooms and card games. The uniformed policeman, who represented law and order, was not a respected officer. He was feared and circumvented. Max became a defender of what he came to consider his freedom of action. If that meant hiding or scurrying here and there in his and other neighborhoods, he did just that. To Max law did not inspire respect but fear. Whom men fear, they do not respect.

It was not long before the earnings of Max's unsteady employment did not suffice for his avocations in gambling and pool rooms and loose women. He drifted naturally toward petty stealing. He drifted just as naturally to a reformatory.

On his discharge he returned to his old neighborhood. Many doors of possible employment that might have been open to him before his conviction were now closed. Clean association was barred to him. But the old gang welcomed him with open arms. Max must live. He went forth to find his living. His course led him to prison where he remained for several years.

354

Still a young man, he was discharged. He had advanced no further than when he was sent up to the Big House. The world treated him with its former disdain. Three times was this repeated.

And now Max stood before the court awaiting the word that was to send him away for life.

But there were periods when Max thought he had found himself. During those periods he worked at honest employment. During one of those periods he married. Children were born. Max was now a father with real responsibilities. But he could not easily unlearn the things and ideas that had been implanted during the years of his confinement.

As Max stood facing the Judge, three women sat in the rear of the courtroom. One, almost middle aged, was his wife; two young girls were his daughters. They sat quietly with tear-stained faces, their eyes fixed on the Judge who was about to pronounce the judgment. The words are spoken and Max is led away, followed by three pairs of eyes.

A few weeks ago Max was in the Chapel at Sing Sing during one of the performances of the prison annual Christmas show. At his side stood a young girl. Her hand was in his. I passed by and the prisoner stopped me. There was pride in his voice as he said, "Warden, I want you to meet my daughter." I talked with her for a few moments. Finally she took hold of her father's arm and looked up to me. "Warden, please take good care of my Daddy," she said, with eyes that were suspiciously moist.

Is Max an isolated case? Hardly. For the records of Sing Sing show that ninety-seven percent of our prisoners were never associated with any Boys' Club, or any of the other juvenile associations where boys learn how to spend their leisure in wholesome recreation. Seventy-five percent of our prisoners are not skilled or learned in the mechanics or trades. Ninety-nine percent were not actively interested in church organizations. Seventy-five percent came to us with previous institutional experiences. That is true of first as well as fourth offenders. For our present methods of handling offenders are developing fourth offenders out of first and intermediary offenders. Seventy-five percent of our prisoners make good, at least negatively. The wonder is that it is not otherwise; that the same ratio are not returned.

Persons between the ages of fifteen to thirty constitute fifty percent of the population of the United States, yet they contribute seventy-three percent of our criminals. The problem is, therefore, with the young. Unless society can show that it has done its full duty toward its youth and adolescents, it cannot be heard to say, "We did not send for them." Its hands are not clean. It is not free from guilt.

America spends large sums on education. But its bill for luxuries is three times as high. It is niggardly in providing for social advancement which is left almost entirely to charity and private contributors. A well-known educator promised a decade ago that with the opening of every school he would close a jail. His promise has not been fulfilled. He did not appreciate the importance of regulated and well-supervised leisure. He did not appreciate the fallacy of an education that taught the child to read but neglected the opportunity to teach him to work or even to play.

Vocational training and guidance is a proper subject for school administration. Many children are manual minded, and do not respond to book learning. There should be some method of determining inclinations and fitness for definite vocations during childhood, and school careers should be moulded accordingly. Among the important prerequisites for the educated man, I regard most important the one "that an educated man must have not only general culture but also training for a specific occupation." With vocational training there will be less truancy and less work for the juvenile courts.

Police clamp down the lid and clean out illicit pool rooms where boys in their 'teens congregate amid companionship and associations that presage ill for their future. But no substitute is provided where these boys may re-group under more favorable auspices. That leisure is an important factor in schooling has been recognized by educators throughout the ages. The ancient Grecian philosopher taught that "preparation for the right use of leisure should be the chief end of education." It is a potent influence in encouraging a clean outlook on life. Boys as well as adults will play in groups. The boy who is a member of a gang cannot be effectively treated, except in relation to the life of the group of which he is a part. Mental snarls can best be avoided and ironed out in informal but healthy social relationships. Educators and social workers know from actual experience that juvenile delinquency gives way before supervised playgrounds and well organized boys' and kindred organizations. Some of our larger centers of population report that whereever new playgrounds are opened juvenile delinquency in that neighborhood drops perceptibly. And yet reliable authority has it that three out of every five children in our greatest cities are without adequate opportunity for wholesome play.

Most of our municipal governments are planning to eradicate their slums. They are widening narrow streets and demolishing dark and shabby tenements to replace them with homes where the sun and air will safeguard health and insure simple comforts of decent living. Equally important is the adequate provision for extra-educational activities for the young. In every city square of congested areas, I should like to see a Boys' and Girls' Club House, publicly subsidized, on a par with any other part of our elaborate system of education. This may be a large undertaking. But it is a worth-while investment. It is an insurance premium against delinquency, the cost of which is almost negligible in comparison with the toll, in life and property, of even ordinary crime rates. Operation of Boys' Clubs is estimated at about $15 per capita annually, whereas maintenance alone of a prisoner in Sing Sing and all other penal institutions is well beyond $400 a year.

All this has to do with prevention. There are other factors. There is the Church. Does the minister know his congregants? Does he know how they live and how their children are growing up? Does he invite the confidence of the young? Or would he prefer to be the crusader for "all" the people and neglect those who live around the corner from his church and who need the intimate touch and guidance to save not only their souls but their minds and hearts. One of the reasons why men and women do not take their religion more seriously is that the church and the pulpit have gone in for polemics and controversialism rather than as sowers of seed in their local communities. Ninety-nine percent of our prisoners at Sing Sing are religionists in name only. They have never been actively interested or affiliated with their churches. Who is to blame? We hear, now and then, of church workers convicted of crime, and I wonder how much the emphasis of ritualism over socialization has to do with it?

It has been estimated that twenty-five percent of all children in the United States live in broken homes, broken by death, desertion, separation or divorce. But the studies of the various delinquent groups show that from forty to seventy percent come from broken homes. An established rule of modern civilization is that the world owes no man a living. But society surely owes every child a home. Our practice of sending children to juvenile institutions where experience guides inexperience in the ways of vice and filth is one of the tragedies of our national life. Of 1,393 new admissions to Sing Sing during 1931, 343 are graduates of juvenile homes and reformatories. Compare these figures with the records of 3,307 dependent children in New York City, who were given individual treatment, all of whom were under sixteen years of age. They remained in private homes for periods ranging between one and five years between January 1, 1900, and January 1, 1910. Of these only eleven were arrested for serious offences.

The average citizen is impatient with these figures and thoughts. What has all that to do with crime? Look at the gunmen who turn our public thoroughfares into battlegrounds for their private feuds; or the young rascals who rob and kill without mercy. Those ideas may help in the future, but how deal with the present problem?

Aside from the fact that many of these rascals are the products of our own inadequate facilities of supervision and guidance in childhood, it would be interesting to look them over. The police have their orders. "Shoot to kill." A news film shows police rookies at gun practice. They are running with hands grasping revolvers. Facing them is a row of dummies. As each man passes he empties his gun, taking rapid and careful aim at the heart which is plainly marked on the figure. They seem to be learning fast, for those hearts are soon perforated with shots. These men are developing good marksmanship. We read in the day's news of a running battle with a gang of rowdies. Innocent by-standers are killed or maimed. It ends in the death of all the gunmen. The public smiles contentedly. Our first line of defense is holding fast. We can depend on those fellows. Those gangsters got what they deserved. And it saved the state the job of putting them to death later on.

Yes, it is a serious problem. Especially so, since most of the younger prisoners now at Sing Sing were convicted of robbery. In 1920, crimes of violence constituted a little over 13 percent of our prisoner population. Prior thereto the rate of sentences for robbery fluctuated between 3 percent in 1850 and 7 percent in 1910. This year it exceeds 42 percent. The figures for the month of August, 1931, are the highest in the history of Sing Sing—44.7 percent.

In 1931, our admissions for robbery were 532, and of these 155 were between the ages of sixteen to twenty, inclusive. Contrary to general notions there were no records of either drug habits or other narcotic charges against these men. As a matter of fact, the youngest conviction of robbery showing drug habits was thirty-two years.

One hundred percent of our sixteen-year-old prisoners were robbery cases; the balance as follows:

17 Years of age—91.7 percent for robbery
18 Years of age—70   percent for robbery
19 Years of age—81.7 percent for robbery
20 Years of age—74.7 percent for robbery

The records of the Police Department of the City of New York show a like percentage. Of 1,079 cases of robbery with guns in 1930, 410 were committed by young men, boys in fact, between the ages of sixteen and twenty. There has been no appreciable diminution of this type of crime despite the fact that the percentage of convictions is higher for robbery than any other crime and despite the further fact that prison sentences have been extended for robbery and generally enforced.

Wherein lies the answer to all this? What has brought this plague among us? Where will it end?

Once more we must return to the lure of easy money so well advertised in the accounts of rum runners and bootleggers. Again we are faced with the high standard of living—wine, women and song come high in these days of generally higher levels. Difficult budgets must be balanced. Lack of the necessities of life does not urge these boys to crime. As a matter of fact, many of them are gainfully employed in honest labor at the outset of their careers in crime. Jobs are abandoned only when the first attempt is successful and "getting away with it" encourages further depredations.

It is remarkable how persistent has been the neglect of our State and National legislators in dealing with the problem of the manufacture and sale of firearms. Postal officials are exasperated to a frenzy in discovering an allegedly obscene pamphlet in the mails. Prosecutions are instituted, fines and punishments inflicted. Yet the law permits the mailing of guns and revolvers—to be used only for illegal and dangerous purposes. And in most jurisdictions there is no restriction in the distribution of firearms. It does not require many hours' journey from New York, where there does exist a form of restriction, to nearby states and cities where guns are available for a price.

The unregulated and unchecked manufacture and sale of firearms is one of the major causes for violent crime in this country. Federal legislation is in order. Public spirited citizens have urged it for years. Why not leave reparations and international debts—yes, even Prohibition—long enough to permit us to tackle this pressing problem? The police are doing as well as can be expected. Lives have been sacrificed in the performance of their duties. High-powered automobiles, machine guns, revolvers—all work against them. For the purpose of the robber is to avoid detection and escape his pursuers. Yet the majority of robbers are finally captured.

Thus we have the man in custody. Our failure in prevention during his childhood and adolescence has developed a type—the wayward. Our failure to strengthen the hands of our police has encouraged the wayward to become the criminal. He is now in our hands. Prosecution takes a hand.

The prosecutor is, generally speaking, an honest man. He has been elected upon a platform that promised to drive the criminal out of his jurisdiction. He is not concerned with the adjoining jurisdictions which will be enriched by the promised exodus. The time will come when the prosecutor in other counties or states or municipalities will also be suddenly aroused to extraordinary activity. He too will make a drive against crime and criminals. Word will go forth that if there is an exodus from his jurisdiction he will be satisfied. There will be a return trek. And so this shuttlecock policy of law enforcement will continue merrily on until —but we are getting ahead of the story.

Our young criminal paces nervously the narrow cell in the city jail. He has sent word to his parents or friends. If he is of good family who were not aware of their offspring's escapades the fond parents get busy. Their boy must be saved. Bail is expensive, but there is no hesitation in tapping savings of a lifetime for bail and high-priced counsel. The fellow with good "connections" is likewise freed on bail pending indictment and trial. Meantime the prisoner without friends, or with parents who cannot afford to obtain bail or hire counsel, awaits the earlier disposition of his case. Public sentiment demands prompt action. It is given to the fellow who cannot afford the privileges of bail or competent counsel. A lawyer is assigned by the court. Attorney interviews his client.

"I've looked up your record, boy," he tells him. "It's your first offence. I think I can get the District Attorney to accept a plea for robbery in the third degree."

The sixteen-year-old boy, inexperienced in law or courts or procedure, waves him away. "Nothing doing," he exclaims, "it's first degree or nothing. I'll stand trial."

The lawyer regards him curiously. He does not bother to explain the differences in degrees. "I think I can get you what you want," he smiles.

The prosecutor is gratified. The defendant will take a plea. The court is gratified. No time wasted in useless procedure.

"How do you plead?" the boy is asked by the clerk of the court. The lawyer assigned by the court speaks up. "The defendant pleads to the indictment. Robbery in the first degree."

Judgment is swift. Fifteen to thirty years for the robbery. Five years additional for the gun.

Only when he arrives in the Big House and talks with his newly-found friends, will this simple boy discover that he could have chosen better.

That robbery in the third degree, while a higher number, carried with it a lower sentence. And while he is doing his time, he will learn that the two other fellows are still out on bail. That they are back in the bosom of their families, or have resumed their previous associations without restraint or supervision. That witnesses have disappeared or public fury has died down. Perhaps years will pass before their cases will be called for trial. It may be that both boys have learned their lesson and during the interval have adjusted themselves. They do not need further punishment. It may be that they have acquired new friends and have climbed higher in their criminal avocations. Whatever the facts are, they do not join the poor, ignorant prisoner who will be thirty-six before he can be considered for release on parole.

Justice is not stern when it permits situations like these. It is not equitable. It is not honest.

The Penal Law of New York State contains about nine hundred and sixty sections. The Code of Criminal Procedure contains many more. Almost every offence is divided into degrees of crimes and punishments. How much simpler and more equitable would it be if our Penal Law could be simplified? A man either commits a crime or he does not. He is either guilty or not guilty of wrong. Why make a distinction between the larceny of one hundred dollars or less—one Grand Larceny punishable with five years or more of imprisonment, the other petit larceny, a misdemeanor punishable by a term in the workhouse or reformatory? Is the man who is convicted or given a plea to robbery in the second degree less vicious or less dangerous to the peace of the community than the one who is charged and convicted of robbery in the first degree? Why not say to the boy or man charged with crime, "You have done wrong. Let us find out about you. We are concerned not only with your particular act, but also with your personality. Perhaps we can ascertain the exact nature of your delinquency. Are your home influences bad? Is your environment unsavory? Have you been led and influenced by bad companionship? Would teaching you a trade help? Is there something wrong with your physique? Or, is your mentality so warped as to necessitate your permanent segregation?" Let us be equitable about this.

A judge of one of our cosmopolitan districts was confronted recently with a peculiar situation. A boy of six shot his playmate with his father's hunting gun. There was no question of the boy's guilt. One editor reasoned that the father was equally guilty for having allowed the gun within easy reach of the youngster. However that may have been, the six-year-old boy stood before the court awaiting his fate. Should the boy be sentenced to death, to life imprisonment, or be confined for an indefinite period? The judge did something novel. He called together a conference of several of the public-spirited citizens of the community. He laid the problem before them. "You help the court decide this case. What shall be done with this boy?"

Strange to relate the boy was sent back to his parents. The committee of citizens decided that though he had actually committed a murder in shooting his playmate he was not really a criminal. He could be made one if sent to an institution where he would be compelled to associate with other young but experienced delinquents. His life would be blasted almost beyond repair. Back at home, with more careful supervision and guidance, he would live a normal life and develop his better traits. Naturally he would thenceforth be subjected to close scrutiny. His conduct would have to be exemplary, better than the average.

The youngster with a gun, be he six or sixteen or twenty, is dangerous only when he is in possession of the gun. Generally he is not vicious. Put the gun beyond his reach and he will not be tempted or run riot. Without arms there will be no necessity or purpose for his stealing automobiles, in which crime the youngster predominates. Of 2,509 automobiles stolen from the public highways of New York City in 1930, over 50 percent, or 1,414 were taken by boys between the ages of sixteen and twenty.

The judge who called in the committee of his fellow citizens to help him in the disposition of his case, hit upon a theory that would work well in all our criminal courts.

The prosecutor has done his work. He has established the guilt of the accused. The judge has seen to it that the defendant had a fair trial. Thenceforth the convicted defendant, whether he be juvenile or minor or adult, should be dealt with by an impartial board of experts whose duty and responsibility shall be to determine the mode and method of further procedure.

The thoughtful citizen is hardly impressed with the periodic and often meteoric popular acclaim that promotes a mediocre public servant to high office merely on the basis of his reputation as a prosecutor who relentlessly insists upon long prison sentences or as judge who follows out the letter of the law in imposing them. In doing so, they may temporarily rid society of dangerous criminals, but their work is never ended. An example is the crime of kidnapping, which is a serious offence, punishable by sentences of extreme severity. Yet in New York City, 1930 shows an increase of over one hundred percent in convicted kidnappers over 1929. This, despite the fact that a prison term of fifty years is not uncommon for the convicted kidnapper.

Before a convicted offender is sent to prison or reformatory, all surrounding circumstances should be carefully investigated to determine whether the interests of society and the possibility of readjustment of the individual would not be better served if he were permitted to do his time outside the walls in supervised employment and in more or less normal environment. Whatever else we do not understand about this crime business, we do know that sending one man to prison does not in itself deter another from attempting similar crimes, nor does a term in prison cure the prisoner of his criminal tendencies where his philosophy of life leans toward criminality. By differentiating between the criminal act and the philosophy of criminality we can determine more readily the promising personality which would respond to guidance rather than to punishment.

Doing time outside the prison walls after conviction but before the imposition of a prison sentence is what we have come to know as probation. Not all offenders approve of probation. Many of them would prefer to do their "bits," and thus pay their debt to society for the violation of what they cynically term "the eleventh commandment," that of being caught. They do not take kindly to supervision. They would rather wipe the slate clean and on their emergence try over again. Nevertheless, the records of our probation departments throughout the country show that between eighty-five and ninety percent of men on probation make good and are not returned for new crime. It is a remarkable showing in view of the generally inadequate probationary personnel, lean budgets and lack of uniform and centrally controlled methods of supervision.

Probation removes sensationalism from criminality. For it compels the offender to continue to support his dependents; it regulates his every act; it determines the kind and character of his employment; it asks questions about his associates; it holds the threat of immediate incarceration, without the prolonged and expensive procedure of Grand Juries and district attorneys and courts, in the event of a lapse from conditions imposed, whether of omission or commission. Probation withholds the stigma of prison from the offender who can be saved to society. Probation recognizes the failures of association, of environment, of home life; it aims to rectify them. Its hands should be strengthened by competent personnel, by ample budgets, by strong and determined policies.

The Sentencing Board will naturally find here and there an individual who needs special attention. He may be the mental defective and should be cared for in an institution for the criminal insane or a home for mental cases. He may be a hopeful case but requires training for a definite vocation—a failure of our public school system—or he may be suffering from a physical ailment. It may be that he lacks social responsibility beyond hope of early correction. These need institutional care. They should therefore be segregated. No human mind, be he judge, prosecutor, psychologist or psychiatrist, can determine in advance how long it will take to correct these faults.

Whatever the purpose of segregation, two objectives must be ever apparent. The offender should be made to realize that his obligations to society continue despite his imprisonment; society must appreciate that its duty to its ward is also a continuing one. One of the most farcical of all our penal traditions is that of maintaining the prisoner in comparative idleness and at the same time supporting his dependents on quasi-public charities. The prisoner loses all sense of responsibility.

I would make the prisoner work. I would pay him a living wage, which should maintain him in prison and provide for his family on the outside. To accomplish this end, it will be necessary to re-write our prison labor laws. Public institutions should be compelled to purchase their supplies from prisons and other correctional institutions. Union labor has been heard to complain about prison labor. It forgets that the cost of maintaining thousands of men in idleness, and at the same time supporting their dependents at public expense, is great and ultimately more hazardous from the point of view of economy and public security.

I would not keep a man in custody one day longer than is necessary to establish the fact of his ability to resume his responsibilities outside the walls.

Society must deal with this problem in a human, understanding way. But it should always have that punch in reserve. The hopeless pervert, the man definitely headed for unending battle with society, the gang leader who lives on vice and filth and misfortune—these and kindred characters are proper subjects for lengthy, if not permanent confinement and segregation.

Release from prison does not necessarily mean, as a matter of fact it should never mean, freedom from all supervision. No prisoner should be discharged from physical custody and be permitted to resume his place in society without some measure of moral restraint. Some paroled men need more, some less intimate guidance. But, having once succumbed to delinquency and crime, and his weakness having been established, he should be made to prove his capacity for self-restraint and his corrected attitude toward conformity and authority. Thus parole comes into being as an important branch of correctional methods.

Here also prisoners do not always approve. We have had cases in Sing Sing where prisoners have preferred to do their maximum sentences rather than chance parole on discharge at the termination of their minimum terms. Most prisoners will, however, welcome the opportunity for freedom under the conditions imposed by the Parole Board. Successes on parole (keeping out of further trouble) have averaged from seventy-five to eighty-five percent. An encouraging result, even if the successes are largely negative, when we remember that prisons harbor the failures of all intermediary institutions and the apparently more vicious types of first offenders.

Parole acts not only as a restraining influence on the discharged prisoner. It is as well his guide and protector from persecution. The man who emerges from prison has a double burden. He is a convicted criminal and also an ex-convict. He is at the mercy of every ill-intentioned member of the police force and personal enemy. It is not often that we hear sentiments like the one expressed by a public-spirited citizen who was told that his next door neighbor was a discharged prisoner. "He's a better man than I. He has paid his debt." More often the attitude of the public is expressed in the words of a merchant who greeted one of our civilian clerks with a cordial "Hello Sing Sing," and later apologized that he had informed the curious gentlemen within hearing that our clerk was an official and not an ex-prisoner. Not infrequently do we meet the complacent gentleman who nods toward a serious-minded worker or clerk with the remark, "You wouldn't think that man is an ex-convict." As if it were beyond all imagination for a discharged prisoner to engage in honest labor or employment! Or the man who turns on his heel from the applicant for a job, without bothering about qualifications or responsibility, when informed that the man has done time in prison.

As an important division in the scheme of correction, parole deserves considerably more encouragement than it has been receiving. Four thousand six hundred and forty-nine discharged prisoners are now under the jurisdiction of the Division of Parole of the State of New York. The total budget for this department for 1931 was about $400,000, or $80.67 per man. The cost per capita of our prisons and reformatories is about $410 per year. As a matter of pure economy, parole is to be preferred to institutional confinement. As a corrective influence it could become far superior. Parole should be administered by men of strong and independent minds, uninfluenced by politics or hysteria. It should not hesitate to restrain the doubtful applicant, and should have the courage to discharge from physical custody the man who appears to be a good risk, regardless of the kind or character of his crime. Nor should it hesitate to recall any of its wards if there is a definite challenge against the peace of the community or where lapses occur. Parole supervisors should be capable, socially minded and well trained.

But above and beyond all these, prevention, police, prosecution, probation, prison and parole, in the order of their sequence as related to the problem of behavior, is the attitude of the public. There must be a more popular response toward preventive measures; less desire for the bizarre and glorification.

We should encourage and sustain the efforts of all agencies that have to do with detection, correction and supervision, and extend a willing and helping hand to the boy or man seriously determined to come back. Therein lies the way.

CHAPTER 11: GROPING ...

FOUR hundred thousand men and women fill our prisons and jails throughout the country; one hundred and twenty-five thousand of them in our major state and federal prisons. Every prisoner has been tried and convicted of a criminal act. The law decrees the manner of his atonement. During the period of atonement he must be segregated from kith and kin. He must do hard labor; he must become a penitent. The theory of the law is that the convicted prisoner shall return to society straightened out in thought and vision: repentent of his sins; respectful of authority; with the desire for conformity. The law aims still further. It has evolved an elaborate system of procedure and penalties intended to act first as warnings and admonitions, secondly as chastisement and punishment; thirdly as reformative influences.

Has the law attained its objectives in all or any of these purposes? The answer is to be found in the ever-increasing number of penal and correctional institutions, and in the constantly increasing ranks of prisoners within their walls.

What is this thing Law that brands man with the indelible insignia of shame from which he can never escape?

Law is the process by which one section of the people tries to impose its will upon another.

In the name of the Law, a crimson trail has established itself in the wake of our civilization.

Law is the product of lawyers whose breath of life is precedent and tradition to which they have pinioned government in an ever tightening knot.

Law has encased itself in lifeless tomes, in marble palaces wherein funereal garbed intellects pronounce its decrees in solemn monotony.

Law seeks to regulate human conduct. It is failing in its objective because it disregards and is utterly insensible of human emotions. It has set itself up as the symbol of authority, demanding respect and obedience, not because it is just and honest but because it is the Law. To put it more clearly, Law has lost its moral tone. That, more than anything else, is responsible for our climbing crime rates.

A warden ponders on this while observing the men whom the Law has given into his care. The wheels of justice grind unceasingly. With each turn a new prisoner is dropped within his domain. Who are these men? What is their fault? Wherein have they failed? What to do with them?

In the quiet of my chambers, I call a meeting of shades—not ghosts—but opinions. It is an august assembly. The Law is there. So also the Church, the School, and all the Sciences, Medical, Social, Mental. All that have to do with the human mind and body.

We are organized into a clinic. We shall try to do our analyzing and dissecting together. Our subject stands before us. He has been tried by a court and found guilty of crime. He has been sentenced to prison. I open the session.

"Let us have a complete record," I suggest. "Let us find out first who this man is. Not merely his name

375

and pedigree. We want to know his thoughts, his ideals, if he has any, his views on life and its problems."

The Law is fidgety. Shakes its head in impatient disagreement.

"We are not concerned with all that. This man has broken the accepted precepts of government. I don't care about motives, or thoughts or ideals. He does not fit in. He has been found guilty and deserves his punishment. So far as I am concerned, I am through with him. I am no longer interested."

A chill descends upon the meeting. The Law settles down into its seat, unconcerned with the reactions of the conference toward its view. Cold glances are exchanged. Each waits for the other to take the floor. I prompt them on.

"I believe a word or two from our colleague, the Church, might be in order."

There is no immediate response. The Church is meditating. It seems to be lost in thought. It turns its full gaze upon the subject standing before the meeting.

"I deem myself hardly competent to discuss this situation. I have never seen this man before. He has never entered the portals of my sanctuary. He was never, apparently, a regular attendant. I might have seen his mother at services, but I could not have known of her intimate troubles. You see, we did not have time for that sort of thing. We have all we can do to take care of the routine of the Church organization. It has become so large and our overhead is so big. No, I do not think I can help.

"Now, if he were a regular communicant—— But we seem unable to get the young people to come to us."

We progress slowly. There is no enthusiasm. My guests are wary. They need coaxing. I turn toward a complacent member of the group. He seems well satisfied with life. And unworried. "How about you, School?" I ask. "Can we hear from you?"

This guest rises quickly in his place.

"I know this fellow. He gave me quite some trouble. He was one of our bad boys. Was absent a great deal. Played truant. We had to send him to truant school. Then he came back to us and he got into some difficulties and he was sent to a Protectory for a time. He returned again but in a short while was sent to a Children's Home. After a year or so he was discharged and we had him once more. We let him go as he pleased. We had no interest in him. We anticipated that he would come to no good end and I am not surprised to find him here. We hurried him through school to the eighth grade and then he dropped out of sight. Now, I guess, he is too far gone. There is nothing the School can do for him. If he had attended his classes regularly and been a good boy, he would never have been here."

School sat down with his usual complacency. His remarks were followed by a low murmur among the rest of the group. Each turned to his neighbor and engaged in serious conversation. I noticed that School and Law talked with each other, wholly ignoring Church who sat between them.

There was a sudden hush as the Doctor asked to be heard. "I want to ask a question," he announced.

"Has this man ever been examined for his tonsils? Is he in perfect health? How about his glands? Are they functioning normally? I would like to look him over. I am quite sure you will find something wrong

377

with him physically. And if we do, I would like to correct it. He will be rejuvenated. You ought to give us a chance. I am anxious to try."

He hesitated a moment, then added: "And don't think I am looking for business. I really want to accomplish something."

He finished with an encouraging smile and looked hopefully toward our subject. The rest of the meeting looked up with interest. They gazed at the subject curiously. I knew what was in their minds. They would like the Doctor to try. Perhaps those glands did not really function right. That would relieve everybody and settle the problem at once and for all time.

Another voice interrupted us. It came from a youngish looking fellow in the rear of the room. There was an enthusiastic appeal in his request for a hearing. "May I say a word?" he asked.

"Surely, Mental Clinic. We would all like to have the benefit of your observations."

"The trouble with this man is that he has not been able to adjust himself. He is not responsible. A sort of moral imbecile. Can't distinguish between right and wrong. I think the Law is wrong. You cannot punish or hold an irresponsible man accountable for his mistakes or crimes. Had I been called in during his childhood I would have been able to diagnose his case and perhaps straighten him out. As it is, it may be too late. But I am willing to try. But I don't want anyone else to interfere with my work. I can handle this all alone."

The speaker looked around at the others with a frown. They stared back at him with answering frowns.

378

He shrugged his shoulders with a helpless gesture and sat down.

Seated in the corner was a modest gentleman. He had not joined the others in their low and hushed comments. He had listened carefully to all the speakers. He made a move as though to rise, then changed his mind. I called to him. "Mr. Social Service, how about you? Have you studied this man? What do you make of him? Let's hear from you."

"Yes, I have given this some thought. He is the result of inequality of opportunity. This man never had his chance in life. His home life was unsatisfactory. His parents had no restraining influence on him. He did not have the right kind of supervision or companionship. He is now without aim or purpose in life and lives only for the present. He is the product of the slums. Before we can do anything with him we shall have to help him change his mode of living. I am willing, even anxious to help along, that is, if the others will help too. I cannot work alone."

He looked toward his hearers for an encouraging reply. They smiled at him indulgently. All but the stout gentleman in the opposite corner. He seemed to be lost in thought. I looked closer at him.

"Mr. Public," I called, "you are the only one left to be heard. We shall all be glad to have your opinion."

He sat up suddenly and then I noticed for the first time that he had been dozing. He stared blankly around. Then, apparently recollecting his surroundings, he looked toward me. "I beg your pardon," he drawled, "I didn't quite catch your question."

I repeated it for his benefit.

"Well," he said, as he rose lumberingly to his feet.

"I don't see why I was called here anyway. I don't know a thing about this. I am perfectly willing to leave it all to you gentlemen. You know I am a very busy man."

He looked over at Law. "I did hear what Law had to say. I think he's right. I don't see why we should spend so much time on this fellow. He is just no good. And he ought to be punished. If you Doctors think you can do anything with him, it's all right with me. But so far as I am concerned I'll wash my hands. If he is a tough guy, the sooner we get rid of him the better; if he is insane, put him in an asylum; if he is just a plain boob, a sap who tried something and——" Mr. Public coughed in his hand, "and got caught, why he'll have to take the consequences."

While he talked he hadn't looked at the man who was the subject of this discussion. But as his voice rose in volume and assurance, the subject suddenly looked up at him, and started. To the surprise of the meeting, he ran toward the speaker and clasped his arm. "Dad! What are you doing here?"

The older man looked at the sallow-faced youth. He swayed for a moment, and would have fallen but for the support of his son.

"Bob! I didn't know it was you. How did you get into this mess?" He laid his hand on the boy's shoulder and looked him over carefully.

"God! But this is terrible. Here I am, thinking all the while it was some poor boob from nowhere."

There was anger in his voice as he turned toward the group. His words sounded harsh and his fist swept the group of astonished faces.

"What are you all doing here? Didn't you know

380

this was my son? Couldn't you have saved him from this disgrace? I support all of you. I pay your living. I maintain your courts and judges, I pay fees to lawyers, and doctors, and contribute toward the upkeep of the Church. I pay enormous school bills. I give to charity. What do you all give me in return?"

He paused for breath. Then he turned toward his son. "Come, lad, I'll take you home with me."

I walked over toward Mr. Public and his son. "Sorry," I said. "He can't go home. He will have to stay here with me until his term is ended. But you may rest easy. I'll take good care of him. I shall see that he leads a clean life. He will be taught a trade. We shall guide his reading and encourage him to play. We shall have him tell us of the things that trouble his mind and weigh upon his heart. After all, Mr. Public, you had your chance and threw it away. The Law has had its opportunity. The Church likewise. So has the School. They have all failed. Perhaps, together, we can find a way."

The father took hold of my hand and clasped it firmly. He walked slowly away and out of the room. Simultaneously the group vanished. I was left alone.

Four hundred thousand sons. Four hundred thousand fathers. Four hundred thousand mothers. A million brothers and sisters. They come and go. Today it is Mr. Jones'; tomorrow Mr. Smith's. The next day it is yours. Another day it may be mine. Breaks, temptations, accidents, situations . . .

CHAPTER 12: THE GREAT AMERICAN DETERRENT

NEVER before in America has there been such wide discussion of crime and prison problems. Never before has there been such ebullition of emotions on the status of the criminal. If it were not so serious the scene presented throughout the country, with its many commissions and investigating committees, numbering into the hundreds, each intent upon finding its favorite, preconceived, hobby-ridden solution of these problems, would present an amusing situation. Very much like the dissecting room of the old medical school where groups of students would probe and cut into particular portions of a cadaver in the hope that therein each would find the answer to the riddle of life and death.

What has been the sum total of these investigations? Have the numerous committees found a method to overcome the congested conditions of our prisons and jails and reformatories? Have they discovered a plan to restrain the criminal? The general verdict (with few exceptions) is that the only cure is—more and larger and safer prisons.

It has been estimated that the four hundred thousand prisoners now confined in the various penal and correctional institutions throughout the country represent but eight percent of those actually engaged in criminal practices. That would make a total of about five million people in the United States who, judged by our present standards, belong in one prison or another.

"Lifers" were there, men doing sixty years, fifty years, as well as prisoners about to be discharged. . . . There was not a shady or ominous thought in all that crowd. (*Page 410*)

I encourage prisoners with long "bits" to play on our various teams.   (*Page 409*)

What would happen if, by a fortunate or perhaps unfortunate chance, all these criminals could be put behind the bars today? Would not the morrow yield another crop of new criminals equally determined in the paths of violence and unrighteous acquisition?

Attacking the problem of crime and criminals through prisons is to approach the problem hind-end foremost. The answer does not lie in "more and larger and safer prisons." It is rather in ascertaining some method of diminishing prison populations; of reducing them without danger to the peace and security of the public; of turning these prisons into plants where human impulses and the desire for normal living can be recharged with vigor and encouragement.

The difficulty has been that most of us regard the criminal in terms of prisons and institutions. As a prisoner he is often an object of sentiment, either of hate or pity; as a convict he is dangerous, feared, caged, fettered, stared at in morbid, perhaps sordid curiosity. He serves the purpose for those who find pleasure in hating and of those whose abundant sympathies must have emotional outlets. His emergence from institutions removes him from both categories. He is no longer an object of sympathy or hatred. The moment he becomes a definite personality he loses his emotional value, but he does not regain his social standing. The age-old tragic caste system of Brahman India, which the British Government is trying hard to destroy, is in a large measure reflected in the attitude of the ordinary citizen toward the ex-convict. Without social standing, generally without means, the doors of respectability and equal opportunity are closed to him.

Except where he is intimately concerned, the average person is hard-boiled in his attitude toward offenders. The judge who from the bench demands the return of the whipping post pleads for mercy and leniency when he himself stands at the bar, a defendant convicted of crime.

A distracted father came to me one day. I had known the gentleman for years as a relentless foe of law breakers. He was always unsympathetic. He invariably applauded a sentence of five, ten or twenty years. "Serves them right," was his reaction. But this time he was plainly worried. He was a gentleman of good reputation, of independent means and a devoted parent. Yet one of his young daughters had become involved in a shoplifting escapade. She was arrested, tried and convicted. The distracted father moved heaven and earth to prevent his child from being sent to an institution. He succeeded and probably saved the girl for her present fine womanhood. It was a deserving case, for the girl was not inherently bad. It is only when circumstances strike home that we become keenly aware of the necessity of invoking the rule of individuality in dealing with offenders.

Society's attitude toward the criminal will continue nebulous, without form or definite plan, unless it can ascertain first, who the criminal is, and secondly, how he became one. It is idle prattle to maintain that punishment is not necessary for a certain class of violators. Punishment, however, is always relative. One of our New York Supreme Court Justices stated recently that when he sentenced a man to hard labor he meant "exactly" that. Yet it is a fact that what is hard labor to one man is comparatively an easy task to another. The rock pile does not offer a difficult task to the laborer. A job at a desk where he would have to push a pen with calloused fingers would for him be hard labor indeed. Judges trained in the law, having to do with legal precedents or technical rules of procedure, do not understand prison management. It might not be amiss for every aspirant to the bench in the criminal courts to take a post graduate course in actual prison experience.

What, for instance, can be in the mind of the court that disposes as follows of four young men convicted of participating in the same crime? All were under twenty-one, with similar social background; one is sent to the New York County Penitentiary with an indeterminate sentence of not more than three years (he will probably be released in one year, with the approval of the same judge); one is sentenced to the State Reformatory at Elmira, to serve probably fifteen months; another is sent to Sing Sing with a sentence of two and a half to five years; the fourth to the same prison with a term of five to ten years.

What basis has the judge for such disparity in sentences? Does he expect to reform each boy within the time specified? If the penitentiary can reform in one year, why not send all four there instead of saddling the State with the expense of prolonged imprisonment elsewhere? If Elmira is better, why not send them all to the reformatory? If five years are necessary for effective reform, Sing Sing may be the proper place for all.

The truth is that very few judges consider the possibility of reform.

What are prisons expected to make of these men? If they are irredeemable, why set a definite date for release? If they can be saved, how does the legislature, or the judge, know that five, ten, fifteen or even fifty years will do the trick? In my opinion, if a man cannot be made to respect authority, if he cannot be made to understand the supremacy of the law in ten years he is hopeless and should not be released at all.

In 1926 we were aroused by a "crime wave" which sprang full-grown from the minds of "investigators" and sensational headlines. We rushed to legislate, and amended our penal laws to provide longer terms of imprisonment. We further provided fixed limits to a man's criminal career. Four felonies—and life! Yet to-day, six years after the adoption of that law, I read of a man whose career shows thirty-one previous convictions, invariably followed by short terms in the workhouse, penitentiary or prison. He will now come to Sing Sing for life as a "fourth offender." He probably deserves life imprisonment as one of the hopeless cases. Intelligent penal administration would either have segregated him many years ago as mentally deficient or subjected him to closer supervision after release. Does not the law border on the specious that permits thirty-one trials and convictions before deciding definitely upon a delinquent's final status?

Our defective penal system has broken many spirits beyond all hope of readjustment to normal life. It is quite possible, too, that among prisoners throughout the state there are more than the present number of "lifers" who should be retained for their natural lives. I maintain, however, that a fourth offender law like the one now in effect in New York State is not the proper measure of a man's "qualifications" for a life sentence. There are some first or second offenders to be released within the next few years who will surely be returned for new offences. There are those who, though guilty as fourth offenders, have reached the end of their criminal careers and can, with adequate supervision, be restored to society, reconstructed and rehabilitated.

Society's attitude toward crime and criminals is reflected by the laws on its statute books. As long as it views these problems through prisons and fixed sentences that permit little if any discretion in releasing or discharging delinquents and prisoners, there will be no permanent solution.

Time was when a person with smallpox was lashed through the public streets as "possessed" of evil; when the disordered mind was tortured to free it from the devil. We have passed also through the periods of theoretical, hereditary crime; of criminality due to physical deformities, of limitation of will, of freedom of will, of glandular defects, and the many other pet notions of theorists and investigators.

We are beginning to realize that in a larger sense, none of us is immune from the possibility of falling from grace; that in more cases than we care to acknowledge a criminal career has its origin in unforeseen and unexpected situations that drain men's strength and courage and prompt them to seek the "easiest way out."

Does violation of law, followed by fixed punishment, actually determine the offender's anti-social attitude? The hard-boiled and puritanical among our citizens nod vigorously in affirmation.

Has it ever occurred to these puritanical friends that the Decalogue as written on the tablets of stone under the direct supervision of the Deity carried no penalties for the violation of any of the Commandments? It was only when mortal man began to tinker with the law that punishment was devised. Death was decreed for violation of the Sabbath. Lo, and behold! there was a violation and the first stoning. "Obey these precepts and you will have long life and be happy," is the substance of God-made law. "If you violate any of these inhibitions you will be tortured, maimed and killed," is the mandate of man-made laws.

Immortals among mortals were not lawyers. They were moralists and teachers of social justice among men. Moral suasion was to them far superior and more effective than fear and intimidation. Yet their ideals and spirituality and their personalities have survived through the ages while "strong" men who sought to impress their wills on history with blood and iron and the mailed fist are fading with receding years.

Theologians make distinctions between sin and crime. Government differentiates crime from morals. Hence not all that is sinful is criminal, nor is all that is criminal unmoral. Statesmen are notoriously unmoral in their views and actions affecting international relations and policies, yet we would hardly call them criminals. The average citizen daily violates the code of accepted morals, yet he continues in the respect of his fellows.

Crime is a mongrel born of the illicit union between expediency and opportunity, both of them invaluable to our accepted standards of life and happiness. And it is because expediency and opportunity have become so important in law enforcement and social regulation that crime continues on with unabated vigor.

388

"Thou shalt not steal." How simple a code that is! And yet how all-inclusive. Think what an easy task for a jury to decide on a single question of fact. Did the act of the defendant at the bar constitute a theft? Was he unjustly enriched at the expense of his neighbor? Judgment accordingly. But the complex life that man has built up for himself through the years demanded complex rules. And so we have devised penal codes with variations and variances of offences, starting with simple theft and including unintelligent blue laws that find spasmodic enforcement in the courts. Codes that serve as expedients to point out to the unscrupulous the moralities they may violate with impunity, thus affording them the opportunity to wrong their fellows as long as their acts are "within the law." Is it not a fact that the law profession, as a whole, concerns itself with advising clients how to circumvent law and precedent? And is not the successful practitioner the man who can keep his client out of courts and prisons by guiding him over rough edges in his quest for fortune by means that clearly violate the simple code against theft? The law cannot object because his particular method of operation is not specifically mentioned in any of the minute subdivisions of established penal codes. Is the man who was wrongly advised or who was unable to purchase the services of astute counsel and finds himself eventually beyond the line of safety and expediency and face to face with courts and prisons more vicious and dangerous than his more successful and more fortunate brethren? The law says yes. He is a convicted criminal, dangerous to the peace of the community and must therefore be segregated. That man might really be dangerous and should be segregated. Not because he has violated a law, but because the measure of his viciousness is rather his indifference to the welfare of his fellows and his incapacity for corrected vision. Judged by that standard, how utterly futile are the intricate methods of punishments provided by a static code of laws which life and emotion cannot penetrate.

The measure of a man's criminality, under our arbitrary conceptions of right and wrong, is the length of a prisoner's sentence. I had occasion recently to witness a man's self-appraisement in this respect. It was during the Christmas show week at the prison and I had picked him out as one of the trusties in the chapel. He sent word that he felt he should refuse the designation. "I've got fifty years, Warden," he reminded me. I insisted and he more than fulfilled his trust as I anticipated.

To insure its normal development and growth, organized society must have planning and guidance and leadership. For these, rules are necessary. Hence we have laws. Laws, as well as their makers, must have a social consciousness. Else they become tyrannical. Then come rebellion and revolution. The failure of Eighteenth Century England to understand that, brought on the American Revolution. The conflict in social thought that developed among the peoples to the north and south of the Mason and Dixon line resulted in the Civil War that established the inviolability of the American Union, but left the problem of the southern negro still unsolved.

Social consciousness is, therefore, far more essential to good government than respect for law. There are many laws for which the average citizen has little or no regard. The neglect by legislatures and administrators of problems of social welfare and improvement invariably leads to their recall.

Law is not inviolate, except as it interprets the social impulse that led to its enactment. That is why law enforcement differs in degree in the various states of the Union. And that is why similar laws, or even the same law, will provide a severe penalty in one community and a lighter one in another. Law that does not reflect the social conscience is unenforceable. As a prison administrator having to do with law violators I am interested in the law's effectiveness. I am interested, too, in the kind of men and women who have elected to do it violence.

Outstanding among the results of our prison and penal policies is the fact that prison populations have steadily increased. Of interest, too, is the fact that the head of a building corporation that specializes in prison construction is the largest tax-payer in his community. Thinking citizens are troubled about these conditions and wonder: What are all these men doing in prison? Why keep them there? When do they depart? And whither?

There is wide sentiment among well-intentioned men and women that prisons should reform criminals. "It is difficult to reform a child," spoke a prison wag, "when he is sixty." It is just as difficult to reform a man of thirty, or a youth of sixteen or nineteen, when he knows that he is "paying" for misdeeds in terms of years. "Paying his debt to society," or "wiping the slate clean," is the language of current penology. In barter men look for bargains. This may be good business, but very bad for social reconstruction. Yet few,

391

if any judges in sentencing criminals have anything in mind but punishment for offences. Otherwise, long prison terms are sublimely ridiculous.

For it is idle to suppose that a boy of nineteen, convicted of a serious crime as a first offender, cannot be reformed until he shall have attained the age of forty-four on completion of the minimum of a sentence of twenty-five years and upward. A prisoner facing those years of imprisonment is not a fit subject for reform. He will be a middle-aged man on his discharge. A great many things happen in a quarter of a century. On his release he will either falter his way helplessly into a home for the indigent, or resentment will burst forth in calculating and desperate crime.

During his twenty-five years within the walls he will see men, hardened in crime but lucky in court, serve shorter sentences and return again and again for new violations and crimes. Others with moderate sentences for lesser offences, having made their peace with society, will leave never to return. He will greet old-timers, fifty or sixty years of age, as they come in for their last stretch. He will observe the inequalities of sentences—two men convicted of the same act, one with the sentence of twelve and one-half to twenty-five years, the other five to ten. Men will tell him of their lucky breaks because they were able to hire the "right" lawyer.

But he will be encouraged to attend church services; to join the library where books are available for the asking; and if his education is still elementary, to attend school; he will be permitted to write home regularly. And with the passing of the years there will come the moment of regret and hope. It may be an unconscious reaction, resulting in the urge to do better things.

Caught at that moment and given sympathetic impulse among normal influences that prisoner might be saved to society as a social and economic unit. Years before, however, an impersonal and rigid code pronounced its judgment. It was to be a "warning" to others. The warning passed unheeded, for crime continued to be. The sentence could not be shortened, except by cumbersome proceedings, nearly always hopelessly futile. Yes, twenty-five years is a long time within which to effect the reform of a prisoner.

Why not face the facts about this thing frankly, discarding, if we can, thread-worn notions and personal prejudices? I take my job seriously, first, because it has to do with living, feeling, emotional human beings made of the same stuff as you or I. Second, because the public has entrusted me with a valuable property measured in dollars. For, if the estimate of $2,000 as the cost of detection, arrest, trial and conviction of every prisoner is correct, the public treasury has spent almost $5,000,000 to bring my wards to these prison gates; and it is now spending more than $2,500 a day for their maintenance!

What profiteth all this, if these men are to be kept within walls, their labor restricted, one day exactly like the other; where, in the very nature of things, trivial interests loom large and unreasoned and untrained vision becomes constantly more defective? Prison is the easiest way out for authority, as locks and keys are the warden's simplest tools. It does not require strong imagination or unusual ability to keep men in their cells.

There is no single measure of prisoners' psychology. I have still to find two prisoners exactly alike in thought and reaction to prison routine. Our psychiatric department reports that for the year 1929-1930 only 25.36 percent of our prison population were normal; the rest were either dull-normal or lower down than the scale of intelligence. And yet 654 men—about one third of our last year's population—made frequent use of our research library which contains books for vocational training and several thousand volumes of the best in literature and philosophy. In this connection it is interesting to note that only 0.26 percent, or four out of 1,526 examined, were found to be pathological liars. A favorable showing indeed, as compared with the general population outside the walls, if the daily papers are to be believed.

In prison, every moment is supervised, every act regulated. At work or at play there is ever-present vigilance. Letters, incoming and outgoing, are censored. Prisoners are locked in during prayer, at school, when they eat, sleep or relax. Style and quality of dress are regulated. Neighbors are nearly always the same; faces that bid one another good-night are the same that greet one another in the morning.

All this takes place in a circumscribed area, where men numbering in the thousands crowd and jostle one another continuously. Naturally there is stress and strain among these men. Uppermost in their minds is the moment of release. It becomes their all-consuming passion, their main topic of conversation, their ever-

394

present thought. Advance that moment and hope returns; retard it, there is despair and despondency.

The things that seem ordinary and natural to the average citizen are looked upon with suspicious nervousness if they occur in prison. Emotional outpourings among free men are translated into evidences of hate and revenge and downright brutality when associated with prisons.

At ball games, umpires sometimes render unpopular decisions. From the bleachers come hoots and howls, not infrequently followed by barrages of empty bottles and other missiles. Such demonstrations are not ascribed to criminal instincts. They are emotional outbursts.

A popular entertainer meets with disfavor among impatient and disappointed auditors, and he becomes a target for unsavory edibles. The incident is passed off humorously and with grace. It is not an indication of viciousness. When similar incidents occur within prison walls, we call it mutiny, deserving of severest repression.

It is well recognized, since Napoleon's famous phrase, that "an army marches on its stomach." It is natural and reasonable. Yet we are disturbed when prisoners ask for wholesome food. We decry their unruly spirit.

A delay of a few moments in the subway and waiting passengers become violently abusive. Time, to the ordinary individual, is very precious and he resents any interference. The crowd may be boisterous, but hardly criminal; yet we carve years and decades out of men's lives, and if they chafe and are bitter they are untamed brutes who should be isolated in "solitary" on bread and water.

I am surfeited with this constant emphasis on punishment and still more punishment. Mere boys handed out twenty and twenty-five years; older men guilty of an only and single offence, five or ten or more years! Investigators who know no more about the psychology of prisoners than about Einstein's changing theories of the cosmos decide that the trouble is in the kitchen —we add to the bill of fare; that prisons are overcrowded—we plan new and expensive cell blocks; that prisoners are receiving too much liberty within the walls—we curtail the possibility for mental development and individual attention toward promising personalities.

An uninformed public nods assent to these proposed remedies. But tell a prisoner that he will have to go on a lean diet, suffer isolation in cramped and crowded quarters, be unable to read books and newspapers, be deprived of radio and talking pictures—yes, even of visits from dear ones—all in exchange for a substantial reduction in his sentence, and his choice will not be long delayed. He will barter quickly. Give him all these and more—but add to his term of confinement— and you will have surliness, with resignation that often ends in what is known among prisoners as "Box A" at the Dannemora State Hospital for the Criminal Insane; and, at one time or another, distemper will show its head amid riot and bloodshed.

Not many understand the workings of a man's mind (I speak now of one of our prisoners) that painstakingly prepared a calendar to designate every day of a twenty-five year sentence, and who daily at sunset crosses off another day from his term. Psychiatrists or psychologists can only guess at his mental makeup. Theirs may be a good guess, but after all only a guess.

If this method of handling crime were at all effective there might be an excuse for it. But we know that it is not. With the advent of long prison terms crime increased; it is still increasing. Crimes of violence are more prevalent today largely because men are made more desperate at the prospect of long prison terms—that statement is based on personal study and observation. The trouble is that "we are holding fast to the tail of the dog, afraid to let go and unable to check his antics."

An arid, desert patch cannot be transformed into a fertile, fruitful garden by a spasmodic spraying of its surface. It requires irrigation; a constant, unending supply of water, often drawn from great distances, that will seep into the earth and bring fecundity where, theretofore, was only sterility. In a similar sense it is idle to talk of prison reform and reforming prisoners merely by dealing with the prison as a distinct institution standing alone in the whole gamut of agencies that have to do with social control. The prison is only a part of our intricate system of dealing with misfits. If the sources that supply its ranks remain polluted, efforts for reform directed at the prison will have little if any appreciable influence.

More than a century ago well-intentioned and socially-minded people began the campaign for reform in prisons. Prisoners were cowed with the fear of physical torture for non-submission to rules and routine. They were put to hard tasks "to sweat out corruption";

they were preached to and secluded in isolation to reflect on past performances and brood over new ones. All this in the cause of reform. If prisoners did not die as the result of this "reform" treatment and if their charges were no worse on their discharge than when they were admitted the authorities thanked their lucky stars.

Except for a negligible number of "lifers" all of our four hundred thousand prisoners will be discharged to resume their places in society. If they and their successors go forth "no worse than they came in," and no better, there is no point or purpose in our elaborate programs for diminution of crime. To build "bigger and better prisons" is to aggravate the problem, for the greater our prison populations the more difficult will be the task of absorption.

The majority of our prisoners are the failures of intermediary institutions. Corrective and reformatory influences made no impress upon them during adolescence or early manhood. They come to us already steeped in viciousness and depravity. What the juvenile home, the penitentiary and reformatory have been unable to accomplish the prison is now asked to complete.

Ordinarily I would say the job is impossible. Believing, as I do, however, that these failures are due to faulty objective rather than to defective material I am willing that prisons should be made to answer to the demands put upon them. Provided with the proper sinews of accomplishment, I see no reason why prisons should not turn out men better than they came in, wiser for their experiences, corrected in their views of life, more widely equipped to attain and retain their places in society and the desire to assume normal responsibilities.

In the hodge-podge of our criminal law and procedure we find this curious circumstance: so-called first offenders are often sentenced to longer terms than hardened criminals. Naturally young men will take chances that old hands will avoid, and so the first offender dares the rash and violent deed while his older and more experienced pal remains secretive behind the scenes. Since the law concerns itself with particular acts rather than with motivating forces, and since rationally minded judges appreciate this fallacy the resulting sentences are often imposed apologetically.

"My hands are tied; the term is fixed by statute," is the explanation given from the bench. The young fellow of sixteen or twenty, facing a prison term of fifteen or twenty years handed out with due apologies, nurses a grievance. He is not easily amenable to reform unless he can be made to understand that his discharge from prison depends upon his corrected attitude toward authority and his urge, adequately expressed, toward restoration to normal life.

Then we have the prisoner, a second offender, with a definite sentence. The date of his discharge is fixed. His previous criminal record, no matter how long; his institutional behavior, no matter how bad, never greatly retard his exit. He has made the rounds of almost every intermediary institution, from juvenile delinquent home to State Prison. He knows the ropes. He appears before the Parole Board sullen, defiant, even brazen. "I don't have to answer your questions," he reminds its members. They shrug their shoulders and bid him farewell, but not good-bye; they are sure to meet him again. When we think about reform in prison we must consider this type of prisoner. A difficult case, indeed.

There is also the prisoner doing life. The records show that judicial apologies are most frequently extended to "lifers." "I'll write the Governor in five years, or ten, recommending a commutation of your sentence. I hate to give you this sentence, but it's mandatory under the law." We have men in Sing Sing doing indeterminate sentences as first offenders in the face of a record of convictions spreading over two long typewritten sheets. Their previous sentences were for misdemeanors and were served in workhouses and penitentiaries. The amounts stolen either did not exceed one hundred dollars in each instance or the charge was reduced by consent of the court and district attorney. Not a few of our "lifers" are fourth offenders under the Baumes Laws, because in each of their four offences the property involved exceeded one hundred dollars. A first offender (so-called) may have fifty-one convictions on his record, the fourth offender only four. Yet one will do four years and the other is doing life (with apologies). Both are in the same prison, and that prison is expected to adjust both individuals with the view toward reformation.

We have, too, the occasional offender: the man who gives way to stress of circumstance, either of passion or business, or actual want; the man guilty of a crime, committed in a drunken frenzy or stupor; the man who loved well and often, or who could not (or would not) support his dependents. One-crime men, all. These men may not be really anti-social in their attitude.

400

There are men of good background as well as men
who "just growed up" in slums and back alleys; men
of fine education as well as illiterates; skilled mechanics as well as men without vocations or trades; old
men, fathers, grandfathers, and boys just beginning
to shave.

All these types are pitched into the prison melting
pot. We spice the concoction with a sprinkling of
idleness, shiftlessness, irresponsibility, over-crowding,
ill-chosen food (in most prisons), hopelessness—and
produce in all its sad glory the pride of our penal
system: The Great American Deterrent!

The net result is a gastronomic disturbance that
threatens to develop into a serious organic disorder.

If prisons are to prepare men for normal life outside they must be administered as far as possible on
a normal basis inside. That cannot be accomplished
unless there is more homogeneity in population. Classification, yes actual segregation of prisoners, therefore,
becomes a basic necessity. It should begin immediately
on conviction and before sentence is imposed.

It is, of course, conceded that a definite type of
criminal (some convicted and in prison, others indicted and awaiting trial, still others not yet apprehended or even detected) is a menace to the community
and should be sent away for life. But there are a great
many boys and men who could best be saved to society
by not sending them to prison. These boys and men
are usually without funds or friends or influence. Unable to procure bail, they languish in jail until they
are glad to accept the plea offered them by the district
attorney.

Inequality before the law is the sore spot of our entire philosophy of penal administration. Prisons feel it most because those whom it keenly affects ultimately find their way to prison where they nurse their grievances, sometimes silently, sometimes articulately, at other times vociferously with dire consequences.

One of the factors that destroys all semblance of equality before the law is that of bail. The Illinois Crime Commission points to the large percentage of bail cases that never reach the trial court. High bail means little or nothing to the wealthy malefactor or to the gangster with millions at his command, or to the henchman whom he sponsors.

It seems to me that we have outgrown the constitutional provision for bail, excessive or otherwise. We are agreed that first and foremost in crime prevention is certainty of detection and celerity of trial. The man who is indicted by a grand jury is entitled to an early trial. Neither he nor the prosecutor should be permitted to delay it unduly. To insure equality before the law and to avoid miscarriage of justice it would be more seemly to restrict the right to bail after indictment for a felony, whether it be for a first or fourth offence, and fix a mandatory time-limit for an early trial. To carry this into effect we may need additional judges and larger prosecuting staffs.

Prison administration is concerned with this phase of procedure because of the generally accepted notion —in and out of prisons—that money can get away with anything. A most unwholesome influence when your objective is to kindle a proper respect for law and conformity among men doing time within the walls!

Prison administration is vitally concerned with the method of sentencing criminals. Not years but accomplishment should be the measure of a prisoner's confinement. In essence prison terms should be based upon the prisoner's ability to make himself useful to society —the unskilled worker to learn a trade; the illiterate to acquire the education needed to hold a job; the wanderer to find for himself a home and responsibility; the deficient mentality to attain a better understanding of the values of life; the cynic and perverse to adopt a saner attitude toward society and government.

The transformation of men's minds and souls cannot be determined in advance. No court or judge or other human agency can tell how long it will take to improve the intellect or restore normal vision. In some cases it can never be done. Twisted mentalities may have been twisted too long and cannot be straightened out. For them there can be nothing but permanent segregation from society just as we segregate the insane or the leper. But most cases will answer to proper treatment. For them we need institutions that will suit their needs and give society the best possible returns in rehabilitated men and women. These prisoners do not need hospitals. They do not need armed camps or guns or bludgeons. They need workshops and schools.

That is what we should make of our prisons. Many prisoners have to learn to work just as others have to learn their alphabet. Doing tasks rather than doing time must become the objective of every prisoner if our corrective measures are ever to serve their purposes.

Every task assigned to him should be treated with an eye toward vocational training. He must appreciate the importance of tasks well done in their relationship toward his physical well-being. In other words, he should be paid for his work, and the amount of his earnings ought to govern his mode of living within the walls, just as the worker outside the walls adjusts his life in accordance with his economic status.

Every prisoner should be made to pay for his keep. Clothing, food, entertainment and other incidentals should be charged against him, and in addition a certain proportion of his earnings should be retained for the benefit of dependents. There should be nothing paternal about prisons. As in an industrial plant wages should be graded according to the importance of the job in order that ambitious workers might improve themselves and rise to higher type work and greater responsibilities.

Like an industrial plant the prison should be provided with the best possible machinery so that prisoners may become accustomed to handle the kind of work they may be called upon to do after their discharge. Most prisons throughout the country are provided with secondary outfits in their shops. The material used is old-fashioned. If we are to train a prisoner for normal life everything within the prison must be made to conform with normal requirements.

The man who has served his time and who, in the judgment of the authorities, is competent to face the world with every chance of success should not be deprived of the opportunities offered to men in ordinary walks of life.

There is no good reason why, under limitations, the man who has rebuilt himself in prison should be barred from civil service examinations or any other opportunities that are open to his fellows on the outside. You cannot expect to send a man out into the world and

404

demand that he go straight if you close the door to employment for which he is fitted. Training the prisoner for normal life must be supplemented with provision for normal chances for right living.

Prison administration is concerned with prisoners' contact with the outside world. Prisoners should be encouraged to keep abreast of current events. We did not find it necessary or desirable to restrict newspapers from Sing Sing Prison in the latter part of 1929 when prisons in New York State and throughout the country were restless. We felt it better to be frank with our men about conditions, and by pointing out the futility of uprisings and discussing local problems in man-to-man fashion attained results which elsewhere had to be impressed with guns and clubs.

I encourage decent correspondence—not promiscuous letter writing of the amorous type with soft-minded women or matrimonial agencies. But letters to wives, parents or brothers and sisters, or male friends are always encouraged. Who can say that these constant contacts are not helpful?

Normal expressions of emotions within prisons are important. If prisoners want to laugh while they eat, let them. If they have the urge to discuss politics or economics or the latest talkie or recent sport events, or even the prison menu, at the mess table, what harm is there in that? If wearing a tie helps them retain their self-respect, why not? If any popular radio number makes for kinship among the public at large I want my men to be a part of that kinship. If depressed emotions can be revived by a baseball game or soothed by a game of checkers or chess or an occasional talking picture, why not supply those things that help to keep men normal? Certainly if we are to return men to society we do want to send them out as normal human beings, keenly alive to all that is of interest to man and to the particular communities to which they are to return.

We shall have strenuous opposition to any change in the former traditional method of prison government. In more recent years baseball was considered an ill-advised luxury for prisoners. As a matter of fact all outdoor recreation was frowned upon, and, in many quarters, still is.

I can understand the theory of the Nineteenth Century penologist or administrator whose sole thought was for the punishment of offenders. To him the prisoner was as a man forgotten. "Put him in a cell, lock him up and throw the key away," is a theory that can be sustained from the standpoint of mere punishment for crime. But when we are asked to maintain a high standard of health, when we are cautioned to return men to society better than they come to us, when we are directed to rebuild characters and remold men's minds, we must have material to work with and the proper latitude to apply the best known methods.

It has been my theory that these objectives can best be obtained by teaching the prisoner, first, the art of thinking; second, the art of forgetting. Clear, clean thinking about his future and forgetting about the devious ways and dubious plans that led him toward crime and prison. If these two objectives can be obtained, prisons will have justified their existence and wardens will feel a measure of satisfaction in their work.

When men are kept occupied with normal tasks,

suited to individual capabilities, they can be trained for gainful labor. This feature of the prison program is now receiving the serious attention of every responsible social and governmental agency. I believe that we shall, in the course of time, be able to work it out. Equally important, however, is the prisoner's ability to forget.

The hospitals for the insane are filled to overflowing with patients who could not forget. Intimate problems, financial burdens, harrowing experiences all contribute to the mental strain. Vital statistics of every community show constantly increasing numbers of suicides —men and women who had not learned the art of forgetting.

Prison life is peculiarly attuned to the state of mind that does not permit forgetfulness. Intimate relationships that may have dimmed with the years; the passing of loved ones; the inconstancy of friendships; the helplessness of dependents; the blindness of justice; the inequality of laws' determinations—all these and more loom large in the eyes and the mind of the man behind the walls. Leisure to him may become the very curse of his existence. It may give him time to brood. It has been suggested that this leisure should be spent in remorse—the remorse that leads to repentance. But periods of remorse must not be unduly extended. The sincere repentant finds himself during the early years of his prison life; thereafter the burden of imprisonment is his cross and it rests heavily on his shoulders.

Innumerable scripts have been written about the beautiful panorama of the majestic Hudson as it can be observed from the barred windows of the new cell blocks on the hills of the new Sing Sing; much comment has been made about radio earphones in individual cells, talking pictures, occasional lectures by interested and public-spirited laymen with a message to the prisoner; a Thanksgiving or Christmas dinner calls for a column in many newspapers. To the prisoner with a sensitive mind—and there are many such prisoners in Sing Sing, as in all other prisons—these so-called luxuries bring increased punishment. They emphasize the fact of his imprisonment.

A very human letter passed through our correspondence department not long ago. It was from a husband to his wife. A church service was to be broadcast over the air and the prison radio was to tune in on it. "I would like you and the children to listen in on that program," this prisoner wrote. "I'll be in my cell hearing the service. It will be a comfort to know that we are all attending the same service and praying at the same moment. We shall be together even though far apart."

The writing of that letter, the listening in on that church service accentuated that prisoner's prison life. I would like to accomplish two things with that man: influence him toward a sensible, sane and sober perspective of life with an acute understanding of his responsibilities toward those who are waiting for him, and at the same time enable him to do his time within the walls without brooding about the years he still owes the state.

We have, also, the prisoner who is considered definitely and irredeemably bad. Solitary confinement will not make him better. Permitting him to roam aimlessly about the prison yard will enable him to

408

emphasize and spread his evil influence. It has been well said that recreation in prison is futile unless it leads to re-creation. By keeping his attention fixed on tasks and giving him the opportunity to wax enthusiastic during leisure hours over athletics or other normal interests, his "badness" will generally wane with the years. It is the law of human nature.

That is why I make every effort to assign my prisoners the kind of work that will interest them. That is why I encourage these men to adopt hobbies which will occupy their leisure hours; hobbies not inconsistent with the orderly routine of the prison government. And that is why I encourage baseball, football and all other forms of outdoor recreation.

While prisoners are taking their turn on the field; while they argue about their favorite heroes on the diamond or on the gridiron; while they discuss the salient points of a noted ring event or exchange ideas on politics or any other topic of common interest, they are not talking about their "cases"; they forget about length of sentences; they have no time to brood about emotions. They are, during those hours, normal human beings with normal interests.

It is a well-established fact that supervised recreation in congested areas makes for crime prevention. It is equally apparent to every earnest prison administrator that clean, wholesome sports within the congestion of the prison will accomplish more than ordinary institutional inhibitions in maintaining discipline and a contented spirit.

I encourage prisoners with long "bits" to play on our various teams. They have a big fight ahead of them—the fight against despondency. It is a tough fight. In order to regain society's confidence it must be a clean fight.

We have advanced beyond the theory of isolation for prisoners. We should recognize, as well, the importance of well regulated, supervised and helpful worldly contacts. A baseball game or a football contest with reputable outside teams serves a two-fold purpose: visitors learn to understand that prisoners are human, and prisoners appreciate the necessity of playing the game on the square with their fellows. The urge for normal contact which is thus kindled keeps many prisoners to the line of reason and conformity. Its influence is far-reaching.

I have been an interested spectator at football games in Sing Sing. I knew that some of our guests —gentlemen of the press and others—would find here and there an inspiration for a comic strip. That follows in the nature of things when prison affairs or events are discussed or explained for the benefit of the public at large. To me the Sing Sing gridiron always presents a serious and sober thought. At each game more than two thousand men lined up alongside the north wall, intent and enthusiastic about the progress their team was making. They were not compelled to witness the games; they came of their own volition. "Lifers" were there, men doing sixty years, fifty years, as well as prisoners about to be discharged. The field was well policed with officers, but they were hardly needed. There was not a shady or ominous thought in all that crowd of men. They rooted for a clean fight toward the goal.

Our average count shows that we have in Sing Sing twenty-five hundred individual goals. Every one of

Courtesy Fox Movietone News.

Prisons should turn out men better than they came in. (*Page 398*)

our prisoners has to make his own fight. As their warden I am willing to help them reach it, provided they play fair and clean and with common purpose. It was said, during the war, that when a certain London regiment was ordered to charge the enemy a football was immediately punted toward the German trenches and the whole regiment answered as one man. "It was," the account reads, "a wonderful instance of team spirit and true sportsmanship."

Each of our men must make his own play, whether it takes him one year or fifty years, but the community of interest and the clean, wholesome spirit that comes with social consciousness will help him to "play square." That understanding will regain for him the respect of his fellows.

Guidance rather than deterrence is the answer to crime. It is the only course that promises permanence. Prison walls must not be permitted to bar society's primary obligation to its faltering wards.

Our recurrent and short-lived hysteria over vicious and desperate crime should not blind us to basic needs. Violent crime in the United States is a passing phase in American life, just as insanity and suicide, which have more than doubled within a decade; just as Prohibition, or dishonesty in public and civic office, or financial duplicity. "Shoot to kill" is but a temporary measure, even as alms giving can but momentarily relieve unemployment and privation. Probers grow more numerous and panaceas multiply. What are they all but variations of the old "There but for the Grace of God" attitude, ascribed to preacher, poet, statesman and teacher. It brings the whole problem close to us. These men who are grasping for a foothold are stran-

411

gers; they may also be ourselves, our children, our parents, or brothers. We may never produce a world with "Men like gods," but we can at least implant a social consciousness that shall make each of us in truth and in fact his brother's keeper.